A HUMAN RIGHTS BASED APPROACH TO DEVELOPMENT IN INDIA

Asia Pacific
LEGAL CULTURE
& GLOBALIZATION

The Asia Pacific Legal Culture and Globalization series explores intersecting themes that revolve around the impact of globalization in countries on the Asia Pacific Rim and examines the significance of legal culture as a mediator of that impact. The emphasis is on a broad understanding of legal culture that extends beyond traditional legal institutions and actors to normative frameworks and the legal consciousness of ordinary people. Books in the series reflect international scholarship from a wide variety of disciplines, including law, political science, economics, sociology, and history.

Other volumes in the series are:

Sarah Biddulph and Ljiljana Biuković, eds., *Good Governance in Economic Development: International Norms and Chinese Perspectives*
Daniel Drache and Lesley A. Jacobs, eds., *Grey Zones in International Economic Law and Global Governance*
Sarah Biddulph, *The Stability Imperative: Human Rights and Law in China*
Pitman B. Potter, *Assessing Treaty Performance in China: Trade and Human Rights*
Pitman B. Potter and Ljiljana Biuković, eds., *Globalization and Local Adaptation in International Trade Law*

A HUMAN RIGHTS BASED APPROACH TO DEVELOPMENT IN INDIA

Edited by Moshe Hirsch, Ashok Kotwal, and Bharat Ramaswami

UBCPress · Vancouver · Toronto

28 27 26 25 24 23 22 21 20 19 5 4 3 2 1

Printed in Canada on FSC-certified ancient-forest-free paper (100% post-consumer recycled) that is processed chlorine- and acid-free.

Library and Archives Canada Cataloguing in Publication

Title: A human rights based approach to development in India / edited by Moshe Hirsch, Ashok Kotwal, and Bharat Ramaswami.

Names: Hirsch, Moshe, editor. | Kotwal, Ashok, editor. | Ramaswami, Bharat, editor.

Series: Asia Pacific legal culture and globalization (Series)

Description: Series statement: Asia Pacific legal culture and globalization, ISSN 1925-0320 (print), ISSN 1925-0339 (ebook)

Identifiers: Canadiana (print) 20190093471 | Canadiana (ebook) 2019009348X | ISBN 9780774860307 (hardcover) | ISBN 9780774860321 (PDF) | ISBN 9780774860338 (EPUB) | ISBN 9780774860345 (Kindle)

Subjects: LCSH: Economic development – India. | LCSH: Economic development – Moral and ethical aspects – India. | LCSH: Economic development – Social aspects – India. | LCSH: India – Economic policy – 1991-2016. | LCSH: India – Economic policy – 2016- | LCSH: India – Economic conditions – 1991- | LCSH: Human rights – India.

Classification: LCC HC435.3 .H86 2019 | DDC 338.954 – dc23

Canadä

UBC Press gratefully acknowledges the financial support for our publishing program of the Government of Canada (through the Canada Book Fund) and the British Columbia Arts Council.

This book has been published with the help of a grant from the Canadian Federation for the Humanities and Social Sciences, through the Awards to Scholarly Publications Program, using funds provided by the Social Sciences and Humanities Research Council of Canada.

Printed and bound in Canada by Friesens
Set in Futura Condensed and Warnock by Artegraphica Design Co. Ltd.
Copy editor: Frank Chow
Proofreader: Caitlin Gordon-Walker
Indexer: Celia Braves
Cover designer: Setareh Ashrafologhalai

UBC Press
The University of British Columbia
2029 West Mall
Vancouver, BC V6T 1Z2
www.ubcpress.ca

Contents

Tables and Figures

Tables

Figures

Foreword

PITMAN B. POTTER

This volume examines the challenge of coordinating local performance of international trade and human rights standards in the Asia Pacific region, with particular attention to questions about the right to development. The book is part of a group of edited volumes examining different aspects of trade and human rights performance presented by the Asia Pacific Dispute Resolution (APDR) project and published in the UBC Press Asia Pacific Legal Culture and Globalization series. The APDR program began in 2003 with a SSHRC/MCRI-supported project on normative and operational conditions for local compliance with international trade and human rights standards in Canada, China, and Japan. Since 2009, the APDR project has focused on "understanding integrated compliance with international trade and human rights standards from a comparative perspective." This has involved building conceptual understanding and generating policy analysis on coordinating performance of international standards on trade and human rights in the Asia Pacific region, with particular attention to Canada, China, India, Indonesia, and Japan. The APDR project is based at the Peter A. Allard School of Law and the Institute of Asian Research of the University of British Columbia, and involves a collaborative network of colleagues from UBC and from partner institutions in North America, Asia, and Australia.

The challenge of coordinating local compliance with international trade and human rights standards is a critical issue for the globalized world.

International, regional, and subnational disputes over issues of trade and human rights present increasingly serious obstacles to international cooperation. Resolving and, where possible, preventing such disputes will benefit the course of international cooperation in areas of trade and human rights. Such efforts will also help reduce transactional, operational, and opportunity costs resulting from international disputes that make existing relationships more complex and costly, entail significant management costs, and distract public and private sector leaders from other, more productive pursuits.

Coordinating local compliance with international trade and human rights standards has been difficult in part because of conceptual differences and assumed trade-offs between these two regimes. All too often, human rights standards around the right to development, for example, are seen as inconsistent with trade goals of efficiency, economic growth, and private property rights. Conversely, trade policy is often seen as an obstacle to achieving human rights goals concerning health, education, and food security. As well, coordinated compliance with international trade and human rights standards has been elusive because the officials and specialists who manage local interpretation and implementation of these regimes often have few opportunities for institutional collaboration.

Mindful of these conceptual and organizational challenges, this project works to build knowledge and policy support for coordinating local compliance with international trade and human rights standards in ways that are mutually sustaining rather than conflicted. The project has generated policy proposals for building treaty compliance programs, processes, and institutions that are more responsive to cross-cultural differences and aim to resolve and, where possible, prevent disputes over trade and human rights. The results of the research are enabling interdisciplinary scholars and policy makers to better understand the requirements for coordinated compliance and have the potential to reduce and prevent disputes over trade and human rights, thus enhancing international cooperation.

This UBC Press series will publish new volumes edited by leading international scholars in their respective fields on the interaction of trade policy with human rights issues such as the right to development, labour relations, health policy, poverty and inequality, and government accountability. The books are grounded in original empirical research as well as qualitative and quantitative analyses relating to international trade and human rights. The work is characterized by a high degree of interdisciplinarity and focuses on questions of legal culture, international law, and globalization in the countries that compose the Asia Pacific region.

Research for this volume and for the APDR project of which it is a part has been supported by the Social Sciences and Humanities Research Council of Canada under its Major Collaborative Research Initiatives program, for which my colleagues and I are deeply thankful. The APDR project has benefited immensely from input and advice from an International Advisory Board constituted as follows:

Jack Austin (former Government Leader in the Senate of Canada and former president of the Canada China Business Council)
Joseph Caron (former Canadian High Commissioner to India, Ambassador to China, and Ambassador to Japan)
Professor Thomas Cottier (former managing director of the World Trade Institute, Berne, Switzerland)
The Honourable Irwin Cotler (former Member of Parliament; former Minister of Justice)
Professor Ernst-Ulrich Petersmann (European University, Florence, Italy)
Professor John Hogarth (Professor Emeritus, Peter A. Allard School of Law, University of British Columbia)
Jonathan Fried (Ambassador and Permanent Representative of Canada to the World Trade Organization, Geneva, Switzerland).

This project has included a wide range of graduate students working as researchers, analysts, and writers. Graduate students contributing to the work on this volume include Alvin Pei-ting Lin and Arka Roy Chaudhuri.

I have been privileged to serve as Principal Investigator for the APDR project. I am grateful to the many colleagues from across our research network who have contributed their time and expertise to strengthen the work we have done together. Particular thanks go to project manager Rozalia Mate for her stellar contributions to the operational details of the project.

Pitman B. Potter
Vancouver, Canada

Acknowledgments

Many people contributed in one way or another to the long process of writing and editing this book. We are deeply indebted to Pitman Potter, who conceived this Asia Pacific Dispute Resolution (APDR) project, skillfully led the research team, and provided good advice throughout the project. We are also grateful to the project manager, Rozalia Mate, who was in charge of complex administrative operations involved in the research project and kindly assisted all of us. Many thanks are due to Alvin Pei-Ting Lin for his excellent editorial work on the whole volume, and to Arka Roy Chaudhuri for research and editorial work. Funding support was kindly provided by the Social Sciences and Humanities Research Council (SSHRC) of Canada under its Major Collaborative Research Initiative (MCRI) program, and this generous support is gratefully acknowledged. We are also grateful to the editors at UBC Press, particularly senior editor Randy Schmidt. Finally, we owe a debt of gratitude to each contributor to this volume who joined us in this challenging but rewarding project.

A HUMAN RIGHTS BASED APPROACH TO DEVELOPMENT IN INDIA

Introduction
India and a Human Rights Based Approach to Economic Development

MOSHE HIRSCH, ASHOK KOTWAL,
and BHARAT RAMASWAMI

Over the last couple of decades, India has adopted a unique approach to economic development. It has passed parliamentary acts making some crucial desirable developmental outcomes, such as food security, primary education, and even employment, into "legal rights" conferred on every citizen. This approach can run into two problems, however. First, enacting laws is one thing but implementing them in practice through a highly imperfect institutional structure is another. If what is promised as a legal right is not delivered, it damages the government's credibility. Second, the domestic policies required to deliver on the promises implicit in legislating rights to development may run counter to the letter or the spirit of India's international treaty obligations under the World Trade Organization (WTO) or the *Agreement on Trade-Related Aspects of Intellectual Property Rights* (TRIPS).

The chapters in this volume attempt to shed light on both these issues. They ask to what extent it is possible, or whether it is possible at all, to bring about development by making it a legal right. They also probe whether there is a genuine clash between India's right to develop and India's commitment to international agreements.

"Development" is an all-encompassing term. The aspects of development that we tackle in this book are those that we regard as most pertinent to a poor country like India: food security, malnutrition, primary education, rural employment, the impact of multinational corporations on domestic labour markets, and two environmental issues: technology policy (on biotechnology) and climate change. Each of these seven chapters is written by an expert on the topic at hand. First, however, in order to understand why "rights-based development" was adopted in India, it is necessary to review the course of Indian development.

The Course of Indian Development: A Brief History

India has experienced impressive economic growth since the early 1990s, and its path to economic development demonstrates some prominent features of the human rights based approach to economic development.

India began its turnaround in economic performance in the 1980s. The pace of economic growth was sustained and then boosted by a series of economic policy reforms beginning in 1991 that opened up the economy to international trade and foreign investment. Domestic reforms deregulated industry; removed restrictions on the entry of the private sector in banking, insurance, aviation, and other sectors; rationalized the tax structure; and facilitated a competitive financial sector. Indian economic policy continues to emphasize measures that enable foreign and domestic investments in all areas, particularly in the infrastructure areas of transport, energy, and communications.

From 1951 to 1981, the Indian growth rate averaged 3.7 percent per annum. In the subsequent thirty-two years up to 2012, the growth rate averaged 6.2 percent. In the first period, India's GDP growth exceeded 6 percent in only nine years; in the subsequent period, however, it occurred on seventeen occasions. In 2014–15 and 2015–16, when the world economy struggled to grow at rates between 3 percent and 3.5 percent, the Indian economy grew at over 7 percent.

The impressive growth performance has been accompanied by a decline in poverty but the relationship has been variable and inconsistent.[1] The proportion of the population living in poverty (by official definitions) did not change significantly between the early 1950s and 1973–74. In the subsequent fourteen years up to 1987–88, it fell by a third, after which the rate of decline slowed till 2004–05. Poverty went down sharply in the period 2004–05 to 2011–12. According to the currently accepted definition of the poverty line, the poor in India comprise 22 percent of the population (26 percent in rural and 14 percent in urban India).

In absolute numbers, the poor number 270 million. At the $1.90 per day poverty line, India accounts for about one-quarter of the world's poor. For India to achieve near-elimination of poverty by 2030 (in line with the aspiration of the Sustainable Development Goals of the United Nations), not only must India continue to grow but incomes at the bottom end also have to rise consistently. The latter constitutes a particular challenge for India since, as mentioned earlier, periods of growth have not always translated into rapid progress on poverty. Even when poverty fell rapidly in the period between 2004 and 2012, the elasticity of poverty to growth was only –0.9. Compared with other developing countries, India's poverty elasticity is well below the median and toward the bottom third (Narayan and Murugai 2016). Its failure to achieve inclusive growth has been attributed to two failures in its development strategy (Kotwal, Ramaswami, and Wadhwa 2011).

First, India has not been able to create enough productive jobs for much of its low-skilled population (in labour-intensive sectors such as textiles) and thereby facilitate a swift transformation of the economy. Second, India has failed to rapidly upgrade the human capital of its labour force to sustain the expansion of the economy into high-skill–based activities, especially in services.

The discordance between growth and poverty is evident in the relatively slow progress in social indicators. In the twenty years from 1994 to 2014, both infant and under-five mortality rates have decreased drastically, but their levels (39 and 50 percent, respectively) are still higher than those of other poor nations in the neighbourhood, namely, Bangladesh and Sri Lanka. One important proximate cause is that access to improved sanitation and to piped water at home have not improved much and still remain limited to less than half of the population. In 2004–05, as many as 44 percent of under-five children were underweight and 48 percent were stunted. More recent figures indicate that these numbers have moderated to 29 percent and 39 percent, respectively. Nonetheless, international comparisons show that India's progress in these health indicators are much worse than might be expected from its income levels.

India also carries a significant burden of low educational attainment. Only about a third of the population have secondary education or greater.

Nearly one-third of adults are illiterate, while the remaining third has primary or middle-school education. Despite steady improvement, the number of poorly educated people has been so large that the progress has been slow. At the primary level, there are over 95 percent of children in school, but the major problems are middle-school dropouts and the poor quality of schooling.

Research has shown that the public health and educational institutions have failed to cope with the pressures placed on them. The tertiary care segment of the government health system suffers from underinvestment and poor quality. Furthermore, while investment in the government school system has grown substantially, its quality (measured in learning outcomes) has not improved. The private sector has expanded to partly fill these gaps but access to quality remains a concern. A raft of institutional problems that result in a lack of accountability of service providers to users plagues the public health and educational systems (Muralidharan 2013; Das et al. 2014). This means that India's slower-than-expected reduction in poverty is not the only reason for the failure of social indicators to improve rapidly.

These problems are thorny enough to cause activists to promote a legislative approach to imposing accountability on government institutions. In the 2000s, such approaches found favour with the courts as well as the political leadership, which was aware that rising incomes leading to greater aspirations were both a threat and an opportunity. In light of this institutional weakness, India has undertaken a rights-based approach to economic development, which creates legal rights to vital services such as education, food, and employment through parliamentary legislation. This policy constitutes an exemplary case of the "right to development" widely known in international law literature and aims to compel government bureaucracies to be legally accountable to individuals under their jurisdiction. Though various states and international institutions have adopted a rights-based approach to development, India's exceptional policies in this sphere represent a model for other states.

The right to development is a broad normative concept that seeks to hold states and international institutions accountable in particular instances. Philosophically, the rights approach is rooted in the right to human dignity, which in turn implies a right to basic human necessities. As these necessities need economic resources, the right to development implies a redistribution of resources. While a fiscal tax-subsidy framework for redistribution quickly draws opposition, a rights-based approach often has the potential to be backed by a broader political alliance. However, institutions such as an activist civil society, an independent judiciary, and a free press are needed for this approach to succeed in compelling governments to change.

This book reviews, probes, and analyzes India's experience with the human rights approach. By changing the legal environment, a rights approach could also significantly affect markets and compliance with trade agreements. A principal focus of this book is to understand the conflict, if any, between markets/trade and specific rights to development such as food, education, and health. The book also advances the state of policy by suggesting effective ways of designing and implementing the rights to development that minimize conflict with trade and market policies.

The Right to Development

The right to development[2] was officially proclaimed in 1986 by the UN General Assembly as the *Declaration on the Right to Development*[3] and was later included in a series of international declarations.[4] The right does not constitute a legally binding rule under international law and is instead an influential normative concept affecting the behaviour of states and international institutions ("soft law"). Unlike many other human rights, the right to development presents certain unique features (discussed below) and reflects a distinctive humanistic approach to economic development. Some of the principal characteristics of the right are: human-centred development; a right realization process requiring the implementation of a wide range of specific and interdependent human rights; a participatory, non-discriminatory, accountable, and transparent right implementation process; and the involvement of considerations of social justice, including fair distribution of benefits and burdens (OHCHR 2010, 6).

Though the general right to development includes both individual and collective specific rights (including those of states), the predominant component in contemporary literature and practice relates to the individual person as the central subject of development.[5] The rise of developing countries as a significant political bloc and the formulation of the New International Economic Order (NIEO) constituted the historical background to the early stages of the evolution of the right to development[6] (with the 1986 *Declaration* bearing some traces of the NIEO concept).[7] Some Third World countries argued during this period that past exploitative practices justified the imposition of direct obligations on developed countries toward poor ones. Notwithstanding such arguments regarding the collective rights of underdeveloped countries ("the right to development assistance") and ensuing duties of rich countries, and some references to several rights of states and peoples in the 1986 *Declaration,*[8] the widespread conception of the current right emphasizes the human person, the suffering of poor individuals, and their right to human dignity with minimum necessities of life, including access to basic resources.[9] Individuals who are deprived of such basic needs live in both developed and developing countries, but much more so in developing ones.

The realization of the right to development may be impeded by a breach of a broad range of human rights,[10] including political rights such as those relating to transparent and accountable governance and democracy.[11] However, it also tends to emphasize the importance of social and economic rights, such as the right to food, education, health, water, clean environment, housing, and work.[12] The holistic concept underpinning the right to development[13] also refers to the interrelationship between numerous specific human rights involved in the promotion of human development. Unlike the common hierarchy involving categories of human rights (such as peremptory and fundamental rights), the relevant instruments emphasize that the specific human rights included in the broad concept of the right to development are indivisible, interdependent, and mutually reinforcing.[14] Thus, from this perspective, these particular rights are profoundly interconnected and their implementation promotes human development.

The duties emanating from the right to development are attributed to both national governments and international institutions.[15] The governments of countries suffering from a lack of adequate development are required to undertake the necessary measures at the national level for realizing the right to development,[16] while developed countries as well as international institutions are required to adopt complementary measures to promote development in the former countries.[17] Though the implementation of the right to development involves joint and complementary commitments, national authorities bear the primary responsibility for creating conditions favourable to the realization of the right to development.[18] This joint responsibility requires international cooperation to support the efforts of developing countries to solve their economic and social problems, and create an environment conducive to the promotion of human development.[19]

The realization of the right to development involves numerous measures in the sphere of both international economic law and policy. Thus, for example, developed countries are called on to grant significant non-reciprocal trade preferences to poor countries, international institutions to establish adequate intellectual property rules to allow poor people access to life-saving medicines, and international financial institutions to provide adequate assistance to promote human development. From this perspective, the World Trade Organization is urged to adopt a broad range of measures, including the evaluation of the impact of member states' trade policies on the right to development (as part of the Trade Policy Review Mechanism), the expansion and reform of technical assistance programs to developing countries, the enhancement of the role of poor countries and human rights organizations in the negotiations leading to new WTO agreements, the interpretation of trade legal rules in accordance with the right to development,[20] and the establishment of progressive rules of origin to ease the asymmetric impacts of such rules on poor countries (Hirsch 2010, para. 18).

India, Economic Development, and the Right to Development

Exploring the experience of India with regard to the right to development is particularly relevant because, in light of its institutional weakness (discussed earlier), the country has adopted some prominent laws and policies significantly linked with the right to development, such as laws concerning the rights to education, food, and employment.

Several factors contribute to the adoption of rights-based laws and policies in India: an established tradition of "public interest litigation" in the Indian legal system (see, for example, Jacobs and Sen 2012; Cunningham 1987); judicial activism, including an increased inclination by the Supreme Court to refer to the United Nations *Declaration on the Right to Development;* strong networks and campaigns advocating such legislation and measures; and a free press and wide media coverage of these campaigns (Kumar 2013; Wolf 2015). The following chapters address some thought-provoking interactions between the right to development and various statutes and policies undertaken by India, as well as some of the rights-based approach to economic development.

Summary of Chapters

Chapter 1: India's *National Food Security Act* and the WTO *Agreement on Agriculture*, by Milind Murugkar

This chapter addresses the implementation of one of the more prominent rights included in the broader right to development: the right to food. The importance of access to food was underlined in Article 8 of the *Declaration on the Right to Development* and additional major international instruments (such as the *Universal Declaration of Human Rights*[21] and the *International Covenant on Economic, Social and Cultural Rights*[22]). It presents the 2013 Indian *National Food Security Act* (NFSA), which guarantees a certain quantity of food grains at subsidized rates to nearly two-thirds of India's population. This act can be considered as the biggest-ever experiment by any government in distributing subsidized food through a rights-based approach. Murugkar shows that the primary aim of the NFSA (to provide food security to the common citizen) is not at odds with the WTO regime. He analyzes the source of the conflict between the Indian government's commitment to provide food security to its citizens and its commitment under the WTO regime. He suggests that moving from a system of in-kind transfers to a system of cash transfers would mitigate this conflict and help India achieve coordinated compliance with its food security goals and its commitment under the WTO. An important lesson coming out of this study is that what has been thought of as a conflict between the domestic mandate for food security and the obligations under the WTO *Agreement on Agriculture* could be avoided by choosing alternate ways to ensure food security.

Chapter 2: Primary Education in India: Evidence and Practice, by Ashok Kotwal, Bharat Ramaswami, and Wilima Wadhwa

This chapter examines the implementation of the right to education in India and its implications for international trade. Promoting the right to development necessitates protecting the right to education,[23] a right recognized in the *Universal Declaration of Human Rights* (Article 26) and the *International Covenant on Economic, Social and Cultural Rights* (Articles 13 and 14). The *Right to Education Act* (RTE) was enacted by the Indian parliament in 2010. It aims to ensure that all children are enrolled in schools and requires schools to have certain provisions, mostly in terms of physical infrastructure. This chapter presents results from a methodical analysis of learning outcomes and their determinants. It finds that physical infrastructure actually matters very little for learning outcomes; what matters are the pedagogical issues that are not mentioned in the RTE. In other words, the rights-based approach can ensure that every child has access to education but it cannot ensure a satisfactory learning outcome. Education, in addition to being a human right, is a key component of the process of development. Chapter 2 suggests a series of measures that would improve the learning outcomes and spur the process of development. "Right to education" should be interpreted as "right to quality education."

Chapter 3: Ensuring the Right to Work through Better Governance, by Ashwini Kulkarni

This chapter focuses on the right to work as implemented by the *Mahatma Gandhi National Rural Employment Guarantee Act* (MGNREGA). The right to work is internationally recognized[24] in the *Universal Declaration of Human Rights* (Article 23) and the *International Covenant on Economic, Social and Cultural Rights* (Article 6). The *Declaration on the Right to Development* does not explicitly mention the right to employment, but it is certainly related in various ways to the promotion of the human right to development (see, for example, OHCHR 2013, 55, 121, 349, 367). This chapter clarifies that the MGNREGA not only constitutes a significant tool of redistribution but is also an instrument to improve rural infrastructure, as well as increase agricultural productivity (hence, the act is also related to the right to food). Kulkarni aims to explain which mechanisms are more likely to improve the implementation of this federal scheme in various constituent states in India. The chapter presents the result of extensive fieldwork undertaken in two states (Maharashtra and Andhra Pradesh), and concludes that the use of information technology and decentralization in governance structures are the primary reasons why the MGNREGA was better implemented in Andhra Pradesh than in Maharashtra. These lessons are important for improving protection of the right to work and promoting economic development in India, and possibly also in other countries.

Chapter 4: From Cautious Support to Precautionary Paralysis: The Evolution of India's Regulatory Regime for Transgenics, by Milind Kandlikar

There is a popular perception that large corporations like Monsanto have taken advantage of the present regime of intellectual property rights to short-change farmers and consumers from developing countries. Several non-governmental organizations (NGOs) with worldwide influence have raised concerns about the possible harm that the use of genetic modification or transgenic technology in agriculture can inflict on the health of humans and the environment. Whether or not this is true for a specific technology in a given country is a question for scientists to answer. Globalization can have a multifaceted impact on the developmental outcomes of a country such as India. On one hand, it offers productivity-enhancing technology to India's agriculture; on the other hand, it allows international NGOs to influence the domestic technological policy through an excessive and unwarranted use of the "precautionary principle." This chapter examines how India, a developing country with a large agrarian rural population, has regulated and controlled the use of transgenics in the agricultural sphere, focusing primarily on issues relating to biosafety. Kandlikar traces the evolution of the Indian government's policies from tentative support to regulatory paralysis, explaining why India has taken an increasingly precautionary approach.

Chapter 5: Child Malnutrition, Infant Feeding Practices, and Information: Evidence from India, by Nisha Malhotra

This chapter addresses the link between access to food and the right to health against the background of infant feeding and the World Health Organization's (WHO) feeding guidelines for a child's optimal growth. The *Declaration on the Right to Development* underlines the importance of health services (Article 8), and the human right to health has also been recognized in central international treaties, such as *International Covenant on Economic, Social and Cultural Rights* (ICESCR) (Article 12). The particular importance of protecting the right to health of children is emphasized by both the ICESCR[25] and the *Convention on the Rights of the Child.*[26] The chapter observes that child malnutrition is widespread in India and underlines the significance of adequate feeding practices for the reduction of child malnutrition and prevention of severe health consequences.

Malhotra's study indicates that the main obstacle to ensuring proper child nutrition in India is the lack of scientific information about nutrition. It points out that the existing feeding practices in India do not follow the WHO recommendations. The chapter recommends extensive intervention in nutritional practices aimed at educating families about proper feeding practices, including counselling on traditional beliefs. This study illustrates the essential link between the work of international institutions, national policies, and local impediments to the implementation of international agencies' recommendations.

Chapter 6: Foreign Direct Investment and Intergroup Disparities in India, by Ashwini Deshpande

This chapter addresses one of the sensitive features of Indian society: gender and intergroup discrimination. Promoting the right to development requires significant reduction of discrimination along caste and gender lines,[27] and freedom from discrimination constitutes an element of virtually every major international human rights instrument,[28] such as the *Universal Declaration of Human Rights* (Articles 2 and 7) and the *International Covenant on Economic, Social and Cultural Rights* (Article 2). There is a belief that with greater economic liberalization, specifically with the entry of foreign direct investments, caste disparities and gender inequality will decline. This expectation is related, *inter alia,* to the anticipation that foreign agents are less likely to share local prejudices. Deshpande concludes that such an expectation is not supported by Indian data. These findings are significant for India (and other developing countries) and indicate that economic liberalization measures are not sufficient to eradicate intergroup or gender discrimination, and that effective programs undertaken by public institutions are vital to counter such prejudices.

Chapter 7: Climate Change Mitigation: The Indian Conundrum, by Milind Kandlikar and Simon Harding

This chapter sheds light on the complex interactions between climate change, human rights, and economic development. Recent studies and reports have highlighted the negative impacts of climate change on human health and human rights, such as diminished health and access to food, water, and shelter. Low-income countries and people belonging to weaker groups are particularly vulnerable to such adverse environmental and health effects (e.g., poor people, members of minority groups, women, children, and seniors).[29] The authors emphasize the multifaceted interrelationships between climate change reduction measures and economic development in India. On the one hand, in order to lift hundreds of millions out of poverty, the Indian economy needs carbon space to grow; on the other, it is overwhelmingly in India's interest to keep carbon emission paths low (under the 2°C benchmark): one-fifth of the world's poorest people live in India and they form the largest group of individuals vulnerable to climate change within a single nation. Facing this conundrum, the chapter highlights the idea of "co-benefits" as a policy emphasis in India's carbon mitigation efforts. It uses the case of indoor air pollution in rural India to examine how development-oriented policies can have significant benefits for climate mitigation.

Conclusion, by Moshe Hirsch, Ashok Kotwal, and Bharat Ramaswami
This chapter briefly recaps some prominent conclusions drawn from the preceding chapters and emphasizes that implementation deficiencies identified in those chapters are related to some limitations of the rights-based approach to development in general, which, in turn, is related to the institutional weakness of the country. An active judiciary, civil society groups, and a free press are essential for promoting the human rights based approach to development because they may pressure state officials to initiate poverty reduction programs and occasionally supervise their implementation. However, these significant actors do not possess the required resources, such as expertise and capital, to administer large-scale programs, particularly given the vastness and diversity of India. Thus, while these actors are valuable for promoting the socio-economic rights of poor people, they cannot substitute for weak institutions. Finally, this chapter offers some policy recommendations to Canadian policy makers regarding productive dialogue between the two countries and certain joint strategies to enhance human rights based approaches to economic development in India. These recommendations relate to common democratic values, implementation of local legislative measures, support for local actors, joint consultative networks, monitoring and dissemination of information, training programs, and initiatives in multilateral economic institutions.

NOTES

1 Due to a change in the official definition of the poverty line, it is not possible to construct a consistent time series. However, using overlapping periods, it is possible to ascertain trends. We use the findings in Kotwal, Ramaswami, and Wadhwa 2011 and Narayan and Murgai 2016.

2 On the right to development, see Bunn 2000; Vandenbogaerde 2013; Marong 2010; de Feyter 2013; OHCHR 2013; Felice 2009; Kirchmeier 2006; Bedjaoui 2011; OHCHR 2010.

3 *Declaration on the Right to Development,* GA Res. 41/128, UNGAOR (4 December 1986) (adopted by 146 votes to 1, with 8 abstentions).

4 See, e.g., *Vienna Declaration and Programme of Action,* World Conference on Human Rights (Vienna, 25 June 1993), arts. 10–11, 73; http://www.ohchr.org/EN/ProfessionalInterest/Pages/Vienna.aspx; *The Right to Development,* CHR Res. 1999/79, UNCHR, UN Doc. E/CN.4/RES/1999/79 (28 April 1999).

5 See, e.g., *The Right to Development,* art. 3. See also *Declaration on the Right to Development,* art. 2(1).

6 For an analysis of the early evolution of the right to development and the historical background of developing the NIEO, see, e.g., Whelan 2015. See also Donnelly 1985 and Bunn 2000, 1430–32.

7 See *Declaration on the Right to Development,* preamble and art. 3(3).

8 See, e.g., ibid., preamble and art. 5 (concerning non-interference in internal affairs and self-determination).

9 See, e.g., *The Right to Development,* art. 3.

10 See, e.g., *Declaration on the Right to Development,* art. 6; and *The Right to Development,* art. 4.

11 See, e.g., *The Right to Development,* art. 4(f).

12 See, e.g., *Declaration on the Right to Development,* art. 8(1). On the importance of eradicating poverty, see *Millennium Declaration,* GA Res. 55/2, UNGAOR (8 September 2000), art. 11.

13 On the holistic vision that underlies the right to development, see, e.g., *The Right to Development,* preamble.

14 See, e.g., ibid., art. 6; *Declaration on the Right to Development,* arts. 6 and 9.

15 See, e.g., *Declaration on the Right to Development,* art. 10; *The Right to Development,* preamble. See also *Millennium Declaration,* art. 6.

16 *Declaration on the Right to Development,* arts. 3 and 8(1).

17 Ibid., arts. 3(3) and 4(2).

18 Ibid., art. 3.

19 *The Right to Development,* art. 7.

20 On the reforms to be adopted by the WTO, see Howse 2013. See also WTO, *Submission in Follow-up to HRC Resolution 15/25 "The Right to Development,"* http://www.ohchr.org/Documents/Issues/Development/Session12/WTO.pdf.

21 *Universal Declaration of Human Rights,* GA Res. 217(III), UNGAOR, UN Doc. A/810 (1948), art. 25. On the right to food, see also CESCR, "General Comment 12: The right to adequate food (art. 11)," UN Doc. E/C.12/1999/5 (12 May 1999); Mechlem 2008.

22 *International Covenant on Economic, Social and Cultural Rights,* New York, 16 December 1966, 993 U.N.T.S. 3 (entered into force 3 January 1976), art. 11 [ICESCR].

23 See *Declaration on the Right to Development,* art. 8(1).

24 On the right to work in international law, see Nußberger 2007.

25 On the right to health under international law, see also Riedel 2011; and CESCR, "General Comment 14: The right to the highest attainable standard of health," UN Doc. E/C.12/2000/4 (11 August 2000).

26 See the *Convention on the Rights of the Child,* 20 November 1989, 1577 U.N.T.S. 3 (entered into force 2 September 1990), art. 23.

27 See, e.g., *Declaration on the Right to Development,* arts. 5 and 6.

28 On the importance of these rights in international human rights law, see, e.g., van Boven 2007; Chinkin 2010.

29 See Levy and Patz 2015; UN Human Rights Office of the High Commissioner, "Understanding Human Rights and Climate Change," 2015; http://www.ohchr.org/Documents/Issues/ClimateChange/COP21.pdf.

1

India's *National Food Security Act* and the WTO *Agreement on Agriculture*

MILIND MURUGKAR

The United Progressive Alliance (UPA) government that was in power in India from 2004 to 2014 ushered in a series of rights-based legislation aimed at empowering the common citizen. The first act promulgated was that of Right to Information, the second guaranteed a minimum income to poor families in rural India through public works programs, and the third ensured a right to education. On 12 September 2013, the Indian parliament passed the fourth act in this series, the *National Food Security Act* (NFSA). This act guarantees a certain quantity of food grains at highly subsidized rates to nearly two-thirds of India's population – the largest experiment ever conducted by any government in the world for distributing subsidized food through a rights-based approach.

In this chapter, we analyze the dyad of food security and free markets in light of India's commitment to the World Trade Organization (WTO) regime. We show that while the primary aim of the NFSA – to provide food security to the common citizen – is not at odds with the WTO regime, conflicts do arise because of the chosen methods of delivering food subsidies. We then show how moving to a system of cash transfers from a system of highly subsidized grains will mitigate this conflict and help India both achieve its food security goals and fulfill its commitment to the WTO.

The NFSA drew international attention when the director general of the WTO, Roberto Azevêdo, hinted on 25 June 2014 that India might opt for a short-term solution of a "peace clause," which is a provision in the WTO *Agreement on Agriculture*. The peace clause provides temporary protection to any country if its policy is at odds with its commitment to the WTO. In particular, it prevents any member country from challenging the relevant policy of the concerned country for a certain period. The context of the director general's remark was that the NFSA was widely believed to contravene the WTO's limit on domestic support to Indian farmers.[1] Azevêdo later attended a ministerial conference at Bali that was expected to put on track the decade-long derailed process of liberalization of trade in agricultural commodities and build consensus on the WTO's Trade Facilitation Agreement (TFA).

Earlier at the WTO headquarters in Geneva, the US WTO ambassador, Michael Punke, had criticized India's proposal on food security.[2] He alleged that India's policy of offering ever-increasing price support to select cereals led to overproduction, to which the Indian government responded by stocking and dumping in the international market, occasionally harming the interests of not only foreign but also Indian producers who do not receive support. The US ambassador cited some newspaper reports as evidence of such trade distortions by India's food grain exports in the recent past. Some Indian commentators also attacked the government for bringing in a policy that was completely at odds with India's commitment to the WTO (Sukumar 2013).

The issue of India's food grain stockpiling remained the most contentious one at the 9th and 10th Ministerial Conferences of the WTO held in Bali and Nairobi, respectively. In 2013, the Bali Ministerial Decision responded to India's concerns over its freedom to stockpile. Under the ministerial decision, developing countries were allowed to continue food-stockpiling programs, which were otherwise at risk of breaching the WTO's domestic subsidy cap, until a permanent solution was found by the 11th Ministerial Conference in 2017.[3] During talks on the TFA in Geneva in July 2014, India refused to sign the agreement, citing the "slow" progress on finding permanent solutions to the public stockholding as agreed in the Bali Ministerial. However, the 10th Ministerial in Nairobi reaffirmed the decision of the Bali Ministerial about the issue of public stockholding.[4] It is now certain that India's freedom to provide output subsidies to its grain producers through minimum support prices (MSP) would be greatly curtailed if it must live up to the WTO commitment.

The relevant point that needs to be stressed in this context is that the primary aim of the NFSA, to provide food security to the common citizen, is not at odds with the WTO regime. The regime is concerned with facilitating free trade, and the restrictions under that, which aim to end policies that distort trade. However, it does not impose restrictions on any consumption subsidy that a government might provide to its citizens. The conflict between the NFSA and the WTO stems from the fact that the Indian government procures food grains from farmers under a price support regime. It procures food at a minimum support price (MSP) and distributes it to consumers at a subsidized price. It is the producer subsidy that is under scrutiny from the WTO.

The rest of this chapter discusses the *Agreement on Agriculture* and India's commitment under it; provides an overview of the NFSA; discusses the conflict between India's food security regime and its commitment under the WTO; and discusses the role of cash transfers in mitigating such conflict.

The WTO *Agreement on Agriculture*

The *Agreement on Agriculture* came into existence in 1995. It was a result of prolonged negotiations to liberalize international trade in agricultural commodities. It was the first worldwide endeavour to address agricultural trade issues. The agreement aims to lower barriers to international trade in agricultural commodities. The targeted restrictions are related to market access, trade-distorting domestic subsidies, and export subsidies.

The measures under market access entail the conversion of all quantitative restrictions into equivalent tariffs, followed by their progressive reduction. Domestic support was categorized as trade distorting and non–trade-distorting or minimally trade distorting. Trade-distorting support includes payments to farmers by the national governments through price support. This is because with such subsidies, farmers can afford to produce products in which they are not competitive relative to their counterparts in other countries. The principle of free trade demands that, under such circumstances, the products be imported and domestic producers switch to producing goods in which they are more competitive. It was envisaged that WTO member countries would progressively reduce such subsidies.

The *Agreement on Agriculture* also demands phased reduction of export subsidies. It grouped all these measures into amber boxes, blue boxes, and green boxes. Amber boxes comprised subsidies that distort trade and production and that should be subject to progressive reduction. Examples of such subsidies are price supports and other supports that influence the quantity of production. Supports that require farmers to limit their production are placed in the blue boxes. Subsidies in the green boxes are those that do not distort trade, or that cause minimal distortion; they must not include price supports and have to be directly funded by the government.

India did not have to make any commitment to reduce these three types of support when the agreement was signed in 1995. Regarding market access, India claimed exemption from reduction, citing a balance of payments situation. Later, after improvement in its balance of payments, India accepted a ceiling on tariffs, but in almost all cases, its applied tariffs were much lower than their bound levels. India was not required to make reduction commitments, as it did not offer any export subsidies that were not allowed during the implementation period of the agreement.

Finally, in the context of domestic support, India's policy of providing price supports in the form of MSPs and input subsidies came under the purview of the agreement. However, during the base period of the agreement, from 1986 to 1990, India's product-specific and non–product-specific domestic support was well below the bound level of 10 percent of the production value. Thus, India was not required to make any reduction commitment and, barring a few small changes, it did not have to change its domestic policies. It was only in the recent past, just before the Bali Ministerial, that India's domestic policy emerged as a contentious international issue. This was also the period when India debated the NFSA, which later became the focal point of international discourse as it was thought to magnify the distortion in the international food grain trade.

The *National Food Security Act*

The NFSA includes many measures to tackle the issue of malnutrition by making nutritious food more affordable. It includes initiatives such as offering midday meals in schools, running *anganwadis* (i.e., shelters providing supplementary food for six-month- to six-year-old children) to combat child malnutrition, providing financial assistance to pregnant and lactating mothers, and distributing subsidized food through the Public Distribution System (PDS).

The PDS, a vestige of the rationing system from the Second World War, is the current vehicle for delivering food subsidies in India. The Food Corporation of India (FCI), set up in 1965 as a government agency to procure food grains, is responsible for procuring food grains for state governments for ultimate distribution to consumers through select retail outlets known as "fair price shops." For a while, PDS coverage was universal, but between 1997 and the enactment of the NFSA, the PDS targeted categories of households labelled "Above Poverty Line" (APL), "Below Poverty Line" (BPL), and "Poorest of the Poor" (POP). Eligible beneficiaries received 35 kilograms of food grains at subsidized rates, with the lowest level of subsidy going to APL households and the highest to POP households. Distribution of food depended on the availability of grains with the FCI. While the supply of grain to the POP and the BPL categories was a firm commitment, supply to the APL category was contingent on available supplies.

This targeting system had disastrous consequences for the poor due to several administrative and local political factors. A major absurdity lay in the method of identifying the poor. The number of poor in a state in India is fixed based on estimates from sample surveys, while the number of poor who are entitled to subsidized food is determined by door-to-door identification. Since the latter is much larger than the former, many of the identified poor are excluded from coverage – they are simply not on the list. In addition, a sizable proportion of the eligible poor did not participate in the program for reasons such as a lack of cash to purchase the monthly rations all at once. According to Jha and Ramaswami (2012), only about 30 percent of the poor (in 2004 and 2005) derived some benefit from the PDS.

The NFSA has attempted to address this issue by expanding the coverage of the PDS. Now there are only two categories of beneficiaries: "Priority" households and the Poorest of the Poor (POP) households. Priority households are entitled to 5 kilograms of food grains per person per month, and POP households are entitled to 35 kilograms per household per month. The combined coverage of these two categories comprises 75 percent of the rural and 50 percent of the urban population. Rice, wheat, and millet are supplied through the PDS at three, two, and one rupee per kilogram, respectively. The prices are to be revised after three years. To support these entitlements, the government would procure and distribute about 62 metric tonnes of food grains annually. This is about 30 percent of the total food grain production of the country.

The PDS, now backed by the NFSA, involves stocking of the food grains procured from the farmers at the minimum support prices and their distribution to the poor. Issues of the compatibility of the NFSA with India's WTO commitment seem relevant at all these stages. To ensure the food security of its poor people, the measures undertaken by the WTO member states fall under the green box provision, but this comes with important caveats; the guiding principle is that such measures must not end up being protectionist and trade distorting.

NFSA and the *Agreement on Agriculture:* Areas of Contention

Calculating Aggregate Measure of Support (AMS)

The PDS plays a dual role of ensuring price supports for farmers and supplying subsidized food to the poor. The *Agreement on Agriculture* places no limit on the subsidy to consumers, but it has bound the price support offered to farmers. This issue falls within the amber box as it distorts international trade, according to the WTO.

The *Agreement on Agriculture* requires that food grains be procured at market price. The related requirement is that the procurement policy should not be protectionist: that is, the prices offered should not be more than a commodity's world price, which is a predetermined external reference price (ERP).

The measure of domestic support offered through procurement is known as the aggregate measure of support (AMS). The AMS is the difference between the government support price and the fixed ERP multiplied by the total quantity of agricultural products eligible for support. For a developing country like India, the allowable limit for the AMS, also known as the *de minimis* support, is 10 percent of the value of agricultural production. The value of production is assessed at the administered prices, that is, the prices at which the government has committed to procuring the grain. This cap also applies to individual agricultural products and is measured by the product-specific AMS.

The limit on product-specific AMS has important implications for India because even though the government declares minimum support prices for many agricultural commodities, their effectiveness, and hence procurement, is concentrated mainly on two commodities: wheat and rice. These are the principal cereals supplied through the PDS. Thus, for India, along with the challenge of staying within the bounds of total AMS, the daunting challenge is that of honouring the limit for wheat and rice.

The rule limiting the AMS for each product is applicable only to countries, such as India, that had no reduction commitment on total AMS during the base period of 1986–88. Developed countries, however, were above the *de minimis* level and committed themselves to reduce it in a phased manner. Still, they were exempted from capping their product-specific support. Thus, in principle, such countries can concentrate their support on a few select commodities and still stay within the limit of the non–product-specific support. This room for manoeuvre is non-existent for developing countries like India.

Another important issue in the methodology for the AMS is the use of a fixed ERP. The ERP is based on international prices prevailing during 1986–88. There is no economic logic in comparing the current state intervention prices with the international prices prevailing during that period. This methodology hugely overestimates India's support for wheat and rice as international prices during the base period were much lower than those at present.

A related issue is that Article I(h)(ii) of the *Agreement on Agriculture* demands that the methodology for calculating current domestic support should be that used in the base period notification.[5] As it happened, India denominated the ERP in terms of rupees (INR) in its base period notification. However, during later notifications, the fixed ERP was denominated in terms of US dollars. This does not conform to the requirements of the *Agreement on Agriculture* and has since become a controversial issue in the WTO. Canada, for example, has demanded that India should "resubmit its data using Indian rupees, as per its constituent data and methodology."[6]

Narayanan (2014) calculates the levels of price support for rice and wheat by the Indian government under different regimes. She shows that if we follow the Indian government's method of calculating price support based on fixed ERP in terms of US dollars, India's AMS for wheat and rice during the base period was negative until 2007–08. Since 2008–09, however, the price support for rice has turned positive but remains below the 10 percent level. The AMS for wheat remains negative. However, if the AMS for wheat and rice is estimated strictly in accordance with the *Agreement on Agriculture* rule – that is, considering a fixed ERP in terms of rupees – the domestic support for these crops has violated the WTO's limits several times in the past. The product-specific support for rice and wheat breached the 10 percent limit in 1999–2000 and has been increasing since then (Narayanan 2014).

The *Agreement on Agriculture* provides scope for accommodating the effect of inflation on domestic support. Part XI of Article 18 of the agreement mentions the scope for the review of the implementation of the commitments made by the members. The fourth clause under this article states that "in the review process, Members shall give due consideration to the influence of excessive rates of inflation on the ability of any Member to abide by its domestic support commitments." However, the interpretation of "due consideration" is ambiguous. The United States and other countries say that member countries cannot automatically get the benefit of inflation, and that the committee on agriculture must determine what such "due consideration" should mean.

Some economists have estimated domestic support for rice and wheat by factoring in the inflation rate and by considering the moving ERP instead of the fixed ERP. Computations by these methods show that India's domestic support for these food grains was negative during most of the period from 1995 to 2013 (Narayanan 2014).

The key question at this moment is to what extent India might succeed in modifying the method of estimating the AMS. Shifting to moving ERP from fixed ERP might be too radical a change. The implications of such change for other countries are not clear, and such a shift may amount to opening the entire agreement for new negotiations.

Public Stocking of Food Grains

Public stocking of food grains for food security of the poor is allowed under the *Agreement on Agriculture* and falls under green box measures that do not require reduction commitments. Annex 2 of the agreement gives the basis for exempting domestic support from the reduction commitments. Clause 3 of the annex states that the "expenditures (or revenue forgone) in relation to the accumulation and holding of stocks of products which form an integral part of a food security program identified in national legislation" are to be exempted from the reduction commitments. This may include government aid to private storage of products as part of such a program. The fourth clause of the same annex, about food aid, exempts "expenditures (or revenue forgone) in relation to the provision of domestic food aid to sections of the population in need."

These clauses are clear enough to exempt the cost of public stocking for the NFSA from any reduction commitment. However, there are certain important caveats. For example, Clause 3 of Annex 2 also requires that "food purchases by the government shall be made at current market prices." This clause also requires that the "sales from the food security stocks shall be made at no less than the current domestic market price for the product and quality in question." This clearly sets the limit on the procurement of food. This is important because India's present system of food security also incorporates the aim of providing price support to farmers; thus, even if the food is procured for security purposes, the expenditure for procurement will be exempted from the reduction commitment only if the purchase is at market price. The sale from the food security stocks also should be at market price. This puts restrictions on the open market sales of these stocks and has implications for India's policy of public stocking.

There is one more important caveat regarding the above exemption. Clause 3 in Annex 2 also states that "the volume and accumulation of such stocks shall correspond to predetermined targets related solely to food security. The process of stock accumulation and disposal shall be financially transparent." As far as transparency is concerned, it must be noted that India has been regularly reporting its food stocks and relevant maintenance expenditures to the WTO since the agreement in 1995. However, the part of Clause 3 mentioned above demands that, to be included in the green box, the accumulation of the stock must correspond to predetermined targets related solely to food security. This requirement can be at odds with India's food policy, as India has been procuring much more than that needed to meet the PDS requirement. If the government procures just enough to meet the PDS requirement, there would be no stockpiling, but since 1989 procurement has exceeded PDS sales every year (Jha and Ramaswami 2012).

This raises the question of whether there is some relationship between the PDS requirement and the level of stockpiling that may pose a threat to the stability of international markets and be a drain on the exchequer. This relationship is rather complex. One may ask why the Indian government procures grain far in excess of the PDS requirement. Through the FCI, the government is obliged to buy all the grain that anyone wants to sell at the preannounced support price. After the harvest, the government and private traders are in the market for procuring grain; as long as government operations continue, the support price is the market price. A trader's margins come from the difference between expected future prices and the support price. When the government maintains large stocks, future prices are unpredictable. This is because the government can offload the stocks and prices can collapse. The effect is similar to that when the government restricts exports or restricts the activities of private traders.

As a result, private traders withdraw from the market when stocks held by the government build up. The government does not have the option to withdraw as it is bound to purchase all that is offered for sale at the support price. The result is that government procurement (and stocks) increase even more than they would have otherwise, particularly if the initial level of stocks was low (Balakrishnan and Ramaswami 1995).

Table 1.1 shows how the support price and the procurement of wheat have moved over the last decade. From 2001 to 2007, the support price increased by 20 percent, before things changed dramatically. The support price increased by 21 percent in 2007-08 alone and by another 18 percent

TABLE 1.1

Support prices and procurement, from 2001–02 to 2010–11

Year	MSP (INR/quintal)	Amount of procurement (million tons)
2001–02	580	20.6
2002–03	610	19.0
2003–04	630	15.8
2004–05	630	16.7
2005–06	640	14.7
2006–07	700	9.2
2007–08	850	11.1
2008–09	1,000	22.6
2009–10	1,080	25.3
2010–11	1,100	22.5

Source: Food Corporation of India, http://fciweb.nic.in.

the following year. This is the period during which world food prices peaked. India responded by closing off exports to world markets and by hiking support prices so that it could procure enough to maintain supply to the PDS.

Some observers have maintained that the sharp hikes in support prices were populist policies aimed at garnering support from the farmer lobby for the parliamentary election in 2009. Generally, farmer lobbies do succeed in influencing the support price policy, but they are not the only factor. After all, the movement in support prices during the first half of the 2000s was modest despite there being parliamentary elections. The explanation also does not accord with the export bans and the imports of wheat during the 2000s at prices higher than those granted to domestic producers.

A more consistent explanation is the government's overriding commitment to the PDS, which, in turn, derives from the perception that a failure here would have significant electoral costs. Due to this immense paranoia at the top, nobody is held responsible for excessive stocks. Predictably, the errors are in one direction only.

What is surprising is that this situation has continued until now. Why has the government not undertaken open market sales to bring the price down, especially during this period of inflation? One plausible explanation is that the government machinery is simply not set up to sell the excess inventory on the open market. To do so, the Food Corporation of India would have to receive permission from the Ministry of Food as well as the Ministry of Finance, especially if they had to sell below their economic costs, which would have created a nominal loss. In other words, although price stabilization has been one of their primary objectives, there are no streamlined administrative procedures to sell in a timely manner to achieve it. Over the years, the FCI has been quick to buy but unable to divest itself systematically of unwanted stocks, thus leading to high stock levels.

A Promising Option of Cash Transfers

Some staunch supporters of the NFSA have recommended that subsidies could be delivered in the form of cash transfers rather than in-kind support (Kotwal, Murugkar, and Ramaswami 2011), an idea that has gained political traction in India. While such subsidies are compliant with WTO limits, support for the idea is largely due to the potential of cash transfers in stopping large-scale corruption in the PDS.

Cash Transfers and the *Agreement on Agriculture*

The unique feature of cash transfers lies in their ability to clearly distinguish subsidies to consumers from those to producers. This is important because the WTO imposes no limit on the subsidy to consumers; its aim is to minimize the producer's trade-distorting subsidies. If the government procured the grains at open market prices and distributed it to consumers at the subsidized price, the WTO would not be concerned because it would be considered a subsidy to the consumers. However, India's unique food subsidy system blurs this distinction.

The term "food subsidy bill" gives the impression that the amount represents the food subsidy to consumers, but in fact it includes the subsidy to farmers as well. In principle, the subsidy to consumers is the difference between the price at which consumers would have to buy the grain from the open market and the price through the PDS. By the same logic, the subsidy to the farmers would be the difference between the price at which the farmers sell their produce to the government and the price had there been no government intervention. However, since the government is the biggest procuring agency in India, the open market is always distorted, leading to opaqueness in the system. It is also impossible to determine whether farmers are subsidized at the cost of consumers or at their own cost. This is because the huge stockpiling of grains is also associated with frequent bans on the export of grains, which is done to curb inflation in the open market.

However, if consumers are given a subsidy in the form of cash, it will bring about much-needed transparency, which can pave way for reforms and lead the system to efficiency. Cash transfers are perfectly compatible with the WTO because they are subsidies to consumers and do not distort trade. They raise the purchasing power of the consumers without giving any undue advantage to domestic producers. Of course, this assumes that border protections in any form are removed. This is also a requirement of the *Agreement on Agriculture.*

Cash Transfers and Farmers

The option of cash transfers itself does not get rid of the stockpiling problem because the government will still face pressure from the farmers to raise the MSP to levels where the government ends up becoming the main buyer of food grains, driving out private traders as it does today. However, cash transfers help in creating a political space to withstand the pressure from the farm lobby as the government would be under no compulsion to buy food grains for public distribution.

This does not eliminate the necessity of a price floor for farmers. In the absence of any insurance mechanism, in countries like India small farmers will not be able to withstand the vagaries of the international market. Thus, a price floor is essential in the Indian context to provide protection. The original idea of the MSP was precisely this.

Cash transfers can also address the issue of inequitable distribution of resources among farmers. In a system with in-kind transfers, the government needs to engage in procurement, storage, and distribution. Naturally, it is logistically convenient to procure grains in two or three large-surplus states before distributing it. The farmers in these surplus states are generally well-off and receive the benefit of government-assured support prices. They also benefit from the irrigation facilities and subsidies on fertilizer and electricity.

However, a large majority of the farming community toils in rain-fed agriculture. Deprived of irrigation facilities, their consumption of fertilizer is minuscule and they do not consume electricity; thus, the benefits of the subsidy are negligible to them. There is, therefore, a need to correct this policy imbalance by shifting resources that are locked in the support prices for wheat and rice to the creation of irrigation facilities and research for dry-land agriculture. This might not be to the disadvantage of the wheat and rice growers in the long run as they would be encouraged to diversify toward high-value crops such as vegetables and pulses, the inflation of which has been a burning issue in India for quite some time now.

A long-term alternative to price supports to producers could be cash transfers that are delinked from the quantity and type of production. Such support would face no WTO constraints as it would not stimulate any type or quantity of produce. The choice of crop under such a system would be made based on price signals offered by the market. The strongest opposition to such WTO-compatible, market-oriented reforms would likely come from farmers, however.

Cash Transfers and Farm Lobbies

The farm lobbies, especially in the Green Revolution Belt, have always pressured the government for higher MSPs. The growth in political clout of these lobbies can be traced to the Green Revolution of the mid-sixties. The goal of the Green Revolution was to attain self-sufficiency in food grain production, which entailed policies that encouraged farmers to use costly but highly productive inputs. For a long time, price control policies through export bans (particularly bans on interstate movement of grains by private traders) also went hand-in-hand with the MSP. However, the emergence of the farmers' movement since the late seventies has pressured the government to raise the MSPs.

Although it was supposed to provide a price floor for grain producers who had no other protection from the vagaries of the market, over time the support prices were converted into procurement prices, with the government emerging as the largest procurement agency in the market. In fact, the government is the only wheat procurement agency in Punjab. The huge stock of food grains that the FCI has been carrying for many years is also partial testimony to the clout of the farm lobbies.

In the recent past, the government has expanded its procurement operations beyond the states of Punjab and Haryana, the traditional Green Revolution states. Now, the government procures grains from Chhattisgarh, Madhya Pradesh, Orissa, and Andhra Pradesh; thus, many farmers have high stakes in higher MSPs.

The significance of the farmers' political power in Madhya Pradesh and Chhattisgarh, the states where procurement has spread in recent times, can be gauged by the "bonus" amount that has been offered to farmers. The bonus is the procurement price the state government offers in excess of what is offered by the central government. This measure is considered one of the main reasons behind the success of the incumbent state governments in the last two consecutive elections. The new central government (which belongs to the same party as the Madhya Pradesh and Chhattisgarh governments) has taken measures to stop this practice of incentivizing grain production, but the opposition has attacked this reversal by calling it an anti-farmer move.

The politically sensitive nature of the issue of procurement prices can be judged by the fact that the present prime minister of India, Narendra Modi, promised farmers MSPs that would ensure 50 percent profit margins. This promise was made during the 2014 federal election campaign, and the opposition frequently attacks the government for failing to deliver even after four and a half years in power. On the eve of his first year in power, the prime minister claimed credit for safeguarding the interest of farmers in the WTO, by which he meant the government's freedom to offer higher procurement prices. The fact, however, is that there is now no escape from following WTO-compatible reforms that involve moving away from support through market intervention.

Feasibility of Cash Transfers

The discussion of cash transfers, then, raises two more questions: How can cash be transferred? Does a poor country have the systems to implement it?

A cash transfer system is constructed on two pillars: a payment system to distribute the cash and an authentication system to verify the intended beneficiary. Conventional payment systems are brick-and-mortar banks and post offices. Such infrastructure is not properly developed in the poor, remote areas of low-income countries, posing a barrier to the use of cash transfers. However, the digitization of financial systems and the use of the internet and mobile devices have broken through this impasse. For example, Africa leads the world in the use of mobile phones to transfer cash. This has enabled urban migrants to remit money to their families who still live in rural areas.

Effectively, any retailer is a potential point for banking transactions. In India, cash payments in welfare programs (such as those arising from pension and public works) have typically been delivered by post offices. This introduces potential problems with the intermediaries, resulting in both delays and losses. Policies now emphasize the need for direct transfers to the savings accounts of beneficiaries in banks and post offices, a method possible only because of digitization. However, this still does not address the issue of last-mile connectivity.

An emerging model here is the use of intermediaries between the banks (situated in towns and larger habitations) and the beneficiaries (residents in villages). These intermediaries, called banking correspondents, provide withdrawal and deposit services with the help of internet-enabled portable devices that record these transactions in real time using internet connectivity provided through the usual mobile phone networks. These authentication systems require identity verification from the beneficiary, which can be done through a user-supplied numeric code or password in a digital system. More secure systems rely on biometric identification, a system that is supported by a nationwide project in India that stores biometric data of individuals in the country. Although this requires investment in biometric scanners, this technology is easily built into the portable, internet-enabled devices used for recording transactions. Until a decade ago, the feasibility of cash transfers was restricted to areas with a high density of payment systems such as the big cities, but this is no longer true.

What about corruption? One can ask whether cash can be siphoned off just as easily as grain. Indeed, these two questions are related because for cash transfers to be able to reduce corruption, they need to be a part of a well-functioning system. New technologies that enable secure biometric identification and permit access to bank accounts through cellphone networks hold great promise. Any potential beneficiary will then be able to have a bank account in which the due amount can be directly deposited, bypassing the local bureaucracy that is often responsible for siphoning off the money.

Is it conceivable that a system can create and maintain a data bank for over 1.2 billion people and use it without significant errors? This is a reasonable question, and all we can hope for is that there will be many pilot projects and experiments to test the system. The best possible scenario is one where states can experiment with different systems, including cash transfers, reformed in-kind transfers, or hybrid models such as using cash transfers in cities and in-kind transfers in financially underdeveloped regions. Through them, we will learn more about the strengths and weaknesses of various ways to deliver food subsidies, and propagate the most effective ways across the country.

Conclusion

Never since it signed the *Agreement on Agriculture* in 1994 has India been under so much pressure from the WTO to reform its domestic support policy. India's tough stand in the recent WTO ministerial conference and subsequent negotiations has given it the freedom to continue with its present price support policy until a permanent solution to measuring the domestic support is found. However, this freedom appears illusory when we consider the fact that WTO rules prevent the offloading of public stocks of grains in the international market. India's exports have since come under closer scrutiny by the WTO.

In this chapter, we have analyzed the dyad of trade and food security. Following the enactment of the NFSA, the Indian government faces the steep challenge of honouring the right to food security for 67 percent of the

Indian population. However, India's commitment to food security is not in conflict with the WTO regime per se. If the government chooses to replace in-kind transfers with cash transfers, it can avoid transgressing WTO rules and thus achieve coordinated compliance. Diverting the resources from support achieved through market intervention to one that creates infrastructure for agriculture will also address the issue of equity. It can also encourage farmers in the Green Revolution states to pursue much-needed diversification of production. Moving to a system of cash transfers will also reduce the colossal waste of national resources through reduced corruption and improvements in subsidy delivery mechanisms. The technological platform created through unique identification systems is emerging as a promising option for implementing such a move. However, balancing the interests of the farm lobbies and the WTO rules is a formidable political task, one that will require skillful political management by the regime in Delhi.

NOTES

1 https://www.thehindubusinessline.com/economy/india-may-settle-for-compromise-solution-to-food-security-issue-at-wto/article23104251.ece.

2 https://ustr.gov/about-us/policy-offices/press-office/speeches/transcripts/2013/april/amb-punke-statement-wto-tnc.

3 "Bali Ministerial Declaration," WTO document WT/MIN(13)/DEC.

4 "Export Competition," WTO document WT/MIN(15)/45.

5 This can be found in the WTO document G/AG/AG/IND, "Notification," available on the WTO website.

6 The details are available in the WTO document G/AG/W/87, "Points Raised by the Members under the Review Process," available on the WTO website.

2

Primary Education in India
Evidence and Practice

ASHOK KOTWAL, BHARAT RAMASWAMI,
and WILIMA WADHWA

In the last two and a half decades, India has been one of the fastest growing economies in the world. The opening up of the economy after the 1991 reforms enabled businesses to take advantage of the growing global demand for high-tech services; to a large extent, Indian economic growth has been led by the service sector. Exports of highly skill-intensive services have sustained the trade balance since the opening up of the economy. With demand for skilled workers growing, a potential talent crunch could stall the growth process. A shortage of skilled workers might lead to a drop in exports, which would adversely affect India's current account balances, possibly inducing the country to violate WTO agreements and pursue more protectionist policies. Therefore, investment in quality human capital becomes imperative.

The *Right of Children to Free and Compulsory Education Act,* also known as the *Right to Education Act* (RTE), came into effect in 2010 and guarantees enrolment to all children between six and fourteen years old; however, it says nothing about what we expect children to learn in schools. In fact, all the evidence on learning outcomes indicates that children are far below grade competency.

At the same time, there are great hopes that the economy will reap the so-called demographic dividend. The proportion of the Indian population in the age group of 15–59 has been rising steadily, from 53.3 percent in 1961 to 57.8 percent in 2001. Projections for the next thirty years put the working-age population at almost 65 percent of the total population by 2040 (Aiyar and Mody 2011). The United Nations (2009) estimates that in the next thirty years India will gain about 300 million workers, making it the largest contributor to the global workforce. This population bulge can translate into growth through two channels. First, since young workers produce more than they consume, this can lead to generation of savings and accumulation of physical capital. Second, as human capital accumulates, the supply of skilled workers rises, leading to innovation and technical progress, which further spur growth. However, for the demographic dividend to actually bear fruit, two conditions must be met: 1) the additional labour force is productively employed; and 2) the quality of the labour force is such that it can be productively employed. Both supply and demand have to be in sync to unleash the benefits of the demographic dividend.

On the demand side, while India has been one of the fastest growing economies in the world, this growth has not created high-productivity jobs for the population at large. As Kotwal, Ramaswami, and Wadhwa (2011) conclude, "there are two Indias: one of educated managers and engineers who have been able to take advantage of the opportunities made available through globalization and the other, a huge mass of undereducated people who are making a living in low-productivity jobs in the informal sector, the largest of which is still agriculture."[1]

On the supply side, India is close to the goal of universalizing education. Over 96 percent of children in the age group of 6–14 are enrolled in school.[2] In addition, the *Right to Education Act,* introduced in 2010, will ensure 100 percent enrolment, improved infrastructure in schools, and reasonable pupil-teacher ratios. While government spending on education remains far less than the suggested 6 percent of GDP, the government has been steadily increasing its spending on primary education under its flagship primary education program, Sarva Shiksha Abhiyan (SSA). In 2007, a similar program for the universalization of secondary education, Rashtriya Madhyamik Shiksha Abhiyan (RMSA), was also launched. Both SSA and RMSA focus primarily on providing school inputs and improving access.

To reap the demographic dividend, we need a well-trained and productive labour force, which raises a few questions: How do we measure the quality of the labour force? Do years of schooling adequately capture this quality? Does enrolment translate into learning? While it is important to build skills at all levels, unless the basic foundations of primary education are built for all, additional human capital accumulation is going to be constrained. Therefore, while improving the state of our educational system may not be sufficient for reaping the demographic dividend, it is a necessary first step, particularly since the available evidence on learning outcomes indicates that India is far away from the goal of guaranteeing education for all children.

We review this evidence from two major sources: Pratham's Annual Status of Education Report (ASER) surveys (2005–14) and the Inside Primary Schools study. We then present some of the interventions this evidence has prompted and discuss how successful they have been in improving learning outcomes. Finally, we provide some recommendations for the RTE.

The *Right to Education Act* (RTE)

The focus of the RTE is to ensure that

> every child of the age six to fourteen years shall have a right to free and compulsory education in a neighbourhood school till completion of elementary education.
>
> No child shall be liable to pay any kind of fee or charges or expenses which may prevent him or her from pursuing and completing the elementary education.
>
> Where a child above six years of age has not been admitted in any school or though admitted, could not complete his or her elementary education, then, he or she shall be admitted in a class appropriate to his or her age.[3]

With enrolment levels already as high as 95 percent in most states, the RTE in its current form really addresses the "last mile" problem of enrolling the remaining out-of-school children. The RTE also gives detailed norms for availability of schools and teachers, pupil-teacher ratio (PTR), and infrastructure in schools.

The following are some of the main norms in the RTE with which all schools have to comply:

- Access:
  - Appropriate government/local authorities shall establish, within such areas or limits of neighbourhood as may be prescribed, a school, where

it is not so established, within three years from the commencement of the act.
- For children in classes I–V,[4] a school shall be established within a walking distance of one kilometre of the neighbourhood.
- For children in classes VI–VIII, a school shall be established within a walking distance of three kilometres of the neighbourhood.

- School infrastructure:[5]
  - at least one classroom per teacher
  - office cum-store-cum-headteacher's room
  - barrier-free access
  - separate toilets for girls and boys
  - safe and adequate drinking water facility for all children
  - a kitchen where the midday meal is cooked in the school
  - a playground
  - arrangements for securing the school building with a wall or fence.

- Teacher learning material (TLM):
  - There shall be a library in each school providing newspapers, magazines, and books on all subjects, including storybooks.
  - Play material, games, and sports equipment shall be provided to each class as required.

- Teachers:
  - maintain regularity and punctuality in attending school
  - complete entire curriculum within the specified period of time
  - assess the learning ability of each child and provide additional instruction accordingly
  - hold regular meetings with parents and guardians.

- Pupil-teacher ratio (PTR) in school:
  - up to 60 children for 2 teachers
  - 61–90 children for 3 teachers
  - 91–120 children for 4 teachers
  - 121–200 children for 5 teachers
  - >150 children for 5 teachers + 1 headteacher
  - PTR excluding headteacher shall not exceed 40.[6]

- Learning and evaluation:
  - The child's knowledge, potential, and talent should be built up.
  - Medium of instruction shall, as far as practicable, be the child's mother tongue.
  - No child admitted in a school shall be held back in any class or expelled from school until the completion of elementary education.

While the RTE specifies clear norms for enrolment, access, school infrastructure, teacher appointment, teacher learning materials, and pupil-teacher ratio, it is not that clear in the area of children's learning achievement. Ambiguous phrases like "building up child's knowledge, potential, and talent" and "development of physical and mental abilities to the fullest extent" are used. In many ways, the RTE's norms continue to build on the government's focus on inputs rather than outcomes. This is not to say that inputs are not important – without inputs we cannot have outcomes. However, as far as the educational sector is concerned, the inputs are by and large in place. It is time to shift the focus to outcomes. If the RTE is to be true to its spirit of providing an education to all children, then it has to go beyond simple input norms. It has to specify what the expected outcome of the education process is – that is, what we expect a child to be able to do at the end of five years of schooling. This translation of inputs into outcomes is often taken for granted. The thinking has been that if enough schools are built, teachers appointed, and curriculums framed, then learning will automatically take place. However, unless children and teachers attend school and instruction takes place, learning, however defined, will not take place, no matter how many classrooms, toilets, and playgrounds are built.

Evidence on Learning Outcomes: 2005–14 Annual Status of Education Report

This section uses primary data collected in the Annual Status of Education Report (ASER), the largest annual data collection effort with children in rural India. Since 2005, when it was first introduced, the report has presented annual estimates of enrolment and basic reading and arithmetic learning outcomes for every district in rural India. ASER completed ten years in 2014.

ASER uses a two-stage sample design. In the first stage, 30 villages are selected from each district from the 2001 census village listing using probability proportion to size (PPS). In the second stage, 20 households are sampled randomly in each of the selected villages. All children in the age group of 3–16 in the selected households are surveyed, and children in the age group of 5–16 are tested. This gives a sample size of 600 households and approximately 900–1,200 children per district. At the national level, ASER visits about 16,000 villages, 300,000 households, and 700,000 children each year.

Every year, the core set of questions in ASER regarding schooling status and basic learning levels remains the same; however, a set of new questions are added in order to explore different dimensions of schooling and learning in the elementary stage. In 2006 and 2007, ASER tested reading comprehension for different kinds of readers. ASER 2007 introduced testing in English and asked questions on paid tuition; ASER 2008 had questions on telling time and oral math problems using currency, and incorporated questions on village infrastructure and household assets. Investigators were asked to record whether the village visited had a tarred road leading to it and whether it had a bank, ration shop, and so on. In the sampled households, information on assets (type of house, telephone, television, and so on) was also recorded.

Recent ASERs have brought together elements from previous ASERs. English testing was repeated in 2009, 2012, and 2014; questions on paid tuition and household and village characteristics have been retained since 2009. While some of the information available in ASER, such as enrolment, is available from other sources, it remains the only annual exercise in the public domain to provide data on learning outcomes, which makes it a valuable policy tool.

The instruments used for the ASER survey test language and math skills of children in the age group of 5–16 years. The tools have been extensively used and piloted and provide good estimates for learning levels at the state and district levels (Ramaswami and Wadhwa 2010). Each test takes about five minutes to administer and is done on a one-on-one basis. There are five levels in each of the ASER tests of language and math: the highest level in the language test is reading at the Grade 2 level, while the highest level in math is being able to do a simple division problem, which in most states, is part of the curriculum for Grade 4 or earlier.[7]

ASER tests are floor-level tests in the sense of testing minimum learning standards; the same tests are administered to all children, regardless of which class they are enrolled in. Once a child is at the highest level, the tests do not

TABLE 2.1

Percentage of children who can read a Grade 2–level text

Year	Grade 3	Grade 4	Grade 5
2006	20.02	37.65	53.06
2008	22.34	41.01	56.27
2010	19.58	37.92	53.69
2012	21.80	34.72	46.86
2014	23.62	37.28	48.03

TABLE 2.2

Percentage of children who can do at least subtraction, by grade

Year	Grade 3	Grade 4	Grade 5
2008	38.94	57.38	69.91
2010	36.34	57.65	70.91
2012	26.38	42.33	53.64
2014	25.36	40.25	50.55

tell us what else the child is capable of. Thus, although they are useful for evaluating early reading and math abilities and are able to capture changes in these parameters, they do not capture the full spectrum of variation or progress within each of the competency levels (Vagh 2009).

The availability of ASER data enables us to track trends over time. The ASER tests are designed for children in Grades 1–5. As children in Grades 1 and 2 are too young for testing to be reliable, we examine the learning outcomes for Grades 3 and 5. Three clear trends emerge from ten years of ASER data.

Learning Levels Are Low and Remain Low over Time

In 2005, about half the children enrolled in Grade 5 were unable to read a Grade 2–level text. This number was virtually unchanged in 2014. If anything, there are some signs of decline in basic learning levels since 2010 (Table 2.1). In other words, about half of all children are completing the primary stage of schooling without basic skills like reading. These findings have serious implications for what children will be able to do when they are in upper primary and secondary school. For instance, in 2014, even in

FIGURE 2.1

Percentage of children who can read a Grade 2–level text

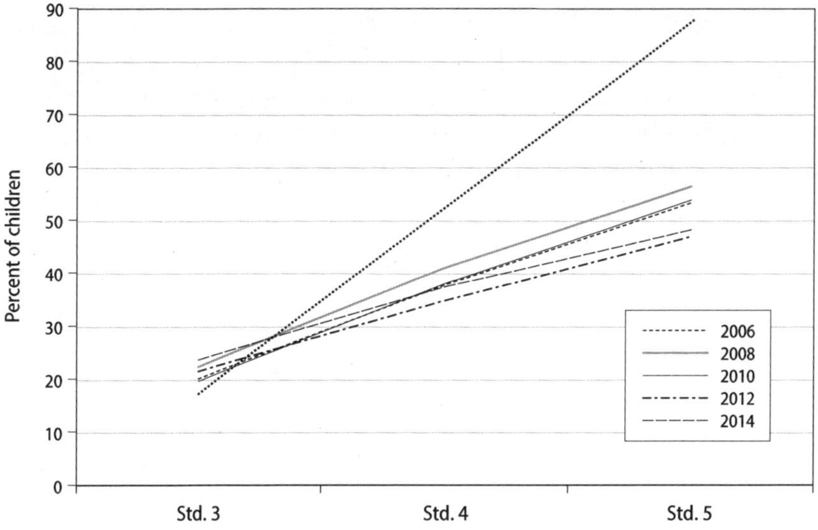

Grade 8, close to 25 percent of children were unable to read a Grade 2–level text. The arithmetic numbers are even more worrying (Table 2.2).

Learning Trajectories Are Flat over Time

Children do learn as they proceed to higher grades, but these learning trajectories are relatively flat over time, as is clear from Figure 2.1. For example, if one of the goals of the school system is to ensure that all children can read a simple text fluently by the time they finish Grade 5, then the learning curve over time needs to be much steeper (as shown by the dotted line). Pritchett and Beatty (2012) have a similar finding. This implies that if a child does not learn some of the basic skills in early years, it is unlikely that he or she will learn them later. Thus, learning delayed is learning denied. This is an issue of concern because it implies that, for the majority of children, each year in school does not lead to much "value added."

Each Successive Cohort Does Worse than the Previous Cohort

Ideally, to measure change in learning outcomes, the same children would be tracked over time. While ASER does not track the same children each year, data from successive years can be used to create artificial cohorts in order to see how successive cohorts are faring as they move through the system. For example, a cohort that was in Grade 3 in 2009 would be in Grade 4 in 2010, and Grade 6 in 2012. The next cohort would be in Grade 3 in 2010 and Grade 6 in 2013, and so on. Table 2.3 presents learning outcomes in arithmetic of three such cohorts over time. Of the first cohort – those who were Grade 3 in 2009 – 39.1 percent could do subtraction, compared with 36.4 percent of the next cohort, which was in Grade 3 in 2010. Of the children who entered Grade 3 in 2011, about 30 percent could do the same kind of subtraction problem.

Two trends emerge from the data in Table 2.3, where each column can be interpreted as a learning trajectory for a particular cohort of students. First, learning trajectories are flat even when cohorts are tracked over time. Secondly, and more importantly, learning outcomes of each successive cohort are a little worse compared with the previous cohort. For instance, by the time the 2009 Grade 3 cohort reached Grade 6 in 2012, 61.7 percent could do subtraction. In contrast, 59.1 percent of the next cohort, which started Grade 3 in 2010, could do subtraction by the time they reached Grade 6 in 2013, and 58.1 percent of the following cohort, which started Grade 3 in 2011. In other words, the learning trajectories of successive cohorts lie below those of previous cohorts (Figure 2.2). What this means is that each additional year of schooling adds less value for successive cohorts.

The analysis presented here includes children enrolled in both government and private schools. A similar analysis of government schools only shows that learning levels are lower compared with private schools. However, two things need to be kept in mind while comparing learning outcomes between these school systems. First, it is well known that the demographic characteristics of private school children can be quite different from those of government school children – these need to be controlled when comparing learning outcomes. Second, even children in private schools are far from grade-level competency.[8]

Inside Primary Schools

ASER is a large, nationally representative survey of learning that gives reliable estimates of learning levels at a point in time. Since its tools are comparable, it can also be used to study changes in learning outcomes over time. However, given its rapid-assessment nature, it is not designed to answer

TABLE 2.3

Percentage of children who can do at least subtraction

	Year that cohort started Grade 3		
Class	2009	2010	2011
Grade 3	39.09	36.38	29.99
Grade 4	57.68	48.52	42.33
Grade 5	61.20	53.65	52.34
Grade 6	61.68	59.11	58.14

FIGURE 2.2

Cohorts over time, Grade 3 to Grade 6: percentage of children who can do subtraction

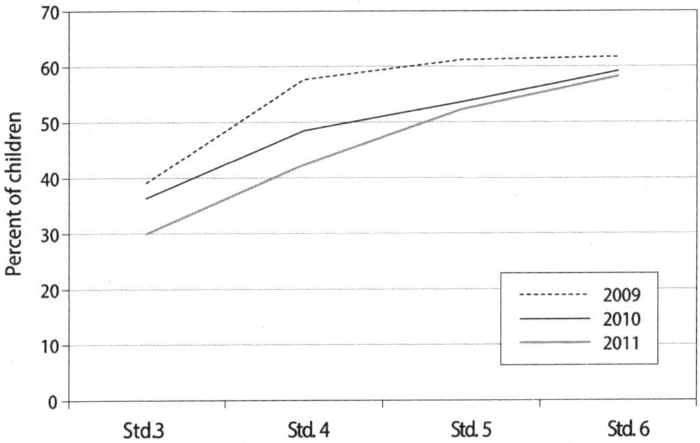

such questions as “Why are learning levels so low?” or “What can we do to improve learning outcomes?” For that, a much more detailed dataset, with information on child, household, classroom, and school characteristics, is needed.

This section is based on a study titled “Inside Primary Schools,” done in 2009–11. The study tracked 30,000 children in Grades 2 and 4 across five states (Andhra Pradesh, Assam, Himachal Pradesh, Jharkhand, and Rajasthan) over fifteen months. Learning outcomes in mathematics and language skills were measured by giving a baseline test at the beginning of the year and an end-line test near the end of the period. The sample was restricted to government primary schools and students only. Within each state, three districts were selected on the basis of geographical location and socio-economic indicators. In each district, sixty government schools with primary sections were sampled, and up to twenty-five students each from Grade 2 and Grade 4 were then randomly sampled from the enrolment registers of each of these schools.

The study also consisted of one student household visit and three school visits in order to observe classroom activity, classroom environment, and teaching styles (e.g., using local examples). Furthermore, teachers were administered an assessment that they agreed to take anonymously. In summary, the sample was drawn from fifteen districts located in five states, consisting of 900 schools and nearly 30,000 students; however, teacher characteristics and competency data can be analyzed only at the school level.

Learning outcomes could depend on the characteristics of children (e.g., age, gender, whether they were receiving outside tuition); households (e.g., parental interest, wealth status, caste, mother's education, dependency ratio, the number of literate adults in the family); classroom experience (e.g., availability and quality of classroom supplies, teacher competency, attitude, style); and schools (e.g., physical assets, basic facilities, teacher education, provision for midday meals). The survey collected data on all these variables so that we could see which ones would be significant in explaining the variation in the learning outcomes across the sample. In addition to the direct measurement of the learning outcomes, there were some other distinctive features of this dataset. Teacher competency was calculated by giving teachers a test that required no more knowledge than what they taught in Grade 4. Teacher attitude and classroom behaviour were recorded through direct observation made on random visits to the classroom.

Though our methodology does not allow us to establish causality, we can ascertain that some factors would indeed play a role in determining the learning outcomes, while other factors emphasized by the RTE, such as physical school assets and teacher educational qualification, do not seem to matter. Some of these factors (e.g., household characteristics) are outside the control of educational policy; however, among the factors that can be influenced, a prominent one is teacher competence, as revealed by the test scores on elementary-level material as opposed to qualifications in terms of degree certificates.

It also matters what teachers do in the class – whether they have a friendly attitude and whether they are spending their time teaching rather than performing non-teaching activities. Student attendance matters but that, in turn, seems to be affected significantly by the teacher's attitude: the friendlier the teacher, the higher the attendance. It is unfortunate for policy makers that the learning outcomes seem to depend much more on qualities that are more difficult to measure.

Descriptive Statistics

Before presenting the results of the regression analysis that links characteristics of children, households, classrooms, teachers, and schools to learning outcomes, we present some descriptive statistics from the dataset in Table 2.4.[9] As the table shows, there is a lot of variation by state.

Attendance was measured in three ways: from the attendance registers on the day of the survey; from the attendance registers for one day previous to the day of the survey; and by taking an actual head count on the day of the survey. For each sampled school, this was done on all three visits during the survey period. We found that attendance by register on the previous day was always greater than the attendance on the day of the survey.[10] This could be because schools inflate attendance in retrospect in order to get higher attendance-based entitlements such as supplies for the midday meal program. The more reliable measure of attendance, therefore, is that based on actual head count.

For our analysis, we aggregate the information for the three visits by dividing children into two groups: those present in school on all three visits versus those who were not. This is the measure we present in Table 2.4. The highest attendance was observed in Himachal Pradesh, where 79 percent of the children were present in school on all three visits. This was closely followed by Andhra Pradesh at 75 percent and Rajasthan with 60 percent. Finally, in Jharkhand, attendance was the lowest at an appalling 31 percent.

Children were assessed in language and math in the first visit (baseline) and the last visit of the study (end line). Given the evidence from ASER that children are far behind grade competency, the tools of the study were designed so that all the questions covered material that the curriculum would have addressed in earlier grades. The math score ranged from 0 to 21 and the language score was in the range 0–16. The highest math scores were in

TABLE 2.4

Mean attendance and scores for Grade 4

	Himachal Pradesh		Rajasthan		Jharkhand		Andhra Pradesh	
Variable	Obs.	Mean	Obs.	Mean	Obs.	Mean	Obs.	Mean
Attendance	1,853	0.79	1,897	0.60	2,387	0.31	1,798	0.75
Math score								
Baseline	2,144	9.73	2,168	7.67	2,558	9.00	1,950	11.92
End line	2,144	11.52	2,168	8.84	2,558	8.42	1,950	14.30
Improvement (%)	2,144	18.43	2,168	15.19	2,558	-6.41	1,950	19.96
Language score								
Baseline	2,144	5.51	2,168	4.65	2,558	4.98	1,950	6.64
Endline	2,144	6.77	2,168	5.20	2,558	4.37	1,950	8.70
Improvement (%)	2,144	22.94	2,168	11.74	2,558	-12.38	1,950	31.08

Note: Obs. = number of observations.

Andhra Pradesh, as was the largest improvement. The lowest math scores were in Rajasthan; however, by the end-line visit, the state could improve scores by about 15 percent. In contrast, although Jharkhand had higher scores to start with, students there actually showed a learning loss by the endline. This could be due to the particularly low attendance rates in Jharkhand. The results for language are qualitatively similar; however, the average score was only about 50 percent even in the highest-scoring state.

What could explain such large differences across states? Clearly attendance matters, but attendance itself is endogenous to learning outcomes. Table 2.5 displays the data on household characteristics for the Grade 4 children. The table suggests that the only variable in which Jharkhand is noticeably deficient is household assets – it is the poorest of the four states. Judging from the number of literate adults in the household and the dependency ratio, Andhra Pradesh has the smallest size of households. Surprisingly, Andhra Pradesh has the same level of mother's education as Jharkhand, while Rajasthan has the least. In terms of other household variables, Jharkhand does not seem especially handicapped. Similarly, Andhra Pradesh's learning performance is not easily explainable in terms of

TABLE 2.5

Household characteristics of Grade 4 children

	Himchal Pradesh		Rajasthan		Jharkhand		Andhra Pradesh	
Variable	Obs.	Mean	Obs.	Mean	Obs.	Mean	Obs.	Mean
Assets[1]	1,757	2.29	1,363	2.15	1,799	1.66	1,598	2.70
Mother's education[2]	1,407	0.32	1,466	0.03	1,756	0.12	1,418	0.12
No. of literate adults in household	1,478	1.76	1,546	1.19	1,860	1.55	1,498	0.90
Parental interest[3]	2,098	3.70	1,998	3.01	2,370	3.85	1,751	3.50
Commute time (minutes)	2,014	23.28	1,920	17.85	2,306	12.73	1,703	8.86
Dependency ratio[4]	1,290	0.52	1,190	0.51	1,532	0.54	1,364	0.16

Notes:

1 Sum of seven assets observed in the home: TV, radio, phone, fridge, fan, cycle, and tractor.

2 Proportion that are literate.

3 Parental interest ranges from 0 to 15 based on the sum of the following variables: household reading materials (0–6); child reading materials (0–5); whether parents had made a complaint or talked about school problems (0–1); whether they had visited the school (0–1); whether they knew about the VEC (0–1); and whether the child received any help from a parent, sibling, relative, etc. (non-paid help) (0–1).

4 The ratio of non-working adults to total adults in the household.

household characteristics; that is, Andhra Pradesh does not demonstrate particularly exceptional characteristics.

So, is it the case that classrooms and schools are very different across these states? Table 2.6 presents the observed characteristics in classrooms and schools. Jharkhand is an inferior outlier in almost every aspect. The low attendance in Jharkhand could be explained by all other factors related to schools and teachers; however, it is still not the case that Andhra Pradesh is superior in this regard. For instance, it has hardly any teachers with professional education degrees, teachers do not exhibit exceptional performance in the assessments, and school and classroom infrastructure is not very different from other states. However, in terms of the teacher's activities in the classroom, it is way ahead of the other states. This seems to suggest that traditional variables like qualifications and school infrastructure matter less for learning outcomes than how the teacher engages children in the classroom.

No consistent story emerged in a separate multivariate regression for each state where we controlled for characteristics of the child, her family, and her school. Once we controlled for baseline scores, none of the other variables were consistently statistically significant to explain the variation within states. While this analysis is not useful in explaining inter-state differences, we hoped that it would help identify important correlates of learning. Though the dataset is very rich in the types of processes and variables it tries to capture, it does have a fair number of missing observations across variables. Since these are scattered across variables, the sample size is significantly reduced in multivariate regressions that control for a lot of variables.

Furthermore, an additional problem of multi-collinearity exists, since a lot of the variables are correlated within schools – usually "good" schools

TABLE 2.6

School characteristics of Grade 4 children

	Himchal Pradesh		Rajasthan		Jharkhand		Andhra Pradesh	
Variable	Obs.	Mean	Obs.	Mean	Obs.	Mean	Obs.	Mean
Attendance[1] (students)	1,853	0.79	1,897	0.60	2,387	0.31	1,798	0.75
Attendance[2] (teachers)	180	0.76	177	0.81	179	0.68	180	0.84
Meals[3]	174	0.99	170	0.96	173	0.68	176	0.99
Multi-grade[4]	161	0.65	133	0.79	146	0.95	159	0.71
School physical assets[5]	180	7.26	177	7.15	179	5.01	180	5.76
School learning assets[6]	180	3.18	177	2.60	179	2.07	180	3.78

▶

	Himchal Pradesh		Rajasthan		Jharkhand		Andhra Pradesh	
Variable	Obs.	Mean	Obs.	Mean	Obs.	Mean	Obs.	Mean
Classroom assets[7]	174	3.07	167	3.25	168	2.83	171	3.73
Graduate teachers[8]	171	0.44	172	0.70	176	0.57	179	0.78
BEd, MEd[9]	141	0.26	161	0.23	145	0.17	176	0.06
Smiling teachers[10]	163	0.25	166	0.07	168	0.07	171	0.54
Use of local information[11]	166	0.20	166	0.21	168	0.13	169	0.35
Teachers' language score[12]	169	54.76	134	45.25	154	35.18	139	46.88
Teachers' math score[13]	169	72.21	134	66.88	154	60.33	139	67.62

Notes:

1 Proportion of Grade 4 children who were present in all three visits to the schools.

2 Average proportion of teachers who were present in the school in the three visits.

3 Proportion of schools where a meal was observed.

4 Proportion of schools where Grade 4 children were sitting with some other grade.

5 School physical asset is in the range of 0–14 and is the sum of the following seven characteristics that were observed in Visit 1 and Visit 3 in the schools: water was available; it was drinkable; toilet was there; it was usable; separate toilet for girls; it was unlocked; boundary wall.

6 School learning asset is in the range of 0–6 and is the sum of the following three characteristics that were observed in Visit 1 and Visit 3 in the schools: school had a library; children were observed using library books; there was a timetable displayed in the school.

7 Classroom asset is in the range of 0–5 and is the sum of the following five characteristics that were observed in the classrooms: there was a blackboard in the class; this blackboard could be seen from the back of the class; the blackboard was usable; children's work was displayed on the walls; there was teacher learning material in the classroom.

8 Proportion of teachers with a graduate degree.

9 Proportion of teachers with a BEd/MEd degree.

10 Proportion of classrooms observed with teachers smiling and interacting with children.

11 Proportion of classrooms observed with teachers using local information to explain materials.

12 Average percentage teacher score in language assessment.

13 Average percentage teacher score in math assessment.

have all indicators that are superior. We estimate a pooled regression, which uses state-fixed effects to control for unobserved state-level variables, such as state education policy,[11] that are not captured in the dataset. The results from the pooled regression of the four states are as follows:

- Baseline scores and attendance are positively correlated with learning outcomes.
- Girls are slightly better in math.
- Supplemental help improves learning outcomes.
  - Tuition and parental interest variable in math
  - Mother's education in language
- Household asset is positively correlated with learning outcomes.
- School physical infrastructure is not correlated with learning.
- School learning infrastructure is positively correlated with learning.
- Teacher engaged in non-teaching work in the classroom negatively affects learning outcomes (this is the only classroom activity that seems to be important).
- Teacher attendance does not matter.
- Teacher qualifications and competency matters only for math.

Most of the results were as expected, but there were some that are particularly interesting. In our sample of fourth graders, girls have slightly higher math scores, even after controlling for other variables. This finding goes contrary to popular wisdom, but can be explained. We have only government schools in this dataset; ASER and other evidence show that a larger proportion of boys are enrolled in private schools, compared with girls. Rural households will often choose to send their sons to a private school, especially when faced with budgetary constraint. The perception that parents have is that private schools deliver better outcomes, even if it is just in the use of the English language, since it may provide better job prospects. The finding about supplemental help is interesting because it reinforces anecdotal evidence. Math is more difficult than language, so children may need supplemental help that parents cannot provide.

At the school level, whereas inputs related to learning, such as the presence of a library, matter for learning outcomes, physical infrastructure such as toilets does not. Wadhwa (2010) obtained a similar result using ASER data. The fact that the school's physical infrastructure is not correlated with learning outcomes is important, given that the RTE is primarily focused on providing these kinds of inputs.

The study also collected information on a variety of classroom practices. Among these, the only one that was significant was whether the teacher was engaged in non-teaching work. Surprisingly, teacher attendance is not correlated with learning outcomes. Nonetheless, teacher attendance was quite high; in fact, it was higher than that of children, suggesting that the issue of teacher absenteeism is less of a problem than it is made out to be. Similar results for teacher attendance are found in ASER. Finally, while teacher qualifications and competency do not matter for language scores, they do for math scores.

These results represent only average effects, so we also estimated regressions for the top 10 percent and the bottom 10 percent of the class. Given the disparity, in terms of learning levels, age, and other demographic characteristics within Indian classrooms, along with the fact that over 60 percent of classrooms tend to be multi-grade, it is quite possible that some children get ignored in class. The results are as follows:

- Attendance matters only for the bottom 10 percent of learners.
- Compared with boys, girls do worse in language in the bottom 10 percent and better in math in the top 10 percent.
- Supplemental help improves learning outcomes, but far more for the bottom 10 percent.
- Possession of household assets is positively correlated with learning outcomes for the top 10 percent.
- School learning infrastructure matters only for the top 10 percent.
- Teacher attendance matters for the top 10 percent.
- Teacher educational qualifications impact the bottom 10 percent negatively, whereas competency and professional qualifications help.
- Teacher educational qualifications are important for the top 10 percent.

According to these results, different things matter for the top 10 percent of the class compared with the bottom 10 percent. For children in the bottom 10 percent of their class, their attendance and whether they receive supplemental help matter far more than they do for the top 10 percent of the class. There is some evidence that teachers teach to the top of the class; that is, their attendance and educational qualifications matter only for the top achievers in the class.

What Can We Do to Improve Learning?

The evidence clearly indicates that there is a huge learning crisis in India, raising two important questions: What can be done to improve the state of the educational system? What should schools and teachers do to produce better outcomes? Here, it is important to stress a point: the policy prescriptions have to be feasible. Given the size of the country and the fact that it is a poor country, for a solution to work, it has to be scalable and use currently available resources.

Some ideas for what can work come from the field interventions of Pratham, which is the largest primary education NGO in the country, with programs in almost every large state. One feature that differentiates Pratham from other NGOs is that it has always worked with the government within the state educational system to bring about change. Prompted by ASER and even before ASER, Pratham has designed and implemented many learning interventions in rural and urban India. Its largest intervention, Read India, was launched in January 2007 at the release of the ASER 2006 report. Pratham is also one of the most evaluated NGOs in the country. Many randomized control trials (RCT) have been conducted on its interventions; in this section, we discuss the results from some of these studies.

Balsakhi Remedial Tutoring Program (2001–04)

Both ASER and the Inside Primary Schools study show that children are at least two to three grades behind the curriculum. To bridge the gap and, more importantly, to make sure that children do not drop out, children who are getting left behind in class need supplemental help. Usually this help is available from parents at home; however, in the context of rural India or urban low-income areas, this may not be forthcoming because even parents may be illiterate. In fact, according to ASER, 50 percent of children who go to rural public schools have mothers who have never been to school and around 25 percent are first-generation learners. Furthermore, paying for private tutors may not be an option for poor families.

Pratham's Balsakhi program was aimed at providing a tutor – the Balsakhi – in school to help children who had fallen behind. A Balsakhi was usually a young woman recruited from the local community, trained by Pratham, and paid a fraction of the government schoolteacher salary (around US$10–15 per month). She worked with fifteen to twenty children in Grades 2, 3, and 4 for about two hours a day. Instruction was focused on basic reading and numeracy, skills that the children were supposed to have learned in Grades 1 or 2.

The program was evaluated by the Abdul Latif Jameel Poverty Action Lab (J-PAL). The study found that the program showed significant learning gains of 0.14 standard deviations in the first year and 0.28 standard deviations in the second. More importantly, the weakest students, who were the main targets of the program, gained the most. The overall cost of the program was US$2.25 per child per year! Pratham has scaled up this program across the country.

Role of Community Participation: Jaunpur Study (2005–06)

To improve learning levels, it may be necessary to create pressures from both the supply and demand sides. Improvements in schools related to classroom practices or provision of supplemental help are essentially interventions to improve supply. On the demand side, the role of parents is indisputably important as well and has been studied extensively. However, apart from providing help at home, parents can play another important role, especially in the context of low learning outcomes – they can create pressures within the system for better public service delivery since they are the consumers of the services provided by public schools. One way to do this is through community participation in the education process.

In 2001, Uttar Pradesh became one of the first states to establish Village Education Committees (VEC) in every village. These are now mandated by the RTE and all states have them in some form or other. VECs typically consist of the elected village head, the headmaster of the local school, and three parents nominated by the village community. Their responsibilities include monitoring school performance, claiming public funds, and hiring additional contract teachers when necessary. However, surveys have shown that the "members" of the VEC are often unaware that they are part of the committee, and are thus unaware of their responsibilities and their powers made available by funds, especially for appointing additional contract teachers.

In 2005–06, J-PAL, along with Pratham, conducted an RCT of three cascading interventions in 280 villages of the Jaunpur district of Uttar Pradesh.

The aim was to study whether access to more information resulted in VECs and the community demanding better public services, in contrast to the effect of direct interventions on learning outcomes. The first intervention, conducted in 65 villages, involved volunteers having conversations in the village about their state of learning, status of schools, state policies, and funds available for improving education. Villagers were also asked whether they knew about the VEC, its members, and its responsibilities. VEC members also received a pamphlet on their responsibilities. The second intervention, in another 65 villages, had all the features of the first intervention and the community was also trained to test children in basic reading and arithmetic. Volunteers generated a community report card and presented the results at a meeting of the community. The third intervention, once again in 65 villages, added to the first two by teaching volunteers a simple method to help children learn to read in after-school reading classes. The material given to volunteers was designed by Pratham.

In all three sets of treatment villages, there was an increase in VEC members who knew that they could access public funds. Parents were also more likely to know that a VEC existed in their village compared with the control villages. However, this greater awareness did not result in very different performances of the VECs in the treatment and control villages, but more contract teachers were hired in the second-intervention villages. The intervention also did not result in greater engagement of parents with schools; for example, parents did not visit more frequently. Finally, even though only 8 percent of the children in the villages with the teaching intervention attended the classes, there were significant gains in reading ability. These gains were observed for children who were at the lowest and middle end of the reading scale. As expected, the gains were much higher among children who attended the reading classes. No reading gains were observed in villages where there was no teaching intervention.

Thus, simply making communities and parents aware that there is a problem may not be enough – children who need supplemental help gain from actual teaching. However, this supplemental help can be provided by the local communities themselves and does not involve a high-cost intervention.

Read India Evaluation (2008 – Present)

The above interventions and evaluations clearly point to the simple fact that when concerted efforts are made to help children who are falling behind, children learn. This seems like a very obvious statement that would not require complicated and extremely expensive RCTs to prove; however, until the first ASER report came out in 2005, no one in the education establishment was even willing to accept the fact that children who were enrolled in school might not be at grade competency. Fortunately, ASER and other subsequent evidence slowly shifted the focus from enrolment to learning, leading to the acceptance that enrolment does not necessarily translate into learning.

In January 2007, Pratham launched its Read India program in 250 (out of 600) rural districts. The program had various components that had evolved with Pratham's work in different communities across the country. In the initial years (2007–10), Pratham worked large-scale in almost 250 districts across India. In fact, in the summer of 2008, it is said that there was a Pratham summer camp in almost half of all villages in the country. The scale was made possible by mobilizing local volunteers in every village.

By 2010, Pratham decided to scale down so that its impact could be stronger and more sustained. One hundred villages were selected in about 200 blocks across India where Pratham team members, along with local village volunteers, worked for three years. By 2013, the model had begun to deliver "guaranteed results." Even if most of them could not read at first, in 40–50 days' time, Pratham could guarantee that at least 60–70 percent of children between 8 and 12 years old had learned to read and do basic arithmetic. Today, Read India has two distinct models: learning camps and Pratham-government partnership.

Learning Camps: Direct Activity by Pratham in Villages and Schools

Based on Pratham's experience across India in the last few years, "learning camps" have emerged as a promising way to strengthen basic learning levels of children between Grades 3 and 5. Learning camps are short bursts of activities during the school year that are repeated several times a year, each session lasting up to ten days. In preparation for the camp, children are assessed using simple reading and math tools (like the ASER tools) and are grouped according to learning level rather than by grade. During the camp, each child is given a small package of reading materials and each group is taught using corresponding methods and materials.

Teaching-learning activities based on the child's level seems to help the child learn faster compared with the usual organization of schools, where children are grouped by grade and taught using the textbooks and materials of the appropriate grade level. These intensive periods of focused activity help strengthen and build a child's ability to read and do arithmetic. Simple assessment tools are used to track progress across camps and the results are shared with parents, teachers, and the community. Depending on the baseline levels of children's ability to do arithmetic and to read, camps are repeated anywhere between thirty and fifty days during the school year.[12]

A Pratham team member leads the learning camp while local volunteers help run them. An integral part of this strategy is to involve community members in improving children's learning. It is hoped that conducting these camps within the government school during school hours will lead to the adoption of the "demonstration effect" of grouping and of effective teaching-learning practices by the schoolteachers and by the school system so that learning gains can be sustained over time. Pratham team members also rotate through a set of schools and villages to maximize possible outcomes given the time and resources available, thus creating a cost-effective model of learning improvement.

Pratham-Government Partnership for Improving Child Learning

The objective of these partnership programs is to work with schoolteachers and enable them to adopt Pratham methods of grouping, instruction, and teaching-learning practices. By catalyzing the school system, a much larger scale-up and impact is possible than can be done by direct Pratham action.

To start, a cadre of leaders is needed from within the school system; this cadre is often a set of officials called cluster coordinators who are responsible for about twelve to fifteen schools. To become academic leaders who can catalyze the system, they need to be convinced that there was indeed a problem with children's learning, and then "practise" the new teaching method themselves daily for fifteen to twenty days. Pratham trains and orients the cluster coordinators to assess their children and learn how Pratham teaches. After brief training, these cluster coordinators are encouraged to conduct classes daily for a period of fifteen to twenty days. Teaching children daily and seeing their progress first-hand is critical to the adoption of the Pratham method within the system. Subsequently, each cluster coordinator trains all teachers in the ten to fifteen schools in his or her charge, often with Pratham support. The government also prints and distributes the required reading materials. For the rest of the year, the cluster coordinator visits the schools in his or her charge, demonstrates activities, and helps teachers move forward toward the stated learning goals. The strengthening of the capability of cluster coordinators to lead and support teaching-learning has been a critical factor in the scale-up process.[13]

In the 2014–15 school year, such partnerships were seen in Bihar, West Bengal, Madhya Pradesh, and Maharashtra.

Conclusion

In this chapter, we have analyzed the efficiency of the primary education sector in India; in particular, we have looked at what the available evidence tells us about how the provisions under the *Right to Education Act* (RTE) might affect learning outcomes.

The indicators on which the RTE focuses do not seem to be correlated with learning outcomes. For instance, there is a significant focus on improving school infrastructure, which actually seems to have no impact on improving learning. Similarly, the RTE mandates minimum qualifications for regular teachers, but this does not seem to matter for children who are at the bottom of the ladder. In fact, there is some evidence that more qualified teachers might discriminate against children with the most severe learning deficits. Furthermore, the RTE stresses the importance of libraries and the need to maintain a timetable, yet this seems to help only children in the top 10 percent of the class. Similarly, high teacher attendance also helps only children in the top 10 percent of the class.

What seems to work is addressing the needs of the child rather than the curriculum. The RTE provides a great opportunity for the country to renew its efforts to ensure that every child is in school, attending regularly, and learning well. The spirit behind the RTE is to guarantee that, after eight years of elementary schooling, every child in India will receive a good-quality education. Therefore, we need to ensure that this act does not remain merely a guarantee of "schooling" but also a guarantee of "learning."

There is some evidence, as this chapter has discussed, that things that directly aid in a child's learning, such as supplemental help, are more important for improving learning outcomes. Within the school, the overriding emphasis on completing the curriculum has contributed to a neglect of basic learning. Teacher hiring and training must not be based on academic qualifications alone; evaluation should include key elements of teaching ability such as content knowledge, ability to communicate, creativity, and child-friendly behaviours. Parents also need to be involved and empowered. The structure of the government school system does not permit much accountability to parents. In addition, many children in government schools are first-generation learners, and their parents have little clout with the educational bureaucracy.

At the beginning of this chapter, we talked about the importance of education in ensuring that India reaps the fruits of demographic changes that will occur over the next few decades. However, the evidence that we have presented here paints a very dismal picture of the state of education in the country. It is imperative that immediate corrective action be taken to put the educational system in order. In absence of such corrective action, the demographic dividend might turn into demographic disaster and India might suffer the consequences of having a predominantly low-skilled labour force. This would not only hinder India's performance in service-led exports but also weaken the government's efforts to transform India into a manufacturing hub. These adverse consequences might result in political pressure on the government to bring in more protectionist policies, which could further undermine India's economic growth.

NOTES

1 See Kotwal, Ramaswami, and Wadhwa 2011 and Eswaran et al. 2009 for a more detailed discussion of India's growth process.

2 The government of India reported a net enrolment ratio (NER) of 98.3 percent for 2009–10. According to ASER 2011, 96.7 percent of all children in the 6–14-year age group were enrolled in school.

3 *The Gazette of India, Extraordinary,* pt. 2, sec. 1, 27 August 2009.

4 Classes I–V is the terminology used in India for Grades 1–5. Similarly, Classes VI–VIII mean Grades 6–8.

5 Proponents of "low-cost" private schools feel that it imposes an unnecessary burden, in terms of infrastructure norms, on these schools.

6 As can be seen, there is an overlap in the ranges specified in the act between ">150" and ">200." These ranges are generally interpreted as minimum requirements.

7 For more information on ASER tools and processes, see http://www.asercentre.org.

8 See Wadhwa 2009 and 2014.

9 We dropped Assam from our sample because of missing observations in many of the variables, such as caste, that we wanted to control for. Also, we present results for Grade 4 only in this section. We could not get any robust results for Grade 2.

10 The School Tells study also has a similar finding.

11 Education is a concurrent state and central subject in India, so there can be significant differences in state education policy.

12 Evaluations by J-PAL of a program in Bihar in which Pratham worked with Bihar government teachers to raise learning levels showed that a month-long summer camp with children grouped by level produced significant learning gains in both language and math. Moreover, these gains were still visible at the end of two school years.

13 The government partnership program was also evaluated by J-PAL in Haryana in 2011–12.

3 Ensuring the Right to Work through Better Governance

ASHWINI KULKARNI

India embarked on a process of economic liberalization in the 1980s that picked up steam in the 1990s following a balance-of-payments crisis; since then, India has enjoyed impressive growth rates. However, economic liberalization often results in groups of "winners" and "losers" since its benefits often do not reach all sections of the population. In fact, India has one of the lowest rates of growth elasticity of poverty (Lenagala and Ram 2010). In this context, direct intervention to support the marginalized in rural regions was envisaged through a workfare program enshrined in the *Mahatma Gandhi National Rural Employment Guarantee Act* (MGNREGA).

This act is based on an earlier version of the workfare program called the Employment Guarantee Scheme (EGS) that was being implemented in the state of Maharashtra for almost three decades. The basic tenets of the program were to provide work on demand to adults in rural areas by employing unskilled manual labour to construct water and soil conservation structures to support rain-fed farming. The program had two purposes: to provide wage-earning opportunities for unskilled labourers in rural areas and to create durable infrastructure. Thus, this was not meant to be just an income transfer; asset generation was an important dimension as well. Moreover, since it was a workfare program, the demand-based rule ensured that only the truly poor and needy applied for work.

The importance of the MGNREGA lays in the fact that not only is it an impressive tool of redistribution but it also aims to improve rural infrastructure. Despite having a high proportion of its population working in agriculture, India's agricultural productivity rates are one of the lowest in the world; hence, the emphasis on the creation of rural infrastructure is important. The creation of proper infrastructure that aids in rain-fed farming would help increase productivity in agriculture and thus help farmers, especially those who do not have access to irrigation facilities. Furthermore, government support through this route would not contravene World Trade Organization (WTO) rules since there would be no distortion of markets. Hence, the MGNREGA has the potential to transform the agricultural sector, provide relief to marginal farmers through the building of rural infrastructure, and assist agricultural labourers through the provision of employment without violating WTO norms. This is especially important in the context of the recent conflict between India and the WTO over high subsidies provided by the Indian government to its farmers.

In countries like India where governance structures suffer from a myriad of issues such as corruption, red tape, and discrimination toward marginalized sections, it is necessary to understand what kind of systems would lead to better implementation of government programs. One way to understand these issues would be to look at how a program works in different states. India has a federal structure, with constituent states having their own elected governments; by identifying and studying the states that perform better, we can gain insight into the kinds of institutions that we need to establish to ensure that government programs run smoothly and effectively. This chapter carries out such an exercise.

Although the MGNREGA is a national program, state governments and local village councils have an important role to play in implementing it; hence, the implementation procedures differ across states. In this chapter, we study two states, Maharashtra and Andhra Pradesh, which differ significantly in their implementation of MGNREGA. Whereas Andhra Pradesh has seen success, Maharashtra has been a laggard until recently. Extensive fieldwork consisting of interviews with different stakeholders in both states was carried out to identify the differential performance of the two states. We find that the use of information technology (IT) and decentralization in governance structures are the primary reasons why the MGNREGA was better implemented in Andhra Pradesh than in Maharashtra.

TABLE 3.1

Percentage and number of poor in India

Year	Poverty ratio (%)			Number of poor (million)		
	Rural	Urban	National	Rural	Urban	National
1993–94	50.1	31.8	45.3	328.6	74.5	403.7
2004–05	41.8	25.7	37.2	326.3	80.8	407.1
2011–12	25.7	13.7	21.9	216.5	52.8	269.3

Source: "Press Note on Poverty Estimates," Planning Commission 2013. These estimates are based on the official poverty line as defined in 2013.

TABLE 3.2

Landholding distribution: all of India

Size of holding (hectares)	Percentage of farmers	Percentage of total area
0.1–2	85.57	46.82
2–5	11.53	30.86
5–10	2.32	14.01
>10	0.58	8.31

Source: Agricultural Census 2010–11, http://agcensus.dacnet.nic.in/natt1table1.aspx.

The poverty estimates over the decades have shown that there are more poor citizens living in rural India than in urban areas (Table 3.1). Though there is a decline, the number of poor in rural areas has remained consistently higher than in urban India; in fact, according to the Census of India from 2011, 72.18 percent of population still lives in rural India. Thus, not only do the poorest people live in rural areas, but these areas are also the most densely populated.

Rural India is marked by agriculture as the main occupation: according to the same census, 56.6 percent of workers are employed in the agricultural sector. Most of the agriculture carried out in India is rain-fed agriculture, which is dependent on the monsoon since only 40 percent of farmland has irrigation facilities, whole or partial (Agricultural Census 2010–11). The land distribution is skewed as well, as shown in Table 3.2. Most of the poor who live in rural India are likely farmers who own small plots of land, lack irrigation facilities, and are thus dependent on rain.

MGNREGA: An Overview

The *Mahatma Gandhi National Rural Employment Guarantee Act* (MGNREGA), initiated in 2006, is a program with twin objectives of creating wage employment and durable assets. Initially, it covered only the 200 most backward districts of India, but by 2008 it had been expanded to all of rural India.

All adults residing in rural areas who are ready to do unskilled manual work are eligible to participate in this program. Employment must be provided within the same Gram Panchayat boundary.[1] A worker gets paid each week based on work output with task-based rates. The output is calculated at the end of every week and the earnings are deposited by the Block Office[2] into individual accounts opened in the workers' names at a post office or local bank. The worker has to put in "demand" for work to the local authorities, which have to provide employment within fifteen days of receiving it. The daily attendance is maintained on a muster roll. Since the productivity of dry-land agriculture is intrinsically linked with watershed development and the availability of wells, infrastructure created by the MGNREGA projects includes a wide range of assets such as farm ponds, water storage structures, watershed structures, land development, roads, plantations, and other rural assets aimed mostly at water and soil conservation.[3]

The MGNREGA is the most suitable vehicle for facilitating the creation of these assets for three reasons. First, such work is relatively more labour-intensive. Second, most of the material consumed for this is locally available; for watershed treatment structures to be effective, the use of local materials like stones and soil is desirable since the technical design of these structures is usually based on them. Third, to ensure the success of the work, it is desirable that labour from the same area be involved in the construction process, as the workers understand the local conditions well. Furthermore, since the structures are useful to their community, they have a stake in its quality and durability.

As can be seen from Table 3.3, the program has reached out to 50 million households, each averaging 40 to 54 days in a year, instead of the 100 days of work that the program allows. The wage rate differs across states and it increases marginally every year. If they earn US$2 per day (based on the

TABLE 3.3

National overview of MGNREGA performance

Particulars	2009–10	2010–11	2011–12	2012–13	2013–14	2014–15
Employment provided to households (millions)	52.6	54.9	50.6	49.9	47.9	41.4
Person-days generated (millions)	2835.9	2571.5	2187.6	2304.8	2202.2	1661.9
Person-days per household	54	47	43	46	46	40
Expenditure (million INR)	379,052.30	393,772.70	370,728.20	397,782.90	386,724.00	358,689.50
Total number of projects taken up (millions)	4.617	5.099	8.077	10.462	9.414	10.018
Work break-up (%)						
Water conservation	51	48	60	46	33	31
Works on individual land	17	18	11	11	14	14
Land development	14	14	8	6	7	6
Other	18	20	21	37	46	49

Source: "MGNREGA Report to the People 2015 and for FY 14015," http://mnregaweb4.nic.in/netnrega/all_lvl_details_dashboard_new.aspx.

average earning of 121 INR in 2012–13, 133 in 2013–14, and 144 in 2014–15), then the additional earning in a year from this program is in the range of US$80–105. This is seven to nine times the poverty line of 816 INR monthly per capita, which is US$12.75 (at US$1 = 64 INR). This is a substantial income increase for the poor households. The types of projects undertaken are in tune with the objective of creating assets and infrastructure necessary for rain-fed agriculture, especially for small farmers. The total expenditure on this program has been 40–50 percent of the total outlay of the Rural Development Department in a year, which underlines the importance and scope of the program.

Problems in Implementation

There are three dimensions to the MGNREGA implementation problems. First, there are general inefficiencies in the governance mechanisms of all the development programs in India. This can be understood when one looks at the budget outlays and utilization for each of the programs. The difficulties associated with fund flows, information flows, and leakages lead to less utilization as well as inefficient use of program funds. This problem becomes acute when the programs are meant for the poor and marginalized, who lack the voice and wherewithal to interact with the bureaucracy.

Second, the MGNREGA is by design more complex to deliver than most development programs. It is complex because it is not a one-time event like most of the other rural development programs, and it requires the coordination of multiple actors across central government agencies, state government agencies, public sectors, private sectors, public-private partnerships, and more. Furthermore, this is not a program implemented through a single line of hierarchy. The coordination for delivery has to be performed every week for at least half a year across all of rural India.

Third, the MGNREGA is often seen as a make-work program that digs the pits and fills them up in order to create rural employment. Another important complaint is that it has distorted rural labour markets and pushed up the market wages, making farming unprofitable. Large farmers complain the most about the act since they perceive it as a threat against a steady supply of compliant labour. Moreover, it also provides agricultural labourers an alternative source of income, further increasing their bargaining power. Another serious charge that has taken the centre stage in the debate on the

MGNREGA is corruption and the leakage of funds to workers who have never worked on the project. However, the inefficient implementation of the MGNREGA stems not only from corruption; there are systemic problems that we need to understand.

The Case of Maharashtra and Andhra Pradesh

Excellent policies and poor implementation coexist wonderfully in India. A comparative study of implementation of the MGNREGA in Maharashtra and Andhra Pradesh (AP)[4] is presented here; in particular, what made AP succeed in the implementation of MGNREGA in terms of efficiency and outcomes?

To understand the systemic challenges in implementing the MGNREGA, interviews were conducted with government officials at various levels of administration, NGO representatives, and other stakeholders such as bank representatives. Visits to villages to meet MGNREGA workers were made over a period of three years. Information from the MGNREGA website was used for basic comparison of the indicators of good implementation, such as unskilled wage expenditure, number of households getting 100 days of employment as promised, and delays in wage payments.

Good governance can be understood by observing the transparency, accountability, and participation measures, and by studying the achievement of the goals of the program. The management apparatus employed by the government of Andhra Pradesh can be examined with these parameters of good governance.

This case study shows that the use of information technology at all levels of administration seems to be instrumental in explaining the large difference in implementation efficiency across the two states. It also shows the potential of using information technology to address the issues of both mismanagement and corruption.

Performance Comparison

In the first few years, AP did remarkably well in the implementation of the MGNREGA as the state used the central government funds efficiently. In contrast, although it was a pioneer in workfare programs,[5] Maharashtra has not performed well in implementing the act. Figure 3.1 shows the vast

FIGURE 3.1

Expenditure across years: a comparison between Andhra Pradesh and Maharashtra

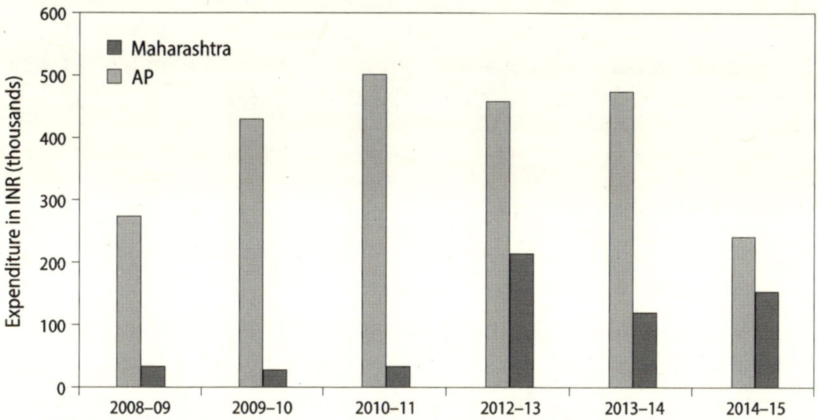

Source: nrega.nic.in

FIGURE 3.2

Rural poverty figures for Andhra Pradesh and Maharashtra, 2011–12

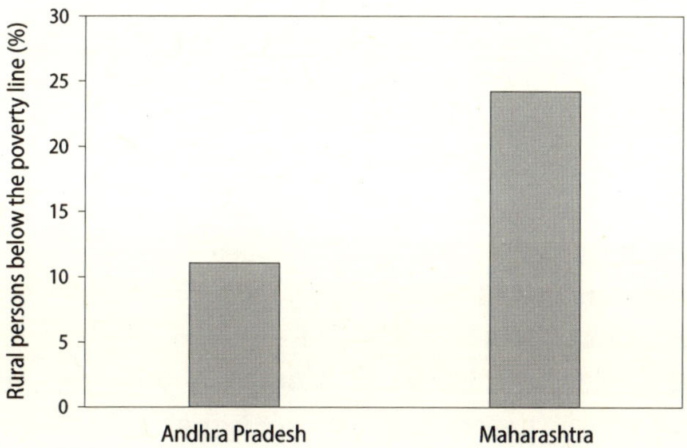

Source: Number and Percentage of Population below Poverty Line by States, 2011–12 (Tendulkar Methodology) from Press Note on Poverty Estimates, 2011–12; Government of India, Planning Commission, July 2013

difference in utilization of funds for MGNREGA by the two states: while AP was quick to make good use of the funds – despite the fact that Maharashtra has almost twice the number of rural poor than AP, as shown in Figure 3.2 – Maharashtra lagged at first before picking up later.

Andhra Pradesh's better performance is not limited to numbers. In their book *Politics and the Right to Work,* Rob Jenkins and James Manor write:

> A meticulous investigation in Andhra Pradesh by a team from the Administrative Staff College of India (Study for Quick Appraisal of NREGA in Andhra Pradesh, 2009) found that numerous members of the locally dominant Reddy caste, who are conventionally considered among the "non-poor" faced sufficiently serious deprivation to seek work under the programme. They were "non-poor" in name but not in reality. And in exercising their right to work and laboring alongside people from disadvantaged castes in NREGA work sites, invidious social barriers between different groups were eroded.

This comes through as a testimony that, if institutional mechanisms are put in place and work effectively, its social impact is also visible.

The Systems

The difference in the implementation of the MGNREGA in AP and Maharashtra is striking. In AP, the administrative unit is the Mandal, which has 20–25 Gram Panchayats instead of the Tehsil/Block[6] in most other states, with around 80–120 Gram Panchayats; thus, for a Mandal officer, implementing development programs is easier, allowing for improved accessibility and communication with the field staff. The delivery mechanism runs from the Rural Development Ministry through the MGNREGA Director to collectors, and then to Mandal officers. The Mandal office has an exclusive team for the MGNREGA, consisting of an administration officer, technical officers, and computer operators. The office is also equipped with computers with broadband connectivity. At the village level, there is a field assistant who is responsible for basic coordination and data recording, especially for the registration and muster records. A technical assistant for a cluster of four to five villages is responsible for recording measurements of completed work. The data are then given to the computer section at the Mandal office, which prepares the payment order.

In Maharashtra, the Employee Guarantee Scheme (EGS) started during the severe and widespread drought of 1972. It was envisaged that since the projects would essentially belong to the state government departments such as agriculture, public works, minor irrigation, and so on, there was no need to create a separate department. Thus, the coordination of work was the responsibility of the Collector's Office and the actual implementation in the villages was managed by the State Departments. This system has continued to the present, and the Zilla Parishad[7] has also been assigned responsibility for delivery of the MGNREGA.

In the delivery system, there is a basic difference between AP and Maharashtra. In AP, there is a single line of command with the development cadre being employed to execute, whereas in Maharashtra, the Department of Revenue has joint responsibility with the development cadre.

The Business Correspondent (BC) model used by AP to make payments to the MGNREGA worker includes people who are not yet in the banking network. The MGNREGA mandates that all wage payments to workers are made to their bank or post office accounts. These are meant to be zero-balance, no-frills accounts, but the bank/postal services are not available in most villages. To overcome this problem, the AP government has entered into contractual arrangements with many banks, both private and public. These banks, in turn, have made arrangements to reach out to the villages through BC private agencies. They have employed a person from the community (usually a member of a women's self-help group) to be the customer service provider who opens accounts and makes payments to the workers. A particular BC private agency can cater to more than one bank and be functional in more than one district.

At the Mandal level, the "muster" and the "measurements of the works" are provided and entered, allowing the software program to calculate the volume of work according to soil type; by applying the rates, the total amount of work done is calculated. The muster details are used to prepare the "payment order" that contains information about job card number, the name of the worker, the account number, number of days of attendance, dates, unique ID of the work, and more. The Mandal officer authorizes the payment, which is deposited into the accounts of the workers.

Once the wages are deposited, the BC agencies make the cash available to the customer service provider at the village for distribution. In some places, on a pilot basis, they have used biometric identification of the worker to ensure that payments reach the correct person. Also, the transaction of payments in cash by the customer service provider is recorded through a mobile phone and uploaded almost in real time. The AP government has piloted different ways of making payments, including the use of Smart Cards and biometric identification devices. This kind of arrangement makes it possible for payments to be made every fortnight, as prescribed by the act.

Conversely, preparation of the payment order is quite cumbersome in Maharashtra. The junior engineer of the Block takes measurements and makes all the calculations with just a calculator. As expected, this prolongs the process of compiling lists and making calculations; with computers, results are obtained not only more quickly but also more accurately. After the payment order is made, it moves within the Block for authorization before being sent to the bank/post office for payment to the worker. There are no last-mile connectivity arrangements such as BC agencies located and operating in villages; thus, someone from the nearest post office must visit the village to make payments by hand. Unsurprisingly, delays are inherent in this arrangement.

Monitoring mechanisms are crucial to any system of delivery – the process indicators, input indicators, outcome indicators, and more all need to be traced for efficient and transparent delivery of the promised entitlements of any program. The MGNREGA website is a very good instrument for providing this transparency; the National Informatics Centre has created a comprehensive website for this purpose as well. The MGNREGA website also provides a facility for complaints to be lodged by a worker or any citizen on behalf of the worker. The AP government has further modified it to suit its needs for transparency and monitoring and made it more appropriate to its implementation systems. It has hired Tata Consultancy Services to create and manage the website, which is updated continuously and uploaded from various Mandal offices. This website provides much better, complete data, with analysis reports too.

Maharashtra, on the other hand, is lagging in this regard. The data uploaded are mainly related to attendance, and work-related data are not given adequate importance. Using the management information system (MIS) for monitoring and corrective measures is not yet a norm for the officers in the delivery set-up, so it neither serves the purpose of transparency nor provides implementers and policy makers with information for decisions regarding delivery improvement.

Furthermore, AP obtains feedback by providing a toll-free number, enabling anyone to register complaints. The complainant is given a number to trace the action taken on the complaint. Furthermore, the AP MGNREGA director appears on the state-run TV channel for an hour every week to take queries, comments, and suggestions. There are periodic (weekly/fortnightly) review meetings at Mandal and district MGNREGA offices, which any civil society organization or journalist can attend. All these measures provide the opportunity for complaints to be addressed, allowing for more open and quicker ways of receiving feedback. No such measures are implemented in Maharashtra.

Social audit is a very important aspect of the MGNREGA as it allows all the records that are generated as part of the program, such as the muster, measurement book, payment order, and all other technical aspects, to be made available to workers and villagers participating in that particular project. These are meant to be read out in a public meeting where any objections voiced are to be noted. These observations are taken as complaints. In AP, there is an elaborate arrangement for social audits to be conducted through a government-initiated directorate. They take the complaints seriously and even lodge police complaints if the irregularities are severe.

In Maharashtra, the fact that record-keeping is not only inefficient but also non-transparent is one reason to doubt the effectiveness of social audits. There, the social audits are conducted primarily by civil society organizations, and no action is ever taken against an erring official.

In AP, the various mechanisms across the entire implementation system have IT support. The website is one example of communication, transparency, and monitoring. The preparation of technical estimates, measurement books, and payment orders are good examples of automation of repetitive tasks. Communication regarding availability, transfer, and utilization of funds among the various levels of administration is facilitated by the IT-based structure. Tracking the flow of funds and payments up to the village and worker level through biometric identification and mobile technology is also a major step in improving efficiency and transparency. The government wants to use IT to trace every household, every rupee, and every project. This is a big accomplishment in itself.

Table 3.4 shows a comparison of the administrative systems in both states.

TABLE 3.4

Status of implementation mechanisms in Andhra Pradesh and Maharashtra

Implementation structure	Andhra Pradesh	Maharashtra
Basic unit of administration	Mandal	Block (at least three times larger)
Human resources	Adequate in number Clearly defined job description Continuous training	Too low Overlapping roles None planned
At the last mile (Gram Panchayat)	Field assistant Technical assistant Customer service provider	None
Extension of bank services	Business Correspondent model with service provider	None
Record-keeping, information sharing, monitoring	MIS (end to end digitization)	MIS (reporting only)
Grievance redress	Website Helpline Ombudsman Social audit	Website

The Makeover of Maharashtra

In 2009 and 2010, Maharashtra acknowledged its dismal performance in and took steps to change from the earlier ways of the EGS to the delivery mechanism of MGNREGA. Operational guidelines were studied and several government orders were issued for better operational clarity. New methods of information flow and documentation were introduced, predominantly in digital form. New formats were introduced to collate information at various levels of administration. To facilitate the transfer of decision making from districts to Blocks, larger overhead expenditure was necessary to build new infrastructure, namely, the computer centres; however, the investment paid off in making the process faster and easier.

To further improve the delivery mechanism, personnel also needed to be recruited and trained. The appointment of a local person as an assistant to the Panchayat secretary in each Gram Panchayat, the formation of special

FIGURE 3.3

Total households participating in the program in Maharashtra

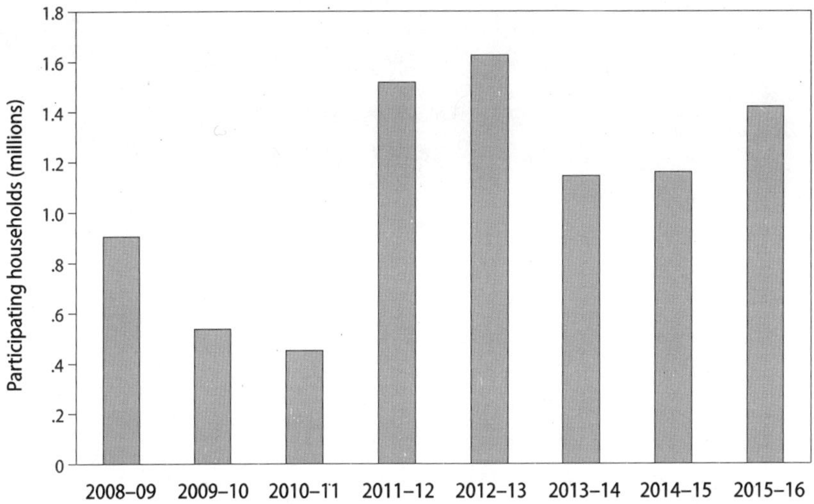

FIGURE 3.4

Total person-days of employment generated by the program in Maharashtra

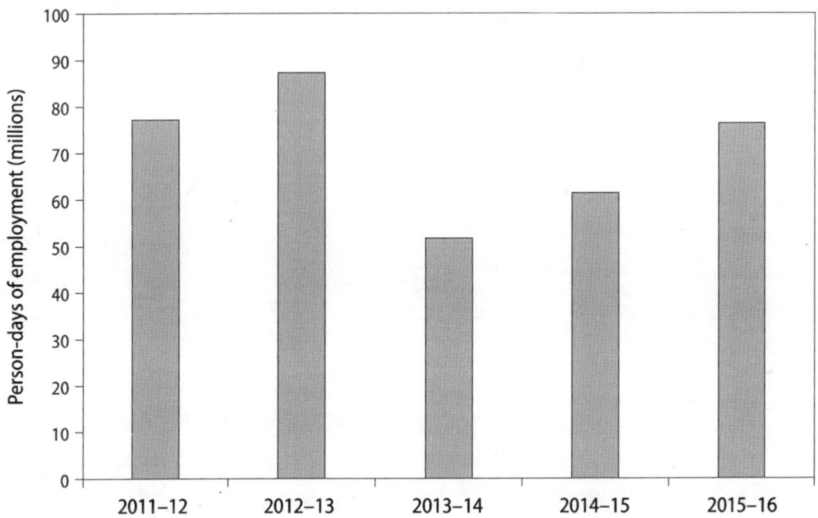

FIGURE 3.5

Expenditure on MGNREGA in Maharashtra

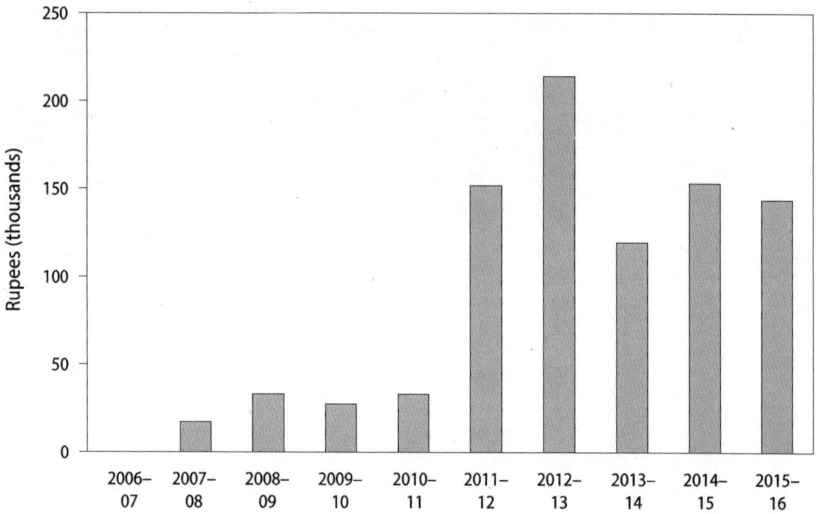

teams in Blocks, and the erection of the special commissioner office for the state were all particularly important actions. The Maharashtra government also created a new website on which all decisions and communication within the state were accessible to all citizens, as opposed to just the bureaucracy. In addition, a helpline for grievance redress was established, an ombudsman was appointed in each district, and a social audit directorate was formed. The development of procedures and rules for paying unemployment allowances, the basic fallback mechanism for the guarantee entitlement, and compensation for delay in wage payments to workers show the accountability of the state government. All such measures have led to some improvement in Maharashtra's implementation performance, as shown in Figures 3.3 to 3.5.

Conclusion

A policy gets formulated into a scheme, and a set of guidelines are prepared from which the implementation system follows. The implementation system has a delivery mechanism, a monitoring mechanism, and a grievance redress mechanism, all of which are important for any development scheme to be implemented effectively. In this chapter, we have studied the details of implementation of one such Indian government scheme, the MGNREGA, in the states of Maharashtra and Andhra Pradesh. Based on extensive fieldwork, we were able to identify the precise implementation procedures in the two states and observe that the use of information technology and decentralization in administration of the scheme are the most important factors ensuring the smooth running of the scheme.

This chapter brings out the importance of institutional knowledge in the appraisal of any government scheme, especially in a federal structure like that of India. While the broad contours of a scheme might be the same across a country, it may be implemented very differently across states, and we shed light on how such differences translate into differences in outcomes. Future research should consider such institutional differences in the evaluation of any government program.

APPENDIX

The *Mahatma Gandhi National Rural Employment Guarantee Act* (MGNREGA) was passed in 2006 with the objective of providing employment to rural labourers who have no alternate source of employment (especially in the slack season). Employment would be provided for infrastructure projects such as irrigation and roads. The MGNREGA, therefore, is also a means of creating productive assets in the rural economy.

The program has the following features:

- It is embodied in an Act of Parliament stating that individuals have the right to demand work. This legislation also makes the program impervious, to some extent, to changes in government at either the centre or the states.
- Universal: All adults in rural India are entitled to the program, with a limit of 100 days per household.
- Self-selection: While the program is not meant for any particular group of households, it offers only unskilled, hard manual labour and corresponding wages; the wages under the program are independent of minimum legal wages (lower in most states).
- Demand-driven: Workers who need employment give a "demand" to the concerned official; as per the act, work has to start within fifteen days of the submission.

- Payment: Workers receive task-based payments, with earnings calculated based on the output:
  - Prescribed in the schedule of rates from each government, each task involved in a particular project has a rate that is fixed by the respective governments and renewed at least once a year to adjust for inflation.
  - Once the work begins, wages earned by the workers must be paid within a fortnight.
- No contractors: Contractors are not allowed to start or supervise work.
- Transparency: This is the first government program that publicizes most information and decisions on a dedicated website (www.nrega.nic.in). Information provided includes: updated progress reports of expenditures, payment, and work on each person, household, and project.
- Grievance redress: This is another first for any development program: the website mentioned above provides a facility for anyone to lodge complaints and to track the action taken on such complaints.
- Social audit: In addition to the mandatory financial audit, there is provision for a social audit conducted by the villagers and the workers in which the Gram Sabha[8] and people of the village question the authorities regarding the lacunae in implementation as well as financial irregularities:
  - The observations and findings voiced during the public hearing of social audits are treated as complaints and an action-taken report is required as part of a completion process.
- Type of work: The rule is that for any project, a minimum of 60 percent of the total expenditure has to be spent on unskilled labour wage component, and a maximum of 40 percent can be spent on skilled labor, materials, and other costs; a maximum of 6 percent of the total cost is allowed on all administrative expenses.
- Worksite facilities: Since the workers do hard manual work, there are some mandatory amenities to be provided at the worksite, including drinking water, shade, daycare for children under six years of age, and first aid for injuries and illnesses.
- Unemployment allowance: If work is not started within fifteen days after the demand has been submitted, workers are entitled to an unemployment allowance, which requires an application.
- Compensation for delayed payments: The government has also promulgated a rule for compensation if wage payment to a worker is delayed. Compensation is calculated at 0.5 percent of the wage per day.

Implementation of the MGNREGA

Registration

A potential worker registers himself/herself and his/her family with the Gram Panchayat.[9] The purpose of registration is to obtain a job card with a unique sixteen-digit number that is used in muster roll attendance, tracking payments, and administering the 100-day limit. However, failing to register prior to working is not a barrier to starting work – registration can also be done on site. If the operations are centralized at the Block level, there can be significant delays in the generation of the job card number.

Demand for Work

A labourer can make a demand for work either personally or in a group. The labourer submits the demand to the Gram Sevak or the Block Development Officer (BDO).[10]

Starting Work

After the demand for work arrives, the BDO issues a work order (with instructions to start the work) to the implementing agency, which can be a line agency such as the Forest Department, Irrigation Department, or Gram Panchayat. The implementing agency or the Gram Sevak issues a "work commencement letter" to the Gram Panchayat and to the demander.

Opening Bank/Post Office Accounts for All Workers

Opening an account for each worker is the responsibility of the administration. Accounts can be opened in the nearest bank or post office, whichever is more convenient for the worker. In practice, such an option is not typically available to individual workers because the entire Gram Panchayat chooses one or the other.

Muster Period, Measurement, and Evaluation

Payments under the MGNREGA are not daily wages: payments vary by tasks and the amount of work accomplished. At the beginning, the technical officer defines the scope of work and assigns it to "gangs" of about five to fifteen workers. A "muster period" consists of seven days during which attendance is recorded. At the end of this period, a technical officer does the measurement and evaluation of work and determines the wages to be paid.

Wages are first calculated by gangs and then distributed (according to the average) across the individual members. This process is repeated every muster period.

Payment Disbursal

From the evaluations conducted by the respective technical officers of implementing agencies, the Gram Sevak prepares a list containing names, job card numbers, account numbers, and amounts payable to all workers. This is normally called a "pay order."

After the pay order is complete, it is sanctioned by the BDO and given to the bank/post office at the Block level. This process is completed electronically; the signatures for approval by the officer and the money deposited into the individual bank accounts of workers are now IT-based as well. The bank/post office then disburses payments directly into workers' accounts.

Back-End Processes

Planning for Works

The different line agencies and Block (Panchayat Samiti) technical officers, along with villagers, first conduct site visits at each village. Walking around the entire village, they identify probable works that can be started according to the village needs, the topography, and the availability of worksites.

The Gram Sabha discusses the works proposed by the team, and a list of approved works is prepared. The list is sent to the Block, which consolidates and approves the lists of all Gram Panchayats in the Block. The lists are then sent to the Zilla Parishad, which consolidates and approves them. Finally, a list of works is sent to each Gram Panchayat. This is the basis for preparing the labour budget.

Preparation of the "Shelf of Works"

The proposed work, along with the necessary approval letter(s), of private landowners goes to the technical team (line agency/Block). The technical officer then takes on-site readings such as initial measurements and weekly measurements of the worksite and prepares a technical estimate. This is approved by the technical officers at a higher level and forwarded for administrative sanction to the BDO. The work then goes on the "shelf of works," a set of works that can be started when the labour demand arrives.

Administration

There are multiple lines of hierarchy in the implementation of this program. Responsibilities of the Block/Tehsil administration include registering demand; starting projects; sanctioning projects (up to a limit); maintaining a shelf of works; keeping records; entering all records through the National Informatics Centre website; keeping expenditures within the guidelines of a 60:40 ratio; and maintaining a maximum of 6 percent administration costs. The cycle from registration to payment with all prerequisites and follow-up actions are all accomplished at this level.

At the Gram Panchayat level, the Gram Sevak is entirely responsible for all aspects of the delivery of the program. For all these tasks, most of which repeat every cycle of work-measurement-payment, the Gram Sevak is assisted by a Gram Rozgar Sevak appointed by the Gram Sabha from among the educated youth of their village.

The district-level authorities are more concerned with supervision, monitoring, and coordination than with troubleshooting and managing of fund flows. Coordinating with the central ministry, the state-level authorities manage fund flows, monitor, make policies, and implement changes for better administration.

Payment Mechanisms: A Closer Look

There is a periodicity in the work and payments mechanism. As mentioned earlier, MGNREGA work is split up into seven-day muster periods, during which attendance is recorded and the progress of work is evaluated and measured (according to the task rate). The approval and disbursement of payments takes place at the end of the muster period.

This is graphically represented in Figure 3.6. It should be noted that there are many functionaries involved in the cycle: Gram Rozgar Sevak, Gram Sevak, engineer, Assistant Program Officer or Block Development Officer, bank/post office personnel, and data entry operator. There are also many locations involved: worksite, engineer's office, BDO office, computer centre, bank/post office. For these reasons, there are multiple points of delay in wage payments.

Presently there are three different methods of wage payment: through the post office, through banks, and through biometric ID-enabled banking payments.

FIGURE 3.6

The work-payment cycle

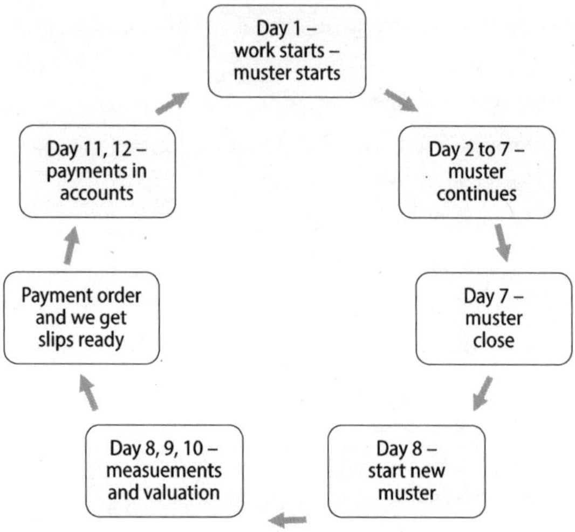

Payment through the Post Office

Funds move from the Collector or Zilla Parishad to the Block office by cheque or e-transfer. This movement is fastest if both offices have accounts in the same bank and if both do e-transfer; otherwise the process takes at least a week. From the Block office, the money is transferred to the Block post office based on the pay order. The sub–post office comes to the Block post office for withdrawals and gives the cash to the respective branch post office for disbursal. This movement takes at least another week. The entire process is inherently ill equipped to make payments to workers within the fifteen days prescribed by the act. The workers have a passbook with a photo that is manually updated by the branch post office. Payments are made based on a withdrawal slip.

Payment through Banks

As with post office transfers, there is the initial movement of funds from the District office to the Blocks. This can take place by cheque or e-transfer. The second-stage transfer occurs when the BDO transfers the amounts to individual bank accounts by e-transfer or cheque. The third stage is the interface between the bank and the MGNREGA worker (the so-called last mile connectivity). This can take several forms, depending on technology.

The simplest form is the use of Business Correspondents (BC) who carry cash to the villages at specified times. Workers make withdrawals based on photographic identity and a bank passbook (where transactions are recorded). A variant of this system is one where the BC carries a portable ATM and the workers authenticate the transactions with a smart card (or biometric ID).

Unique Biometric ID–Enabled Banking Payments

Here, the bank accounts are linked to the unique biometric ID provided by the Unique Identification Development Authority of India. This number is then used to open accounts in a bank that has the back-end infrastructure to access the authentication protocol. The BC makes payments in the villages using a Micro ATM, a portable biometric ID–enabled electronic device connected to a general packet radio services (GPRS) system through the cellular networks. It enables villagers to receive and deposit money and perform a balance inquiry in the village. It generates a receipt for each transaction and has a voice record system that announces every transaction.

NOTES

1 Gram Panchayat is the unit of governance at the village level. It comprises one or more villages and has an elected council of members and a Panchayat secretary who is responsible for delivery of all the rural development programs of the Indian government.

2 A higher office of Gram Panchayat, also known as Panchayat Samiti office.

3 More detailed notes on this program are provided in the Appendix of this chapter.

4 Andhra Pradesh is a state in southern India. In 2014, this state was divided into Andhra Pradesh and Telangana; here, "AP" refers to both states.

5 Maharashtra implemented employment programs as a drought relief measure across the state in 1972. Subsequently, this was better designed and embedded in the *Employment Guarantee Act* by 1978. In 2005, the government of India devised something similar in the MGNREGA. The major tenets of the Maharashtra act can be found in the MGNREGA.

6 The Tehsil/Block is an administrative unit above the Gram Panchayat and below the District Council, Zilla Parishad. The three-tier system of Village-Block-District constitutes the basic administrative structure of the state.

7 The Zilla Parishad is a local government institution at the district level. Within a district, the smaller administrative units are the Panchayat Samiti at the block level and the Gram Panchayat at the village level.
8 Gram Sabha is a meeting of all the voters of a Gram Panchayat.
9 The Gram Panchayat is an elected council for administration of one or more villages.
10 The Gram Sevak is the secretary of the Gram Panchayat. The BDO is the Block Development Officer for a Block, which consists of several Gram Panchayats.

4

From Cautious Support to Precautionary Paralysis
The Evolution of India's Regulatory Regime for Transgenics

MILIND KANDLIKAR

Controversies over the use of genetically modified (GM), or transgenic, crops in agriculture reflect the complex relationship between science, technology, and society in the current era of globalization.[1] Over the past two decades, the growth of molecular biology and applied genetics has led to new technological possibilities in agriculture. Some of these advances have resulted in the improvement of existing areas of research such as plant pathology and conventional breeding. Others, such as transgenic approaches, which enable the introduction of novel genetic traits into commercial agricultural seeds, signify a break from conventional agriculture and open up new possibilities for rapid increases in agricultural productivity not otherwise possible (Gressel 2008). These innovations have come at a time when the debate over globalization has intensified, conflicts over the ownership and control of useful scientific knowledge have become commonplace, and there is growing concern over the health of the natural environment.

At first glance, transgenics appear to be well suited to the needs of developing countries like India. Protagonists, primarily scientists, academic/professional economists, and members of the agricultural biotechnology industry, note that genetic modification could facilitate the development of new crop varieties that can fight disease, combat pests, and tolerate abiotic stresses such as low soil moisture in times of drought. They present evidence that transgenic crops can help reduce costs and/or increase productivity, thus enhancing farm incomes (Qaim and Zilberman 2003).

Transgenics are also seen to be "scale-neutral" – that is, they would not disproportionately favour large farmers over small ones. Designer crops such as "Golden Rice" could be used to tackle nutritional deficiencies by supplementing diets with micronutrients such as vitamin A (Paine et al. 2005). In the long term, transgenic crops may also be used in "pharming," the production of chemicals and pharmaceuticals through agricultural means, thus opening new markets to poor farmers (Ramessar, Capell, and Christou 2008). More broadly, supporters see transgenics as an important component in solving the global challenge of food production – feeding a growing global population at a time when agricultural productivity increases are stabilizing.

Despite India's long history of support and investment in recombinant DNA technologies, including in agriculture, the progress of implementing the use of transgenics in Indian agriculture has been slow because activists have been successful in slowing the adoption of transgenics. Many simply do not trust that the technology is effective; others disagree with the assessment that transgenics are scale-neutral; some even discriminate positively toward small farmers, arguing that the technology favours large and wealthier farmers, and is thus unsuitable for India's needs (Sahai 2003). Others note that research and development (R&D) into and commercialization of transgenics are dominated by a handful of multinationals. They fear that the control of intellectual property (IP) by multinationals renders the use of transgenics in agriculture antithetical to the food security of the poor and the economic interests of developing countries.

These differences in worldview are exacerbated by scientific uncertainty (real and perceived) over the impacts of genetic modification on human health and the environment. On some issues, such as the flows of genetic material from transgenics to their non-transgenic counterparts and wild species, there is genuine scientific disagreement. On human health concerns, such as allergenicity and toxicity, there is an emerging global scientific consensus that current transgenic crops are no more likely to cause harm than other traditional or novel foods (Key, Ma, and Drake 2008). Nonetheless, public perception in many jurisdictions, including India, is ambivalent. More generally, jurisdictions are divided on the choice of policy frameworks for recognizing and managing the risks and uncertainties associated with the cultivation of transgenics. While proponents see it as fundamentally safe and call for regulatory frameworks that enable rapid diffusion of the technology, others invoke the "precautionary principle," according to which transgenic technology is presumed to present a high risk and the onus is on supporters to prove that it is safe, thus requiring transgenics to meet a higher evidentiary bar for safety.

Bt cotton, a type of cottonseed modified to include genetic material from the common soil bacterium *Bacillus thuringiensis,* which is toxic to an important class of cotton pests, is the only transgenic approved for cultivation in India. The experience with *Bt* cotton of India's agricultural sector and most of its roughly 10 million cotton farmers has been positive.[2] Most *Bt* cotton varieties produced in India are under licence from Mahyco, an Indian subsidiary of the US-based multinational Monsanto, and are grown by virtually all of India's cotton famers. *Bt* cotton varieties have proven so popular that small seed companies have produced and sold large quantities of "stealth" varieties that are neither approved by the government nor licensed by Monsanto. These stealth varieties date back to 2002 (prior to commercial approval) and continue to be sold today, albeit in smaller numbers. They represent farmers' grassroots defiance of both IP laws and the authority of the state to monitor and implement its own biosafety regulations.

Agricultural biotechnology in India has an early history of government support. India's Department of Biotechnology (DBT) was formed as early as 1986 to promote biotechnology in health, medicine, and agriculture. Legislative changes in the late 1980s then allowed private firms to engage in the sale of agricultural seed, a move that transformed India's seed industry from primarily state-run enterprises to one involving multiple small and large private firms. By the late 1990s, India's seed sector was competitive, with diversified sales and increasing R&D investment by national and multinational firms (Pray, Ramaswami, and Kelley 2001). In 1997, Mahyco launched field trials of *Bt* cotton.

In many ways, cotton was the most suitable choice for the introduction of transgenic technology to India. In the late 1990s, cotton was planted on 10 percent of India's arable land (Eyhorn, Ramakrishnan, and Mäder 2007) and accounted for almost a third of India's agricultural GDP. Cotton production and associated textile manufacturing was responsible for roughly 30 million jobs in India (Barwale et al. 2004).

The bollworm complex of pests, particularly the Old World Bollworm, or *Helicoverpa armigera,* is extremely harmful to cotton production in India. Prior to the introduction of *Bt* cotton, over half of the pesticides used in India was aimed at *H. armigera.* Despite widespread use of pesticides, however, yields of cotton in India were low, often much lower than those in other major cotton-producing regions (Barwale et al. 2004). A primary reason for this was the growing resistance of *H. armigera* to common pesticides. Transgenics that used *Bt* had been demonstrated to be very effective against this pest and were being used widely in US cotton and corn production. As a cash crop, cotton was also less likely to trigger human health and safety concerns that might have accompanied food crops.

Despite a compelling case for introduction of *Bt* cotton into India, the regulatory approval process was protracted and it took nine years for the multiple stages of negotiation, from the importation of *Bt* cotton germplasm in 1993 to the approval of *Bt* cotton hybrids for cultivation in 2002. The 1990s were a time of contestation over globalization in India. Trade liberalization, particularly in agriculture, was strongly opposed by vocal activists, and many in the government were also ambivalent about Monsanto, which had a history of deep distrust in India and elsewhere. Despite strong endorsement of *Bt* cotton by Indian farmers, no other transgenics have been approved, though firms have made several attempts, both individually and in partnership with public entities, to bring them to the market. The most prominent of these efforts centred on *Bt* brinjal (eggplant) by Mahyco; it came close to approval in 2009 but remains in regulatory limbo, awaiting biosafety certification for commercial use.

This chapter analyzes how India, a developing country with a large agrarian and rural population, has regulated and controlled the use of transgenics in agriculture. The focus is on biosafety and, to a lesser extent, intellectual property, rather than trade in agriculture.[3] Specifically, it examines whether or how the rules governing the adoption of transgenics in India have evolved over time, and how they have been shaped by internal dynamics as well as in reaction to the international policy regimes of biosafety and intellectual property. The Indian story is multi-layered, with international context being important in the initial design of domestic biosafety laws. Yet the explanations for India's policy evolution on transgenic regulation lie within the domestic sphere. Successive Indian governments have responded in sporadic, fragmentary, and often contradictory ways to controversies that have dogged the use of transgenics in Indian agriculture with metronomic regularity. India has moved from a state that, in its early years, supported transgenics to one that has not approved a single new transgenic over the past decade, and one that routinely imposes moratoria on testing and commercialization.

The lack of consistency in India's policy toward transgenics is especially worrying in the context of a globalized economy A key benefit of globalization is knowledge diffusion, which helps less developed or developing economies like India to catch up with the developed economies by using new technologies to which they may otherwise not have access. Transgenics are especially important in India's case since they can play an important role in the country's agriculture, which suffers from low productivity. This chapter traces the evolution of the Indian government's response from tentative support to the current state of regulatory paralysis, and offers reasons why India, a poor country with much to gain from transgenic technologies, has taken an increasingly precautionary approach.

In the next section, we present India's biosafety regulations in a comparative frame vis-à-vis those of the European Union and the United States, and we address the question of how these different regulations handle risk assessments. Next, we describe India's experience with transgenic technologies in two parts. The first part relates to the approval and subsequent commercial cultivation of *Bt* cotton and the regulatory controversies it engendered. The second part relates to the approval processes for *Bt* brinjal and the precautionary turn in India's transgenic policies. We conclude with comments on the future of India's transgenics in the face of precautionary politics.

Biosafety in India in a Comparative Frame

Regulation of transgenics involves two overlapping but distinct national and international policy regimes. First, since transgenic plant varieties often involve scientific techniques and innovations developed in the private sector, IP laws have a bearing on the uptake of transgenic seeds. Firms seek protection for IP in multiple jurisdictions. Second, transgenics are novel biological forms the use and adoption of which are typically governed by biosafety regulations within each jurisdiction. International trade and cross-border movement of transgenics are governed by the Cartagena Protocol aimed at protecting biological diversity from potential risks (De Greef 2004).[4]

IP protection in the form of patents provides firms with incentive to innovate and profit from their investments in R&D. National jurisdictions each have their own patent protection laws and can differ significantly in the IP protections offered to the products of biotechnology. In particular, IP protections related to agricultural biotechnology can be quite complex, and different components might be protected in different ways. In the United States, for instance, novel plant germplasm is offered the more generally used utility patent protection, while cloned varieties can be claimed under a plant patent.

In addition to biological entities, patents can also protect the tools and methods of biotechnology – those used for genetic transformation, selection assisted by genetic markers, and the regulation of genetic expression. Arrangements under the World Trade Organization's *Agreement on Trade-Related Aspects of Intellectual Property Rights* (TRIPS) have sought to harmonize global IP protections for plant varieties, but the actual granting of rights can vary across jurisdictions (Stiglitz 2007). Plant varieties can be protected either by patents or by a unique regime that is wholly indigenous or one based on the *International Convention for the Protection of New Varieties of Plants.* The convention, adopted in 1961 with amendments in 1978 and 1991, established the International Union for the Protection of New Varieties of Plants (UPOV) and grants plant breeders the exclusive right to market registered varieties, with several exemptions for non-commercial and research use (Koo, Nottenburg, and Pardey 2004).

The Cartagena Protocol provides signatories with the legal tools to manage risks from cross-border movements of transgenics. It obligates the parties to ensure that the "development, handling, transport, use, transfer, and release of any living modified organisms are undertaken in a manner that prevents or reduces the risks to biological diversity, also taking into account risks to human health." At its heart, the protocol follows a precautionary approach but permits the regulation of the biosafety of transgenics and trade to remain within national discretion. With its focus on biodiversity, the protocol makes a particular aspect of biosafety – national-level biodiversity – the focal point of in-country regulation. At the national level, biosafety regulations that seek to manage potential human health and environmental risks from use of transgenics can differ (Gupta 2000). In many jurisdictions, including in India, national-level biosafety regulations in their early form predate the Cartagena Protocol. Toxicity and allergenicity of novel forms, and not effects on biodiversity per se, are the primary focal points for regulatory oversight.

Following the success of the Green Revolution in the 1970s, the government of India became an early promoter of biotechnology as a key basis for national development. India's Department of Biotechnology was formed as early as 1986 to promote biotechnology; legislative changes in the late 1980s then allowed private firms to engage in the sale of hybrid agricultural seeds (Pray, Ramaswami, and Kelley 2001). India's regulatory regime for the use of transgenics in agriculture also began to take shape in the 1980s, a time when models for biosafety regulation in the industrialized world were also beginning to emerge. In particular, India and other jurisdictions relied heavily on the recommendations of an Organisation for Economic Co-operation and Development (OECD) task force. The OECD model provided India with a prototype framework required for managing the risks of recombinant DNA (Scoones 2006). Many of the important features of India's biosafety regime designed to address the use of transgenics in research and commerce also derive from the findings of that task force.

There were inherent contradictions in the early Indian responses to biotechnology. On the one hand, one of India's aims was to build a biotechnology sector that would rapidly parlay the gains from the Green Revolution into improvements in agricultural productivity. On the other, the Indian regulatory system concurrently took on a precautionary approach that foreshadowed international agreements such as the Cartagena Protocol by scrutinizing the biosafety of new products to ensure the protection of consumers and marginal producers from technological risks. This tension between support for transgenics and caution over its use mirrors differences between regulatory attitudes in the United States and the European Union. Whereas the former is renowned as "the world's most unambiguously liberal science-based system for the regulation of agri-biotech" (Kleinman, Kinchy, and Autry 2009), the latter takes a more precautionary approach. The Indian approach has been influenced by both systems.

Scientific Risk Assessment and Transgenics

The regulation of biotechnology in the United States is product-based – the assessment of risks focuses on the product and not on the production process. Product-based regulation does not assume that the techniques of genetic engineering, specifically transgenics, are inherently risky. Central to the US approach is the idea of "substantial equivalence": if a new food or food component is found to be substantially equivalent to an existing food or food component, it can be treated in the same manner in terms of safety. This equivalence is typically established by the absence of unexpected changes in a limited set of components such as toxins or allergens that are present in the unmodified food. The US policy, coordinated by the Food and Drug Administration (FDA),[5] thus considers transgenics to be "Generally Regarded as Safe" and does not require approval unless a product is significantly different in structure, function, or composition from substances found in current food.

The assessment of environmental risks is also targeted at the level of a product and within the *existing* framework of environmental protection laws, so transgenics do not require an entirely new regulatory framework to cope with them (Jasanoff 2005). For example, a pesticidal transgenic that the US Environmental Protection Agency is obligated to regulate as a pesticide might be tested for toxicity or impact on soil biota in the same way as other pesticides. Thus, US regulations might require testing but transgenics are not singled out for risk assessments above and beyond those required of the broader class of products to which the transgenic belongs.

The European Union's regulation, by contrast, seeks to regulate the process of genetic engineering. In doing so, it established a firm boundary for transgenics and other ways through which novel varieties are made, such as hybridization or the creation of mutations in germplasms through chemical or radiational attack. Thus, the products of genetic engineering *are not* substantially equivalent to similar products, and transgenics are required to meet a higher regulatory standard for health and environmental risks than other novel varieties. The precautionary principle that underlies the EU approach shifts the burden of proof of safety onto the proponents of a regulatory decision.

In general, the difference is as follows: the US view is that in the absence of demonstrable scientific risk, there is no reason to stop the technology from being introduced, whereas in the EU approach, the product must be proven to be safe to the satisfaction of stakeholders.

Risk assessment as embodied in the US approach quantifies risk in probabilistic terms by assessing hazard probability and the consequences of an adverse event. The EU also relies on scientific means for the evaluation of transgenic risks (Kleinman, Kinchy, and Autry 2009) but since complete knowledge in risk assessment is very rare and it is virtually impossible for the probability of an adverse event to be zero, precautionary approaches such as those in the EU can set an arbitrary (and subjective) bar for approval. Additionally, the European Union regulates transgenics with a broader conceptualization of risk that includes social and political aspects alongside any environmental or health effects. The most recent EU rules (November 2014) have codified this approach and now allow member states to ban transgenics "on the basis of, inter alia, the aims of environmental policy, town and country planning, land use, agricultural policy, public policy, or possible socio-economic impacts."[6]

Indian regulatory directives are at the level of the genetic "event," not the product. Thus, as in the EU case, the production process matters. Consequently, there is reliance on case-by-case biosafety testing, with the onus on the firm to seek safety approval as there is no independent body that does safety testing.[7] Unlike the United States, where testing is not mandatory, firms in India are required to extensively test transgenics before they can be approved for cultivation. The early Indian model drawn from various OECD sources was subjected to multiple pressures over time that helped it "more thoroughly root its form and function within the national context" (Freeman, Satterfield, and Kandlikar 2011). We turn to this transformation next.

India's Evolving and Meta-Stable Biosafety Regime

Prior to *Bt* Cotton Approval (1990–2002)

India's *Environment Protection Act* (EPA) came to effect in 1986 in the aftermath of the Bhopal tragedy, perhaps the deadliest industrial accident in human history. Under the EPA, a newly formed ministry, the Ministry of Environment and Forests (MoEF) was placed in charge of administering and enforcing national environmental policy. In the flurry of environmental legislations that followed, India announced its biosafety rules for transgenics in 1989. OECD guidelines were important in providing the template for the configuration of committees and procedures for the approval of imports, research, monitoring, and commercialization.

Crucial for our case, India's biosafety laws came jointly under the purview of two ministries, the MoEF and the Ministry of Science and Technology via the Department of Biotechnology (DBT). The DBT was to be the nodal unit for providing scientific input into the assessment of risks and biosafety, while the MoEF's focus was the environment. The rules fail to address the roles of other ministries, though the connection of some (such as agriculture and health) to transgenics via seed laws and human health risks are obvious. India's federalist structure also plays a role. Agriculture is a state responsibility under the Indian constitution, and state committees are responsible for monitoring and taking punitive actions within their own jurisdictions in connection with violation of transgenic rules.

The DBT constitutes the Review Committee on Genetic Manipulation (RCGM), a committee of scientists to assess, approve, and monitor the safety of research into transgenics. The RCGM is responsible for approving the importation of novel germplasm, developing protocols for biosafety testing, and approving products through lab and greenhouse experiments and through contained field trials. The bulk of the scientific risk assessment for transgenic approvals is performed under the watch of the RCGM. The RCGM is also responsible for monitoring multi-location and large-scale field trials that are required prior to commercialization.[8]

Approval for commercialization of these trials is the responsibility of the Genetic Engineering Approval Committee (GEAC). The GEAC is constituted by the MoEF and includes bureaucrats and scientists drawn from various ministries. Its purpose is to make the ultimate judgment after assessing the biosafety and commercial performance of the transgenic. Testing for commercial performance is required for all new genetic events, as well as for genetic events that have been previously approved for biosafety but inserted into a new hybrid or variety. Thus, a genetic event requires a single approval for biosafety, but its agro-economic performance is tested each time the event is inserted into a new variety or hybrid. The focus on agro-economic testing is a departure from both US and EU biosafety rules, with the expressed intent being to protect the farmer. Paradoxically, the Ministry of Agriculture was initially not involved in this process.

Transgenics are tested for biosafety by the applicant firm under the watch of the RCGM using a range of studies. With the inclusion of testing for toxicity in mammals and fish, conducting environmental studies of pollen flow and soil micro-biota, or performing laboratory work on the germplasm through genetic analyses, the Indian testing regime for biosafety regulation is comprehensive. The costs of such meticulousness are correspondingly high. Pray, Bengali, and Ramaswami (2005) estimate that the total pre-approval testing costs borne by Mahyco for *Bt* cotton came to $1.8 million, and the cost for transgenic mustard to $4–5 million. Estimates for Indian public sector firms seeking approvals are far lower, mostly because costs incurred in government labs are not included. Regardless, for small firms in India seeking to bring new genetic events to the market, the cost of testing transgenics may be prohibitive.

Biosafety regulation in most jurisdictions has evolved over time. Though outside models are key from the start, the early rules in most jurisdictions have been adapted to shifts in knowledge, emerging public concerns, and other pressures. In India, this process began early in the formation of the bureaucratic machinery of regulation. In the first of many public interest litigation (PIL) challenges in the Supreme Court that have periodically marked India's transgenic regulation, the NGO Research Foundation for Science, Technology, and Ecology (RFSTE) challenged the authorization of field trials for Mahyco's *Bt* cotton varieties provided by the RCGM in 1998. This was due to the RFSTE's contention that the RCGM did not have the writ to authorize field trials, since this was at variance with the 1989 rules that required special GEAC approval for deliberate releases. The legislation was amended to give RCGM such approval authority by creating a distinction between limited/confined and large-scale trials, with the GEAC being responsible for the latter and the RCGM for the former. This change clarified the distinction between scientific aspects of biosafety risk assessment (up to and including limited/confined trials) and the agro-economic aspects needed for commercialization. It also solidified the distinction between the roles of the GEAC and the DBT.

The RFSTE's challenge was only the first by Indian activists. The late 1990s was a time when anti-globalization activism was in full swing in India. Transgenic technologies were regarded with suspicion since they were linked with Monsanto, a widely reviled multinational. Monsanto's purchase of the US firm that held the "terminator gene" patent cemented activist suspicions and led to campaigns such as "Cremate Monsanto" that targeted transgenics and their purveyors. Naturally, more lawsuits by the RFSTE and others followed, eventually leading to the consolidation of an anti-GMO coalition whose opposition to transgenics was as much about multinational takeover of Indian agriculture as it was about risk and biosafety.

Late in the already-contested approval process, controversy related to yields of *Bt* cotton erupted. The commercialization field trials conducted in 2001 by Mahyco showed an 80–87 percent increase in yields for the *Bt* cotton variety compared with the same variety without the *Bt* gene (Qaim and Zilberman 2003). The study also found dramatic reductions in pesticide costs since *Bt* cotton required less pesticides than the non-*Bt* variety to protect against bollworm attacks. Even though it carried the imprimatur of the journal *Science,* the study was criticized as biased because the legitimacy of its findings rested on the acceptance of data from a set of field trials led by Monsanto. The legitimacy of official/state science as embodied by RCGM and GEAC testing was also called into question since Monsanto paid for the trials. The Ministry of Agriculture's Indian Agricultural Research Institute was asked to step in and conduct additional agronomic field trials to verify the RCGM/GEAC trial data so as to provide some legitimacy to the regulatory process.

While India's NGOs were opposing Monsanto's commercial approval, farmers in the western state of Gujarat were busy planting *Bt* cotton in 2001. Mahyco discovered that thousands of them were planting an unapproved variety of *Bt* cotton sold by Navbharat Seeds, a private seed company. By some accounts, this had been going on for over three years. Navbharat's unapproved *Bt* variety was a huge success among farmers since it gave high yields while reducing pesticide costs. In response to a complaint by Mahyco that year, the GEAC requested the Gujarat government to destroy crops that were verifiably *Bt* cotton. Under pressure from the farmers' lobby, the Gujarat government did not comply with this request, but did manage to shut down the sale of contraband seeds from Navbharat. This triggered an unprecedented local response. During the 2002 season, more than a dozen hybrid variants of *Bt* cotton were locally developed and sold in the market under a variety of different names. Local breeders had managed to acquire the parental lines of *Bt* cotton and backcrossed these with locally adapted hybrids to produce *Bt* variants that performed better than Mahyco's legal variety (Shah 2005). Farmers embraced these varieties with enthusiasm.

GEAC approval for the commercialization of *Bt* cotton came in March 2002 after agronomic studies conducted by the GEAC/RCGM and the Indian Council of Agricultural Research showed a clear benefit. However, politics was also at play. As Herring and Kandlikar (2009) have argued, the stringent regulation was one reason why Navbharat bypassed Delhi's GEAC and sold stealth seeds in Gujarat without approval. Ironically, the political impetus for GEAC approval of transgenic cotton came from the astonishing agronomic success of stealth *Bt* cotton. Success in the field galvanized farmers and their unions to protest and to exert pressure on the GEAC to approve the technology.

By the time *Bt* cotton was approved, the battle lines within India were clearly drawn and there was little room for compromise. Since then, the chasm has deepened and the process of testing, approval, and monitoring has been pulled in many directions. On the one hand, advocates in industry and government research labs want a faster regulatory process to approve novel transgenics; on the other, opponents have effectively used court challenges and public consultation processes to prevent the regulatory system from approving field trials or encourage it to impose moratoria.[9] In what follows, we focus on one important tactic used by opponents of *Bt* cotton – the claim that *Bt* cotton (and, by implication, all transgenics) have failed to work in India – and examine how these claims, though incorrect, have furthered an ever more precautionary view of transgenic regulation.

Objective Evidence and Claims of "Failure"

After the approval, controversy related to yields of *Bt* cotton in the first seasons of planting arose. During the first growing seasons, from 2002 to 2003, *Bt* cotton received mixed reports. Whereas industry reports claimed that *Bt* cotton performed well (Barwale et al. 2004) as seed sales of both approved and unapproved varieties were robust and growing, NGOs reported either failure of *Bt* cotton against the bollworm pests or no net positive impact at all (Sahai and Rahman 2003). Furthermore, the claims of failure from Andhra Pradesh in 2004 (Qayum and Sakkhari 2005) and Vidharbha in 2005 (Sahai 2005) set the stage for other negative reports and an unfounded link to mass suicides by farmers that followed.

Conversely, studies by the government and those sponsored by industry were strongly positive regarding the effects of *Bt* cotton on yields and farmer incomes (Herring, Wesseler, and Scatasta 2009). Academic studies were also positive but less so than government and industry studies. Over time, the success of *Bt* cotton was evident in its widespread diffusion and voluntary planting by millions of farmers all over India. By 2011, less than a decade after approval, over 90 percent of cotton grown in India had transgenic *Bt*, and hundreds of seed firms were marketing hundreds of hybrid cultivars of *Bt* cotton.[10] Sales of unapproved seeds have continued, albeit at reduced levels. Despite claims of "failure" by NGOs, the success of *Bt* cotton has persisted.

The failure narrative takes one of two forms (Herring and Rao 2012). First, failure might be agronomic, where the transgenic technology "does not work" and the plants are not protected against bollworm attacks. However, there is no evidence that *Bt* cotton hybrids in India that carry the Cry1Ac gene and its antecedents have failed in this way. Rather, failure narratives have tended to conflate the performance of the trait that confers bollworm resistance with the performance of the hybrid seed (such as response to drought) and the cotton quality (such as staple length and boll size) of the cotton varietal into which the *Bt* gene was inserted. Thus, failures for reasons unrelated to the *Bt* trait (such as the response of a particular hybrid to the lack of rainfall in Andhra Pradesh) have been attributed to the transgenic nature of the seed, and to transgenic technology as a whole. Indeed, an overall assessment of *Bt* cotton's success or failure would need to be economic, namely, determining whether the additional cost of cultivating *Bt* cotton hybrids is offset by the greater income from yield improvements, pesticide reductions, or both. A number of peer-reviewed studies have done exactly this for different *Bt* hybrids from different regions over the past decade.

A meta-analysis of twenty-two field studies sponsored by the International Food Policy Research Institute (IFPRI) found overall benefits to farmers across India (Gruère, Mehta-Bhatt, and Sengupta 2008):[11] average yields increased by 39.1 percent compared with non-*Bt* varieties, and pesticide use declined by 34.4 percent. In fact, the analysis found little evidence for agronomic failure and claimed that the *Bt* trait worked as expected. The variability across NGO, academic, and industry studies is best explained by a number of factors unrelated to transgenic technology – the initial lack of *Bt* varieties tailored for local drought conditions, cases of high seed prices compensating for the reduction in pesticide costs, and inadequate knowledge of the technology influencing agronomic choices. These concerns persist even though the objective evidence from this meta-analysis points to success for *Bt* cotton. Although costs of cultivation increased by 15 percent (as expected), corresponding growth in yields and reduction in pesticide use more than compensated for it. The study found a resulting net increase in average economic returns of 53 percent, a number that is a credibly explained by the rapid uptake of *Bt* cotton in all growing areas. The IFPRI study also disproved another common accusation, namely, that the adoption of *Bt* cotton was responsible for the large number of farmer suicides in India.

A number of more recent peer-reviewed academic studies confirm the finding that *Bt* cotton in India was an agronomic and economic success. Kathage and Qaim (2012) provide evidence that *Bt* cotton led to a 50 percent increase in profits and a 24 percent increase in cotton yield per acre through reduced pest damage. Herring and Rao (2012) also compared *Bt* and non-*Bt* plantings by studying the changes in yields from samples over time, and found that net income from *Bt* crops had doubled, or even tripled in some cases.[12] Pray and colleagues (2011) present evidence showing that, on average, Indian cotton yields almost doubled from 300 kg/ha in 2000–01 to 560 kg/ha in 2007–08. During the same period, *Bt* cotton cultivation increased from less than 1 percent to almost 90 percent of all cotton acreage.[13] In sum, the positive impact of *Bt* cotton on India's yields and smallholder farmer profits is undeniable (Klümper and Qaim 2014).

Around the world, public policy disagreements over transgenics have centred on health or environmental risks, equity concerns related to corporate dominance of agriculture, and the ethics of "tinkering" with nature. Many of these questions cannot be resolved in a straightforward way as they are part of a broader public debate on modernity and a reflection on the zeitgeist of the current era of globalization.

As Herring and Kandlikar (2009) point out, the assertion by those who oppose transgenic technology in India is an empirical claim about a measurable aspect of the technology, and is thus different from ethical objections to the technology or other assertions regarding values. In a series of papers, Herring has argued persuasively that the persistence of the claims of failure is due to a confluence of factors (Herring 2008a, 2008b, 2014; Herring and Kandlikar 2009; Herring and Rao 2012). The GMO frame through which *Bt* cotton is viewed is a stigmatized frame (Herring 2008a); all data, especially field data that are subject to greater uncertainty than laboratory data, are filtered through this frame and are more easily subject to a confirmation bias. Many of the claims of failure are unverifiable and those around the world who strongly oppose transgenics use the internet to spread such claims. The vast amount of peer-reviewed evidence in support of *Bt* cotton is simply ignored by activists or is written off as being constructed by self-interested scientists and economists in cahoots with multinational corporations.

The rapid and universal uptake of *Bt* cotton around India is more difficult to refute and requires the use of a different analytical strategy in order to maintain the narrative of failure. Farmers are framed as dupes who naïvely adopt a technology after a fashion (Stone 2011) and plant the same seeds year after year despite repeated crop failures. The characterizations of the farmer as a naïve agent of his or her own demise, both literal and figurative, reinforce a narrative of profit-seeking multinationals victimizing Third World peasants (Herring and Rao 2012). However, this ignores the fact that farmers around India sought out and bought illegal *Bt* cotton seed, acting as economic agents to further their own interests (Shah 2005).

The claims of *Bt* cotton failure are not without consequence. Broad agreement among vocal activist groups asserting that the technology is harming farmers to the point of driving them to suicide makes it difficult for policy makers to support transgenics. Perceived failure in agronomic performance negates the core justification that transgenics provide benefits that are otherwise unavailable to Indian farmers. A recent example makes this point. In 2012, the Parliamentary Committee of Agriculture submitted a report to the parliament on transgenics in India following a two-year process of consultation. The report focused on stakeholder opinions of long-term environmental and chronic toxicology risks and downplayed the efficacy of the Indian biosafety regulations. The committee's thirty-one members agreed unanimously that the benefits of *Bt* cotton were unrealized, and that it had harmed Indian farmers instead.[14] The fact that a parliamentary committee that included members from a range of political parties unanimously agreed with the failure narrative despite sound evidence to the contrary is a vivid example of how transgenics have come to be widely perceived in India as a risky technology that provides little benefit to poor farmers.

The debate on *Bt* cotton yields follows a well-recognized pattern in the study of technological risk. Objective assessments of the risks and benefits of new technologies are rarely the sole basis on which such technologies are regulated and accepted. Technologies, especially new and emerging ones like transgenics, are also judged by how trade-offs are *perceived.* Psychologists attribute risk aversion to the perceived characteristics of the risk object and to the values and cultural models affiliated with it. Psychometric approaches have found that when a risk object (such as nuclear waste or GMOs) is regarded as dreadful, uncontrollable, unknown, or unfamiliar, that risk will likely capture the public's imagination and lead to risk-averse behavioural outcomes (Fischhoff et al. 1978; Slovic 1987). Numerous studies have also shown that the *perceptions* of risks and benefits are linked. An object that is perceived to have a high benefit might also be seen as having a low risk, and vice versa (Finucane et al. 2000).[15]

This inverse relationship is mediated through positive or negative "affects," or emotions. Thus, the risks from technology with a positive affect (cellphones, for example) and high perceived benefit might be perceived as low or negligible, while the risks from those with a negative affect (such as nuclear power) are perceived as high with little benefit. Similarly, the framing of *Bt* cotton as failing to provide benefits to farmers might influence how risky transgenics are perceived to be.

_Bt_ Brinjal: Paralysis in Action

The vegetable that is variously known as eggplant, aubergine, or brinjal is widely grown and consumed in India, the second-largest producer of the crop worldwide. Regionally, brinjal is grown on small landholdings throughout the country (Choudhary and Gaur 2010) and in many different varieties, many of which are modern hybrids. The brinjal crop is particularly susceptible to pest attack by the Fruit and Shoot Borer (FSB), *Leucinodes orbonalis,* and the Old World Bollworm, *H. amerigera.* In fact, FSB can cause losses of up to 70 percent of the crop (Kumar et al. 2011) and is the main reason for the widespread use of pesticides in brinjal cultivation.

Over the past decade, a number of transgenics (over sixty, by one count) have been in the pipeline for biosafety approval in India. These include applications made by multinationals and their representatives as well as by private and public sector Indian firms. Apart from the four genetic events approved for use in *Bt* cotton, most either did not complete the approval process or the approvals were stopped before the field trials needed for commercialization. *Bt* brinjal, a transgenic containing the same Cry1Ac gene as *Bt* cotton, is the one exception. In 2000, Mahyco began the approval process for *Bt* brinjal by initiating greenhouse studies to test its efficacy against FSB and other target insects. Over the next five years, the company conducted a series of laboratory tests and confined field trials to study genetic expression, pollen flow, toxicity, allergenicity, and sub-chronic effects by feeding goats, rabbits, and cows. Early in the process, Mahyco also established public/private partnerships with two agricultural universities (University of Agricultural Science Dharwar and Tamil Nadu Agricultural University) to develop varieties of *Bt* brinjal hybrids that could, on approval, be available in different regions.

In June 2006, Mahyco applied to the GEAC for permission to conduct large-scale field trials as a step toward commercialization. Anticipating greater scrutiny of the approval, the GEAC set up an ad hoc committee of expert scientists to assess the adequacy of testing, suggest additional tests if needed, and evaluate results. However, its decision was pre-empted by a Supreme Court ruling in response to a public interest litigation challenge brought by Aruna Rodrigues and others. The PIL, which asserted that *Bt* brinjal was unsafe to human health and the environment, resulted in the Supreme Court's issuance of a temporary ban on all trials. The ban was lifted in 2007, and the Supreme Court directed the MoEF to include two senior scientists/bureaucrats, M.S. Swaminathan and P.M. Bhargava, on the GEAC to ensure greater credibility.

In 2007–08, large-scale field trials designed to test agronomic performance and biosafety of seven *Bt* brinjal hybrids were conducted in two public sector research institutions. The trials took into account additional requirements of the ad hoc expert committee and the Supreme Court, and resulted in findings that parallelled those of *Bt* cotton studies: the technology was almost 100 percent effective in preventing FSB infestations. The average increase in marketable yield for the seven *Bt* brinjal hybrids tested at eleven locations (compared with their non-*Bt* counterparts) was 25 percent, and total pesticide use was reduced by 40 percent (Choudhary and Gaur 2008). After almost a decade of safety assessments at multiple public and private research labs, agronomic evaluations, and additional testing to satisfy court challenges, the GEAC approved the hybrids of *Bt* brinjal for cultivation in October 2009.

Unsurprisingly, this was met with immediate and vocal opposition from activist groups. The reasons were familiar – the science behind the regulatory process aroused suspicion since it was paid for by Mahyco, and the long-term health risks were unknown.[16] A well-known member of the GEAC, the Supreme Court–appointed retired scientist/bureaucrat (and overall gadfly) P.M. Bhargava, also voiced his opposition. In response, Minister of

Environment and Forests Jairam Ramesh took the remarkable decision of conducting a public consultation to seek direct stakeholder input on commercialization. In January and February 2010, he took a *Bt* brinjal roadshow to seven cities across the country, with thousands attending. Though stakeholder invitations to each consultation were designed to include a broad spectrum of opinions, the media-savvy urban opposition dominated. Following the consultation, Ramesh decided to reverse the GEAC decision to commercialize, and, in a nineteen-page report, imposed a moratorium on *Bt* brinjal. He backed a European-style precautionary approach that called for further testing using independent scientific studies done to the satisfaction of the public and professionals, safeguarding the diversity of India's genetic stock of brinjals.[17]

In the process of overruling the GEAC, Ramesh also changed the body's name to Genetic Engineering *Appraisal* Committee, signaling that the scientific committee has been downgraded to an advisory one. The GEAC experts no longer have the authority to make an approval decision – that role has been taken over by MoEF politicians.

Science, Precaution, and Development

The manner in which *Bt* brinjal and *Bt* cotton were expected to benefit growers was similar. Both had the same transgene, both were marketed as a means of increasing yields because they protected against a major pest, and both were expected to reduce pesticide costs. Unfortunately, success on the ground from the *Bt* cotton experience did not translate into measurable support for *Bt* brinjal.

Two processes were at play. First, as detailed above, the success of *Bt* cotton was denied; even Ramesh's post-consultation report, which tended toward support, did so hesitantly. Second, in the lead-up to, and especially following, the GEAC's approval, oppositional statements about *Bt* brinjal crops focused primarily on the human health risks for consumers and questions of consumer choice (Freeman 2012). The large body of scientific work that had been done in the approval process and passed muster with a number of GEAC and RCGM scientific experts over the span of a decade, was simply insufficient for many.

The *Bt* brinjal episode reveals different aspects of India's institutions at play. First, and perhaps most critically, federalism was at the centre of the decision to impose a *Bt* brinjal moratorium (Herring 2015). Before and during the consultation process, political leaders in many Indian states expressed reservations about *Bt* brinjal and the risks that cultivation might pose to the environment and to farmers' livelihoods. Since agriculture is a state responsibility in India, widespread discomfort with *Bt* brinjal in the leadership of many states tipped the balance away from approval. Though many farmers' groups expressed support for *Bt* brinjal, vegetable farmers in India are fragmented, geographically dispersed, and poor – they were not organized in the same way as the urban consumers and NGOs, nor were they bolstered by the existence of stealth seeds as the cotton farmers had been in 2002. Federalism in the *Bt* cotton instance lent support to commercial approval, while in the case of *Bt* brinjal it contributed to rejection.

Second, the travails of regulation of transgenics sheds light on the role played by scientific institutions in the development of India's public policy. Scientific institutions need to be authoritative to be heard politically, and independence from state control is a key element of their legitimacy. In the absence of such independence, state science is vulnerable to politics (Herring 2014). The RCGM and the GEAC operate within ministries with specific mandates and interests. As such, they are not independent. The absence of an independent and authoritative scientific body has meant that both the capacity to carry out complex assessments that require syntheses across multiple scientific disciplines and the ability to accurately communicate findings to the public are absent in India.[18] Instead, the courts are routinely called on to adjudicate and make decisions on matters requiring accurate scientific judgment. It is by no means certain that the presence of authoritative science can settle public debates; climate policy in the United States provides an obvious example (Ding et al. 2011). Yet, the absence of authoritative science in India makes it easier to deny the veracity of peer-reviewed science and to deploy arguments about values as matters of scientific disagreement.

How regulatory science is institutionally rooted within the state also matters (Herring 2014), as the manner in which responsibility for agricultural biotechnology is divided in India reinforces existing institutional boundaries. On the one hand, the DBT is meant to promote the benefits of biotechnology industry in India. On the other hand, the MoEF is authorized to prioritize the management of environmental risks. Yet these two groups are mandated to work together toward the governance of biosafety. Other important ministries, such as agriculture, had a single vote on the GEAC, but few other points of intervention. Evidently, finding the balance between risks and benefits of transgenics requires a cohesive effort; a fragmented approach with multiple nodes of authority makes consensus difficult to achieve. Thus, it is not surprising that moratoria that postpone hard decisions are a common outcome.

More broadly, the regulation of transgenics in India lays bare the difficulties of transgenic approvals within the framework of the precautionary principle. Multiple challenges emerge when the burden of proof of a transgenic's safety falls on those seeking approval. There is a definitional challenge because there is no single version of a precautionary principle. Some versions define accepted thresholds of safety while others are silent on the matter. Without accepted thresholds of safety, the precautionary principle can be used to support indefinite inaction. But whose threshold should the regulatory analyst choose? Should it be Ramesh's demand for research to be done to the satisfaction of professionals and the public? Who exactly might this be? In the absence of scientific criteria developed in the laboratory, conferences, and peer-reviewed journals, how might such choices be made? Some versions of the precautionary principle also do not include risk/benefit trade-offs implicit in a decision. In the case of *Bt* brinjal, measures for long-term toxicity risks sought by opponents should reasonably be compared with equivalent reductions from exposure to pesticides. Yet the Indian debate, including Jairam Ramesh's otherwise carefully crafted moratorium statement, is strangely silent on the matter.

In the eight years since Ramesh imposed the moratorium, approval processes for commercial releases have been at a standstill. Despite support within some ministries, there has been no further movement on *Bt* brinjal approvals or on allowing large-scale field trials for any other transgenic. This is in stark contrast to the steady stream of applications and approvals by the RCGM for lab and confined trials that precede large-scale agronomic testing. The applicants are predominantly public and private sector Indian firms, though multinationals and their local arms have also applied. The Indian government now faces a curious paradox – although indigenous and locally adapted studies on transgenic technologies aimed at adding specific traits to a wide range of crops are increasing and enjoying the support of government research, commercialization of these crops remains stymied. In embracing a precautionary approach to the regulation of transgenics, the Indian government is denying its farmers access to a key benefit of globalization.

NOTES

1 The use of GM/GMO is fraught because the term GMO is a politically charged term. In this paper I will use the more neutral term "transgenics" to describe the products of genetic engineering that involve cross-species recombination of DNA.

2 Four genetic events (all using *Bt* genes) have been approved for cotton in India, and include the gene Cry1Ac marketed by Mahyco as Bollgard I, and the stacked gene construct Cry1Ac and Cry2Ab marketed as Bollgard II. In this article, we refer to all approved products with the generic term "*Bt* cotton."

3 Trade disputes over transgenics are a US/EU fight. There is little reason to believe that Indian opposition to transgenics is directly related to trade and protectionism.

4 The *Cartagena Protocol on Biosafety to the Convention on Biological Diversity* is an international agreement aimed at the safe handling, transport, and use of living modified organisms (LMOs) that are products of modern biotechnology and that may have adverse effects on biological diversity.

5 FDA, Statement of Policy: Foods Derived from New Plant Varieties, 57 Fed. Reg. 22,984 (29 May 1992), http://www.fda.gov/Food/GuidanceRegulation/GuidanceDocumentsRegulatoryInformation/Biotechnology/ucm096095.htm.

6 In addition to the local, economic, and political reasoning, the EU law also provides for scientific reasons for banning transgenics and states: "Other reasons should include preventing GMO contamination of other products, persistent scientific uncertainty, the development of pesticide resistance amongst weeds and pests, invasiveness, the persistence of a GMO variety in the environment or a lack of data on the potential negative impacts of a variety."

7 Some of India's government research labs might be contracted to do safety testing for specific sectors.

8 The process is supposed to be decentralized, with district biosafety committees overseen by district collectors throughout the country, although these do not appear to actually exist in practice.

9 A detailed assessment of these changes can be found in Freeman, Satterfield, and Kandlikar 2011; Freeman 2012; and Chaudary et al. 2014.

10 "*Bt* cotton" in India now includes five different approved genetic events, though Mahyco cultivars (Bollgard I and Bollgard II) dominate.

11 A meta-analysis is only as good as the underlying studies it aggregates. Many of the NGO studies do not specify how the sampling was done, nor do they characterize yield increases. The presence of non-peer-reviewed studies raises further questions.

12 Studies of coincident plantings were done in 2004, while the before-and-after study was done in 2006, when all non-*Bt* farmers in the sample had shifted to using *Bt*.

13 Some of the yield increase can be attributed to other factors, such as increased use of fertilizers and irrigation. Conversely, the overall increase in land area under cotton has brought some marginal land into cotton cultivation and may reduce aggregate yield increases.

14 In the committee's own words, *Bt* cotton has "extensively benefitted the industry, as far as the lot of poor farmers is concerned, even the trickle down is not visible," and "being a capital-intensive agriculture practice, investments of the farmers have increased manifolds, thus exposing them to far greater risks due to massive indebtedness which a vast majority of them can ill afford." Ironically the 600-page report that was over two years in the making makes no reference to the extensive peer-reviewed literature on any these topics.

15 The perceived inverse relationship runs contrary to the observed relationship between risks and benefits. Risk and benefit tend to be positively correlated in the real world. Greater benefits tend to be associated with higher risks.

16 In vivo toxicological studies of *Bt* brinjal tested for "sub-chronic" toxicity, i.e., exposure was less than ninety days.

17 Presumably, he meant that the studies were to be independently funded.

18 In the United States, the National Academy of Sciences plays a particularly important role in clarifying scientific debates by convening expert panels to make authoritative assessments of scientific topics in emergent policy interests. The Intergovernmental Panel on Climate Change (IPCC) plays a similarly significant role in global climate policy.

5 Child Malnutrition, Infant Feeding Practices, and Nutrition Information

Evidence from India

NISHA MALHOTRA

Despite a spectacular economic growth over the last three decades, there continues to be widespread malnutrition in India. Consequently, between 2005 and 2006, an alarming 43 percent of children under three years old were stunted, 48 percent were underweight, and 17 percent were wasted – these numbers are worse than some sub-Saharan African countries. It is well known that poor anthropometric indices in children have serious long-term consequences for their development. Much of the literature on this issue has stressed how malnutrition itself is a consequence of poverty (Svedberg 2000; Pryer, Rogers, and Rahman 2004; Fotso and Kuate-Defo 2006). In other words, poverty breeds malnutrition, which then leads to further curtailment of economic opportunity.

Indeed, income constraints can lead to malnutrition, but government policies, cultural norms, and lack of education are also some of the many determinants of malnutrition. I use data from India to demonstrate that information about childhood nutrition also plays a major role in higher rates of child malnutrition.

In this chapter, I survey the literature on the health effects of malnutrition in early years; present statistics on child malnutrition and infant feeding practices in India; and confirm that following World Health Organization (WHO) guidelines on child nutrition makes a significant difference to anthropometric measures. Then based on survey data from the National Family

Health Surveys I argue that poverty alone is not responsible for malnutrition. In fact, 20 percent of parents from the top 40 percent income group do not give supplementary solid food to their six- to eight-month-old infants, which I attribute to a lack of information on sound nutritional practices.

Health Effects of Child Malnutrition

There is ample evidence that nutrition and growth in the early years of life have consequences beyond health outcomes and survival during childhood; in fact, child malnutrition can also have health consequences in adulthood (Osmond et al. 1993; Eriksson et al. 2001). Malnutrition, described as micronutrient deficiency, is a serious concern as it can lead to severe physical and cognitive consequences in a child.

Malnourished children have a higher likelihood of contracting illnesses, lower recovery rates, and a lower likelihood of survival (Pelletier 1994). There is strong evidence that malnutrition at an early age can result in irreversible physical and cognitive damage, even in adolescence. For example, Martorell and colleagues (1996) show that nutrition intake during childhood (younger than three years) plays a key role in future intellectual and reproductive performance. They find that adults who had received a nutritious diet during childhood were less likely to be severely growth-impeded and that nutrition was positively associated with greater adult height, weight, and fat-free mass.

Li and colleagues (2003) find similar results: prenatal and postnatal growth (birthweight, length at fifteen days of age, and length at two years of age) were positively associated with adult body size and compositional measures (height, weight, and fat-free mass) in both men and women. Moreover, several studies have shown low birthweight to be associated with coronary heart disease later in life (Osmond et al. 1993; Eriksson et al. 2001). Eriksson and colleagues (2001) further find that, even after controlling for birthweight, low weight gain during infancy (up to one year old) is associated with increased risk of coronary heart disease.

Furthermore, it has been shown that malnutrition in the early years of life can have intergenerational impacts. In particular, maternal size is shown to be associated with specific reproductive outcomes. A mother's birthweight and growth quality during early infancy not only determines her survival and long-term health consequences but is also related to the likelihood of conceiving a low-birthweight child. Haas and colleagues (1995) use data from Guatemala to show that women with lower nutritional intake during the first years of life were more likely to have children with lower birthweight. Horta and colleagues (2009) use Brazilian data to show that maternal anthropometric measures (weight and length for age Z-score) at twenty months of age are positively correlated with next-generation birthweight as well. Martorell and colleagues (1992) show that the percentage of women with short stature varies strikingly with the degree of stunting at three years of age. A later study (Martorell et al. 1996), finds that short maternal stature predicts not only the child's birth size but also survival.

Guidelines: Infant and Young Child Feeding Practices

According to the Indian National Guidelines on Infant and Young Child Feeding (IYCF) (MOWCD 2006), children should be exclusively breastfed during the first six months for optimal growth and health benefits. During this time, the only important source of food is the mother's breast milk. After this period, to meet their evolving nutritional requirements, infants should receive nutritionally adequate complementary foods in addition to being breastfed. The guidelines also recommend that mothers increase the complementary food offered to their infants while still breastfeeding (breastfeeding is recommended up to two years). Food requirement varies with breastfeeding status: a child breastfed from the age of six to twenty-three months should be fed from three or more different food groups, whereas a child who does not receive breast milk should be fed from four or more food groups while receiving milk or dairy products daily. The World Health Organization (WHO) guidelines on IYCF are similar to the Indian guidelines; thus, the analysis in this chapter will apply to both.[1]

Breastfeeding is nearly universal in India, where 96 percent of children under age five have been breastfed; the issue lies in the prolonged delays in introducing complementary food to the infant. At six to eight months of age, almost half of breastfed children are not being given any solid or semi-solid food. Introduction of such foods around this time is crucial because breast milk is no longer sufficient to maintain optimal growth (Saha et al. 2008; Dewey, Finley, and Lonnerdal 1984; Laskey et al. 1990; Brown, Dewey, and Allen 1998).

In addition to complementary feeding at the right time, a balanced diet rich in both macro- and micronutrients is fundamental to an infant's growth and development. Brown (1991) emphasizes the importance of quality of diet rather than just quantity of intake. There is generally a clustering effect of nutritional deficiency, so the effect of a few nutrients cannot be singled out and a well-balanced, diverse diet is therefore highly important for children (Arimond and Ruel 2004). Sawadogo, Martin-Prevel, and Savy (2006) use data from rural Burkina Faso to show a significant relationship between timing, quality of complementary feeding, and nutritional status. They find a positive and significant association between the mean height-for-age Z-scores and feeding practices for children aged six to twenty-three months.

Data

I used the 2005–06 National Family Health Surveys (NFHS-3) to collect cross-sectional data using a multi-stage sample design. The survey was nationally representative and collected information from 124,385 eligible women aged fifteen to forty-nine, from twenty-nine states. Survey data provide information for children born in the five years preceding the survey, and include demographic and health parameters as well as data on socio-economic and programmatic information at the village, household, and individual levels.

Child Malnutrition

Figure 5.1 reports anthropometric measures for children in the sample. According to the WHO 2006 growth standards, 28 percent of children aged six to eight months were underweight and 23 percent were stunted.

Furthermore, 31 percent of children aged 9–11 months were underweight and 28 percent were stunted. The prevalence of undernutrition increased with increasing age groups – the highest increase occurred in the age group of 12–17 months, where the proportion of stunting increased from 28 percent to 43 percent. This reflects long-term malnourishment in the earlier ages, with 31 percent of children aged 9–11 months underweight. Table 5.1 reports the prevalence of severe undernutrition, with 25 percent of children aged 6–8 months being severely stunted.

Child malnutrition rates differ widely across Indian states (Figure 5.2). Uttar Pradesh has the largest proportion of malnourished children, followed by Meghalaya and Gujarat. Kerala's rates of child malnutrition are the lowest in the country.

FIGURE 5.1

Proportion of malnourished children by age group, based on the 2005–06 Indian National Family Health Survey

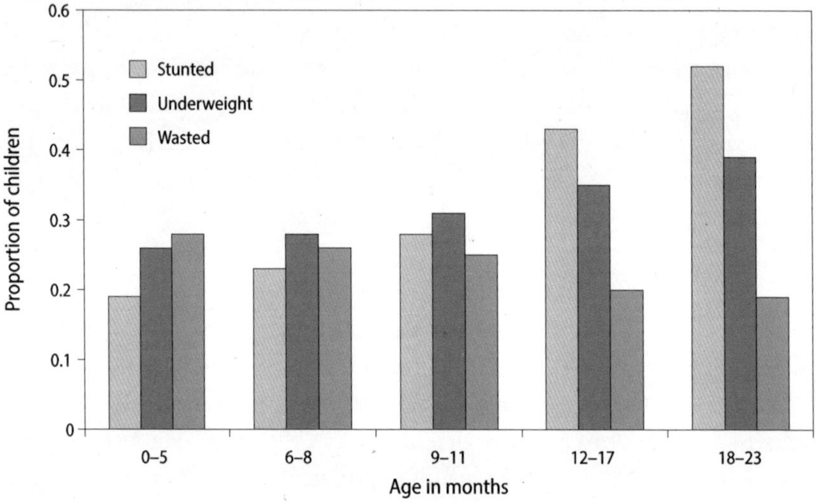

FIGURE 5.2

Child malnutrition rates across states

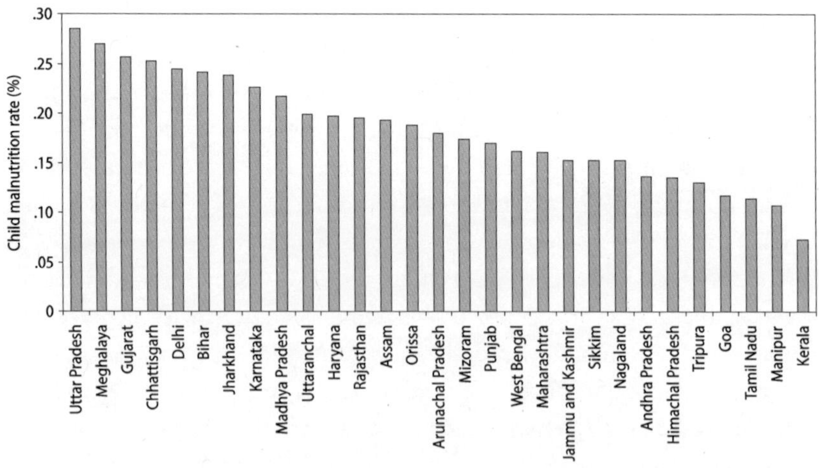

TABLE 5.1

Anthropometric measures (NFHS 2005/2006)

Age (months)		Underweight (WAZ ≤2)	Severely underweight (WAZ ≤3)	Stunted (HAZ ≤2)	Severely stunted (HAZ ≤3)	Wasted (WHZ ≤2)	Severely wasted (WHZ ≤3)
6–8	*N*	2,214	2,214	2,214	2,214	2,214	2,214
	Mean	0.281	0.106	0.228	0.098	0.256	0.092
	SD	0.450	0.308	0.419	0.297	0.436	0.289
9–11	*N*	2,002	2,002	2,002	2,002	2,002	2,002
	Mean	0.311	0.116	0.283	0.117	0.252	0.094
	SD	0.463	0.320	0.451	0.322	0.434	0.292
12–17	*N*	4,224	4,224	4,224	4,224	4,224	4,224
	Mean	0.35	0.12	0.43	0.19	0.20	0.07
	SD	0.48	0.32	0.49	0.40	0.40	0.25
18–23	*N*	4,063	4,063	4,063	4,063	4,063	4,063
	Mean	0.39	0.15	0.52	0.26	0.19	0.06
	SD	0.49	0.36	0.50	0.44	0.39	0.24

Note: WAZ = weight-for-age Z-score; HAZ = height-for-age Z-score; WHZ = weight-for-height Z-score

TABLE 5.2

Feeding practices by age group (NFHS 2005/2006)

Age (months)		Complementary feeding	2+ feeds	3+ feeds	3+ food groups	4+ food groups	Number of food groups	Number of feeds
6–8	*N*	2,213	2,214	2,214	2,214	2,214	2,210	2,201
	Mean	0.63	0.50	0.24	0.08	0.03	0.80	1.52
	SD	0.48	0.50	0.43	0.27	0.17	1.04	1.52
9–11	*N*	1,997	2,002	2,002	2,002	2,002	1,995	1,983
	Mean	0.84	0.67	0.37	0.21	0.08	1.49	2.14
	SD	0.37	0.47	0.48	0.41	0.27	1.31	1.54
12–17	*N*	4,219	4,224	4,224	4,224	4,224	4,215	4,110
	Mean	0.92	0.83	0.52	0.35	0.16	2.10	2.67
	SD	0.27	0.37	0.50	0.48	0.36	1.40	1.47
18–23	*N*	4,053	4,063	4,063	4,063	4,063	4,046	3,704
	Mean	0.92	0.90	0.63	0.43	0.21	2.33	2.95
	SD	0.28	0.30	0.48	0.49	0.41	1.49	1.45

Feeding Practices

As mentioned earlier, 96 percent of children under age five are breastfed, but, alarmingly, nearly half of the infants between ages six and eight months are not complementarily fed with solid or semi-solid foods, putting them at higher risk of malnutrition.

Table 5.2 reports statistics related to the introduction of complementary foods, minimum dietary diversity, and minimum meal frequency. Given that a very small proportion of children received food from four or more food groups (8 percent in the age group 9–11 months) or were fed at least three times (37 percent in the age group 9–11 months), statistics are also reported for a lower score of food diversity (three or more food groups) and a lower level of meal frequency (three times or more).

Of the sample, only 63 percent of children 6–8 months of age were given any solid or semi-solid food, rising to 84 percent of children aged 9–11 months. Even if a child receives complementary food, he or she may not necessarily receive adequate nutrition due to the lack of food diversity or frequency of feedings. Although 92 percent of children aged 12–17 months

FIGURE 5.3

Mean food diversity score: average number of food groups consumed by a child stratified by age group (months)

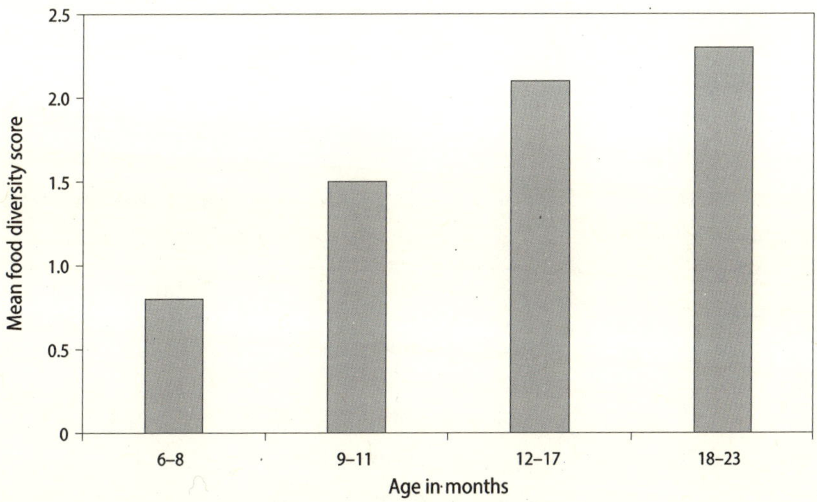

received complementary food, a mere 16 percent of them were fed from an adequate number of food groups and only 52 percent were fed three or more times a day.

Figure 5.3 reports the mean food diversity score, which has a value between 0 and 7. The value of 7 is derived from the seven food groups: milk and dairy products, eggs, flesh foods, fruits and vegetables rich in vitamin A, other fruits and vegetables, grains, and nuts and legumes. The observed low mean food diversity score further highlights the lack of food diversity in the diet of children aged 6–23 months old. While the diversity score does increase with the age of the child, it remains below 3 even for children in the age group 18–23 months.

Role of Information

Information variables were created using questions related to the mother's contact with health professionals. The NFHS-3 survey asked questions about meetings with health professionals in the previous three months and whether respondents discussed or were advised on nutrition and health. Another source of information about nutrition came from antenatal care visits during which respondents were also asked whether they received any nutrition advice. More specifically, they were asked: "In last three months, have you met with an *anganwadi* worker (rural healthcare worker) or other community health worker?" and "Did you see anyone for antenatal care for this pregnancy?" Eighty-two percent of respondents answered affirmatively.

They were then asked about the different matters they talked about. These responses were divided into eighteen categories, one of which was "Nutrition/Health Education and Nutrition Advice." According to this, 43 percent of the respondents who met with a health professional talked about nutrition and health. However, there is no information about who initiated this talk – whether the mother asked the question or the health professional gave advice without any prompting.

Figure 5.4 indicates that wealth or food affordability cannot completely explain the prevalence of inadequate nutritional practices. In the figure, advice is a binary variable that takes the value of 1 if parents received advice from a health professional and 0 otherwise. The wealth index categorizes the households into five wealth quintiles: poorest, poorer, middle, richer, and richest. Figure 5.4 is based on families that belong in the top two quintiles of the wealth index, that is, a household in the top 40 percent of the wealth status.

FIGURE 5.4

Importance of nutritional advice: infant feeding in the top two wealth quintile households stratified by advice and age

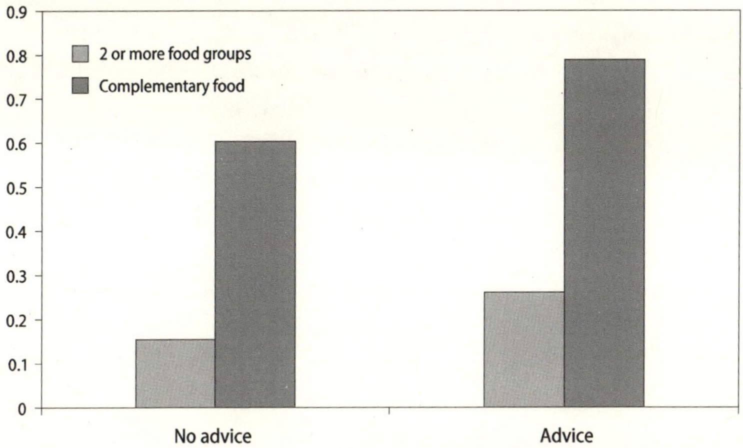

Figure 5.4 shows that 60 percent of parents who did not receive advice gave complementary food to their infants in the age group 6–8 months, compared with 79 percent of parents who received some advice on nutrition. For infants in the age group 9–36 months, 52 percent of parents who received advice gave their child food from three or more food groups, compared with only 31 percent of those who did not receive any advice.

Methodology and Results

Several variables other than food intake that are known to be associated with child anthropometric measures were considered as potential determinants of the weight-for-age Z-score (WAZ). The following variables were included in the regression analysis: gender, birth weight, diarrhea status, breastfeeding status, and fixed effects for state, religion, and caste.

The gender binary variable, male, was assigned the value of 1 if the child was male and 0 otherwise. Since the birthweight of the child was not known, a subjective measure of birthweight was used. Mothers were asked whether the child was large, average, small, or very small at the time of birth. The variable "low birthweight – subjective weight" was assigned the value of 1 if the mother thought that the child was very small at the time of birth and 0 otherwise. A variable for diarrhea was assigned the value of 1 if the child had episodes of diarrhea in the two weeks preceding the survey and 0 otherwise. Diarrhea status controlled for health effects (and, in turn, WAZ statistics) from environmental hazards like unclean water, bad hygiene, or contaminated food. Categorical variables for "Caste" and "Religion" were also included and were based on the identification by the head of the household. "Caste" took "Other" as the reference group and included the scheduled caste, scheduled tribe, and other backward classes. "Religion" used Hindu as the reference group and included Muslim, Christian, and Sikh.

For the second regression, information regarding nutrition and adequate feeding practices was considered separately from formal education. The role of information was captured by variables related to meeting with health professionals, discussion of nutrition, and exposure to media. Frequency of media refers to how often a mother read newspapers, listened to the radio, and watched television. The value ranged from not at all (0), less than once a week (1), at least once a week (2), and almost every day (3).

Another variable related to the mother's knowledge of nutritional importance was the mother's education, categorized by the highest level attained: no education (the reference group), less than primary, primary, middle school, completed high school and above. Work status was also included. Two binary variables pertained to a mother's work situation as these can affect the time she has available to feed a child, and information she might obtain at the workplace. First, if a mother was currently working or had worked in the last twelve months, the variable took the value of 1 and 0 otherwise. Second, if a mother had been working away from home, the variable took the value of 1 and 0 otherwise. The NFHS-3 data did not contain information on individual or household incomes but it did have information about the ownership of assets such as a car, television, and homes. The NFHS-3 has used ownership of assets to create a wealth index categorized into poorest (the reference group), poorer, middle, richer, and richest. Furthermore, the more infants a mother has, the less time she can devote to a single child; this is measured by the "Number of siblings" the child has who are less than five years of age. Finally, "First child" is a binary variable that equalled 1 if a child was the first child and 0 otherwise. The descriptive statistics for all the variables used in the two regressions are provided in Table 5.3.

TABLE 5.3

Descriptive statistics of variables used in the two regression analyses

	Mean	Linearized standard error	95 percent confidence interval
Exposure to health professionals			
Had antenatal check-up	0.6648	0.0034	0.6581–0.6715
Advised on pregnancy nutrition	0.3345	0.0033	0.3280–0.3410
Met healthcare worker in the previous 3 months	0.3910	0.0035	0.3840–0.3979
Discussed nutrition	0.0175	0.0009	0.0157–0.0193
Exposure to media			
Watched TV	1.2521	0.0094	1.2337–1.2704
Listened to radio	0.7597	0.0077	0.7446–0.7748
Read newspaper or magazine	0.4343	0.0058	0.4230–0.4456
Wealth index			
Poorest	0.2592	0.0032	0.2528–0.2655
Poorer	0.2288	0.0031	0.2226–0.2349
Middle	0.2006	0.0029	0.1949–0.2062
Richer	0.1812	0.0027	0.1759–0.1865
Richest	0.1303	0.0022	0.1260–0.1346
Mother's education			
No education	0.5029	0.0036	0.4958–0.5100
Less than primary	0.0707	0.0018	0.0671–0.0742
Primary school	0.0698	0.0018	0.0663–0.0733
Middle school	0.2740	0.0031	0.2678–0.2801
High school and above	0.0827	0.0018	0.0791–0.0862
Mother's employment			
Currently works or has worked in the last 12 months	0.3545	0.0035	0.3477–0.3613
Worked away from home	0.2845	0.0033	0.2781–0.2909
Other variables			
Male	0.5120	0.0036	0.5050–0.5191
Had diarrhea recently	0.1051	0.0022	0.1008–0.1094
Number of siblings aged 0–5 years	0.2093	0.0030	0.2033–0.2152
First child	0.3263	0.0033	0.3198–0.3329
Low birthweight – subjective	0.0589	0.0017	0.0556–0.0622

Importance of Following the IYCF Feeding Guidelines

Results from the Ordinary Least Square OLS regression, WAZ estimates, are reported in Table 5.4. As expected, after six months, complementary feeding is a positive and significant determinant of the WAZ. For a child between nine and twelve months, both complementary feeding and the number of food groups offered to the child are an important determinant of the WAZ. For children older than nineteen months, feeding practices such as the number of feeds a day and whether three or more food groups are included in complementary feeding become significantly important.

TABLE 5.4

Effect of feeding practices on weight-for-age score

	0–5 months	6–8 months	9–12 months	13–18 months	19–36 months
Complementary feeding					
No®	Ref	Ref	Ref		
Yes	–0.04	0.26***	0.17**		
	(0.52)	(4.21)	(2.37)		
2 or more food groups					
No®		Ref			
Yes		0.24***			
		(3.12)			
3 or more food groups					
No®			Ref	Ref	Ref
Yes			0.14**	0.19***	0.15***
			(2.31)	(4.45)	(5.44)
Number of feeds a day				0.03*	0.03***
				(1.79)	(2.87)
Constant	–1.71***	–1.48***	–1.42***	–1.34***	–1.56***
	(7.42)	(6.71)	(7.63)	(9.20)	(17.29)
Observations	3,165	2,111	2,518	3,992	8,646
R^2	0.14	0.17	0.15	0.16	0.16

Notes: Absolute value of t statistics are in parentheses. Control variables: gender, birthweight, diarrhea status, state-level fixed effects, religion-level fixed effects, caste-level fixed effects, current breastfeeding status.

* $p > .10$, ** $p > .05$, *** $p > .01$; ® = Ref = the reference group.

Nutritional Information an Important Determinant of IYCF

Regression analysis was used to assess the role of information. As in the earlier analysis of the WAZ, gender, subjective birthweight, and diarrhea status were included.

TABLE 5.5

Knowledge and adequate feeding practice

Exposure to health professionals	Number of feeds (13–36 months)	Complementary feeding (6–12 months)	2+ food groups (6–8 months)	3+ food groups (9–36 months)
	OLS	Odds ratio	Odds ratio	Odds ratio
Had antenatal check-up				
No®	Ref	Ref	Ref	Ref
Yes	–0.23	2.05*	0.60	1.96***
	(1.60)	(1.79)	(0.62)	(8.61)
Advised on pregnancy nutrition				
No®	Ref	Ref	Ref	Ref
Yes	0.06**	1.32***	1.23	1.29***
	(2.07)	(3.60)	(1.53)	(6.82)
Met with healthcare worker in the previous 3 months				
No®	Ref	Ref	Ref	Ref
Yes	0.11***	1.00	(0.32)	(1.79)
	(3.90)	(0.00)	1.23	1.29***
Discussed nutrition and health				
No®	Ref	Ref	Ref	Ref
Yes	0.37***	1.86*	1.50	1.28*
	(3.52)	(1.85)	(0.97)	(1.93)
Constant		2.83***		
		(19.40)		
Observations	13,352	4,866	2,211	19,379
R^2	0.04			

Notes: Absolute value of the z statistics are in parentheses.
* $p > .10$, ** $p > .05$, *** $p > .01$; ® = Ref = reference group.

The results in Table 5.5 provide evidence for a strong association between information related to nutrition and adequate feeding and the actual feeding practices followed by parents. "Advice" on nutrition during antenatal check-up and during other meetings with a healthcare professional is positive and a significant determinant of adequate feeding practices, even after controlling for the meetings. Thus, among mothers who met with health professionals, those who received nutritional advice were more likely to follow better feeding practices.

Mothers were more likely to give complementary food to their child of 6–12 months and offer food from three or more food groups if they received advice during antenatal check-up than if they did not (odds ratio [OR] = 1.32 and 1.29, respectively). This is true even for mothers who discussed nutrition during other meetings with health professionals (OR = 1.86 for those who did, 1.28 for those who did not). These mothers also tended to feed their child more frequently.

The other set of variables related to information, "Exposure to media," was also found to be an important determinant of proper feeding practices, even after controlling for education. Frequency of listening to the radio seems to be the most important source of information and had a positive impact on all measures of feeding practices. Exposure to all media sources (television, radio, and newspapers) increased the likelihood of parents offering their child food from three or more food groups (OR = 1.06, 1.13, and 1.09, respectively).

The other important factors were the work status of a woman, number of siblings, and whether the child was the firstborn. As expected, having more siblings less than five years of age made it less likely that the child would be properly fed, and a working mother was more likely to follow good feeding practices. A firstborn child was less likely to be fed from three or more food groups or fed more frequently; I attribute this to experience and knowledge. Even after controlling for wealth and education, it was determined that nutritional information significantly increased the odds that a child was properly fed.

Discussion and Conclusion

Despite a common belief that greater wealth would likely translate to proper child nutrition, the data shown in this chapter offer a striking contradiction in showing that the role of information may be superior. However, the pertinent question now is whether the fact that a respondent has talked to a health professional is equivalent to the respondent's having acquired appropriate nutritional information. Should we not take a "Yes" answer in this context to simply mean that the respondent is aware that nutrition is important? If so, should we not conclude that a parent aware of the importance of nutrition does better by the child's health?

If I were making the point that the nutritional information dispensed by a health professional is what makes the difference to nutritional practices, the criticism would be valid. However, I am merely arguing that it is the lack of information rather than income that is the main roadblock in the path of sound nutritional practices in India. "Being aware" means understanding the importance of information – a mother who is aware and therefore raises a question about nutrition while talking to a health professional is searching for information – it is this information that ultimately makes the difference to her child's nutrition and health, regardless of the source. Among those in the richest class, clearly it is the more aware parents (with greater appreciation of information on nutrition) that feed three or more food groups to their children.

Child malnutrition is widespread and poverty is not the only reason for such a poor state of health among India's children. If information diffusion rather than poverty is the main obstacle, the prognosis is hopeful: it is much easier to solve the problem of scarce information than to solve the problem of acute poverty. What is needed is extensive intervention in nutritional practices that aims at educating families in proper infant feeding practices. Nutrition education should be made an integral part of primary and secondary education. Since nutritional advice during antenatal check-up had the biggest impact on feeding practice, early childhood nutrition advice should be made available at every public health facility, not only to mothers but also to pregnant women.

APPENDIX

In a well-nourished population, there is a statistically predictable distribution of children of a given age with respect to height and weight. An international reference population was released by WHO in April 2006 (World Health Organization Multicenter Growth Reference Study Group 2006) and is accepted by the government of India. Standard indices of physical growth that describe nutritional status include height-for-age indices (determines stunting).

Stunted growth reflects a process of failure to reach linear growth potential because of suboptimal health and/or nutritional conditions. On a population basis, high levels of stunting are associated with poor socio-economic conditions and greater risk of frequent and early exposure to adverse conditions such as illnesses and/or inappropriate feeding practices. Furthermore, height-for-age measurements represent the long-term effects of malnutrition in a population and do not vary according to recent dietary intake.

Each of the three nutritional status indicators is expressed in standard deviation units (Z-scores) from the median of the reference population. Each index provides different information about growth and body composition, which is used to assess nutritional status.

$$Z = \frac{\textit{Measured Value} - \textit{Median (reference population)}}{\textit{Standard Deviation (reference population)}}$$

The height-for-age index is an indicator of linear growth retardation and cumulative growth deficits. Children whose height-for-age Z-score is below –2 standard deviations (SD) from the median of the reference population are considered short for their age (stunted) and are chronically malnourished. Children below –3 SD are considered severely stunted. Stunting reflects failure to receive adequate nutrition over a long period, and is also affected by recurrent and chronic illness. Children whose weight-for-age is below –2 SD from the median of the reference population are classified as underweight. Children whose weight-for-age is below –3 SD from the median of the reference population are considered severely underweight. For children in the age group below two to three years old, low height-for-age probably reflects a continuing process of "failing to grow" or "stunting"; for older children, it reflects a state of "having failed to grow" or "being stunted."

NOTES

1 http://www.who.int/nutrition/topics/infantfeeding_recommendation/en/index.html. The recommendation does vary for the developed world. In the United States, the American Academy of Pediatrics (AAP) recommends that a child be exclusively breastfed for the first six months and get supplement food thereafter while supporting breastfeeding for the first year.

6 Foreign Direct Investment and Intergroup Disparities in India

ASHWINI DESHPANDE

There is a belief that as the Indian economy liberalizes, becomes more market-oriented, and increases its integration with the global economy, intergroup disparities (such as those between broad caste groups or between men and women) are likely to decrease, for several reasons: first, because labour market discrimination on account of social identity is expected to decline (Black and Brainerd 2004),[1] and second, because the creation of new and new types of jobs is likely to provide an impetus to members of marginalized groups to acquire new skills to break out of traditional, caste-based, dead-end, oppressive, and stigmatizing occupations (Omvedt 2012). The argument that discrimination is likely to decrease is based on the belief that market orientation will give primacy to profit maximization and, more generally, to efficient allocation of resources – a process in which the social identity of agents ought to be irrelevant (Wilfred 2007). Foreign agents are especially less likely to be concerned with local hierarchies and the accompanying prejudices.

Additionally, theory suggests that gender (or caste) wage gaps should narrow with globalization because greater integration with the global economy could promote competition and less discrimination between social identities (Artecona and Cunningham 2002). Specifically, for women, increase in trade is supposed to drive up relative demand for female labour because female labour supply tends to be more elastic than male labour supply; this effect will be enhanced if women are disproportionately represented in export-oriented sectors (Çağatay and Berik 1991; Wood 1991; Anker 1998; Standing 1999; Ozler 2000).

Contrary to this set of arguments is the view that traditionally marginalized groups might be at a disadvantage even in this new scenario given that they are under-represented at levels of education needed to take advantage of these emerging opportunities. Also, multinational companies (MNCs) do not work in a vacuum – their hiring decisions are made by local employees who are as aware of local social cleavages and as driven by the same prejudices as the hiring managers of domestic firms. Foreign agents are not likely to disturb domestic norms and practices unless it is essential since their bottom line is profits. Indeed, research into the mechanics of the hiring process in urban formal labour markets indicates that, lip service to merit notwithstanding, managers show a deep awareness of the overlapping and complex categories of caste, class, religion, and gender, and of the strong stereotypical beliefs that merit is distributed along axes defined by these social identities (Deshpande and Newman 2007; Jodhka and Newman 2007). This is as true for private domestic firms as it is for MNCs.

This chapter investigates the association between liberalization and intergroup disparities by focusing on one component of liberalization, namely, foreign direct investment (FDI), and its relationship with caste and gender disparities in wages and education using a unique dataset compiled by the author. This dataset combines data on FDI approvals from the Indian government's Ministry of Commerce and other correlates from the quinquennial rounds of the National Sample Survey calculated at the district level. The main findings are as follows: FDI approvals have a small, mildly significant positive association with the wage gaps between the traditionally disadvantaged castes and tribes and everyone else. FDI approvals also have a small but stronger positive association with gender wage gaps. Thus, there is no evidence to suggest that greater FDI inflows are associated with a reduction in wage gaps between traditionally marginalized groups and the dominant groups; on the contrary, there is evidence of some increase. This analysis is done with data on FDI *approvals;* thus it excludes FDI that comes in through the "automatic route," which does not need prior approval, as the exact geographical locations of the latter are not publicly available. Given this very important caveat, the results described here should be seen as indicative and establishing the lack of (or a negative) correlation, rather than as suggestive of any causation.

The rest of the chapter discusses the evidence on the relationship between economic growth, market orientation, and intergroup disparities; reviews the literature on FDI in India; describes the data and methodology; presents the descriptive statistics; describes the empirical results; and discusses the results and some interconnected larger issues.

Economic Growth, Market Orientation, and Intergroup Disparities

Cross-national comparisons of intergroup disparities have highlighted the apparent absence of a straightforward relationship between the relative prosperity of a country, or the level of its market orientation, and the severity of disparities or the prevalence of discrimination. Darity and Deshpande (2003) summarize the major general findings that have emerged from these comparative inquiries. Specifically, they point out that intergroup disparity is persistent and significant in countries at all levels of development, whether development is measured narrowly by per capita income or more broadly by a more encompassing index of wellbeing such as the Human Development Index (HDI).

Also, higher rates of economic growth do not invariably close economic gaps between racial and ethnic groups, nor does lower economic growth inevitably widen the gap. For instance, Malaysia (which had a high rate of growth between 1975 and 1994) and South Africa (which experienced a negative rate of growth over the same period) did not demonstrate opposing movements in terms of intergroup disparity. This is relevant to the Indian discussion in that it suggests that India's high rate of growth in the post-liberalization era might not be sufficient to close the gaps, just as a lower rate of growth would not necessarily widen them.

These findings have strong implications for the interstate variations in intergroup disparities in India, in the sense that they caution against the belief that higher growth will necessarily reduce intergroup disparities. Based on these findings, there is no prima facie basis to expect any systematic patterns in the latter based on whether a state is rich or poor (or fast- or slow-growing). Elsewhere, I have discussed the interstate variations in caste disparity, and it does seem to be the case that caste gaps are not well correlated with either the level of state domestic product or its rate of growth

(Deshpande 2011). All this suggests that even if FDI unambiguously resulted in an increase in the growth rate of the Indian economy or the economy of individual states (a premise that is contested but is outside the scope of this chapter) or in an increase in market orientation, its effects on intergroup disparity would not be unambiguous but would need to be explored.

Literature on FDI in India

One branch of the literature on FDI inflows deals with the choice of location or determinants of FDI at the country level. This literature examines the set of factors that determine the host country's attractiveness for FDI inflows, and accordingly focuses on macroeconomic aggregates (or fundamentals) of an economy in terms of their ability to attract FDI. This chapter takes those sets of issues as given; in other words, given India's desirability (whether strong or weak) as an FDI destination, this chapter focuses on distribution of FDI *within* the country and its likely association with changes in group disparities. Of course, if India ceased to be a preferred destination, or if its attractiveness diminished, then overall inflows to the country would decrease (the decline might be differentially distributed across regions or states) and correspondingly, the potential emancipatory effects (e.g., increase in overall employment, improvement in the occupational profile of the marginalized groups, narrowing of caste or gender wage gaps) of FDI would decrease.

The National Council of Applied Economic Research (NCAER) (2009) conducted a comprehensive national, macro-level study that maps and summarizes FDI in India and evaluates the impact of FDI in India in terms of its linkages with the rest of the economy. Earlier smaller surveys include those by Nagaraj (2013) and Bhaumik and colleagues (2003). Other studies (Athreye and Kapur 2001; Bajpai and Sachs 2000; Banga 2003; Kumar 2005; Ray and Venaik 2008; Palit 2009) have focused on specific issues related to FDI, such as the impact of private foreign investment on broad macro indicators in the Indian economy; problems with India's foreign direct investment regime; the role of government policies in explaining FDI; India's foreign investment policy; how foreign ownership influences subsidiary performance of research and development exports; and royalty outflows.

In a sector-level analysis of the Indian economy, Chakraborty and Nunnenkamp (2008) empirically assess the proposition that FDI promotes growth in the domestic economy. They find that growth effects of FDI vary widely across sectors, namely, that there is a strong effect in the manufacturing sector and no causal relationship in the primary sector. They find only transitory effects of FDI on output in the services sector but find that FDI in the services sector has promoted growth in the manufacturing sector through cross-sector spillovers. Mukim and Nunnenkamp (2010), whose key findings are discussed below, analyze the location choice of FDI projects based on district-level data. Other papers focusing on the spatial concentration of FDI inflows are also discussed below. The relationship between FDI inflows and their impact on group disparities in India has yet to be explored. This chapter attempts to fill that gap to the extent permitted by the data.

Data and Methodology

The dataset used in this chapter is unique as it has been created by the author from a variety of sources. The FDI data relate to approvals of FDI projects from 1995 to July 2010 for 14,627 cases obtained from the Department of Industrial Policy and Promotion (DIPP), Ministry of Commerce, Government of India. These data allow us to identify the location of the project at the district level, thus enabling the analysis to go beyond the state level. These are matched with National Sample Survey (NSS) data at the district level from three large Employment Unemployment Surveys (EUS) (Schedule 10): the 55th round (1999–2000), the 61st round (2004–05), and the 66th round (2009–10). The data from the NSS surveys used in estimation include the following: total population of the district; proportions of men, women, Scheduled Castes (SC), Scheduled Tribes (ST), and Other Backward Classes (OBC) in the district; proportions of each of these groups with at least secondary school education (assuming that is the minimum level of education for employment in FDI-based firms); and proportions in regular wage/salaried (RWS) employment for all groups.

Scheduled Castes, Scheduled Tribes, and Other Backward Classes are designated castes, tribes, and communities eligible for the Indian affirmative action program, which reserves seats (22.5 percent for SC-STs and 27 percent for OBCs) in government jobs and educational institutions. SC-STs also get 22.5 percent quotas in the electoral sphere at all levels of government. These quotas constitute a positive or compensatory discrimination policy designed to counter discrimination and marginalization. While the official administrative nomenclature for the most marginalized castes is Scheduled Castes, "Dalits," meaning "the oppressed," is a term of pride used by members of this group. Similarly, "Adivasis" (literally, "indigenous people") is used interchangeably with the administrative category Scheduled Tribes.

Since the main concern of this chapter is to examine the association of FDI with group disparities, the empirical strategy consists of matching outcomes, calculated from the three rounds of NSS data, to accumulated approvals in the preceding four years. I have divided the total period into four time periods: time period 1 for years 1995–98 (both inclusive); time period 2 for years 1999–2003 (both inclusive); time period 3 for years 2004–08 (both inclusive); and time period 4 for years 2009–10 (both inclusive). Given the three years of data, approvals for the first three time periods (until 2008) are used for the regression in Equation 1 below.

The raw data list each approval separately per year per district to a total of 14,627 observations. Several of these were highly incomplete entries, or duplicates, and could not be used. Retaining the partially and fully complete entries and removing duplicates left 13,592 observations. I aggregated these into total approvals per year for each district, producing a dataset where each observation is a district-year unit. This compressed the 14,627 observations into 1,261 observations. Given the heterogeneity in district population sizes, the estimation uses the "approval rate" per district, which is simply the number of approvals per 100,000 people.

Finally, for most projects, based on their verbal description, I assigned the "sector" of economic activity based on the International Standard Industrial Classification (ISIC) codes used to classify all economic activities, at both the two-digit and three-digit levels. In the regressions explained below, the variable "sector" refers to the two-digit code.

Data on FDI Inflows

From August 1991 to July 2010, the cumulative inflows of FDI into India were US$172,108 million, including equity flows, reinvested earnings, and other capital. Of this, cumulative equity inflows were US$140,020 million.[2] India, along with the other three nations in the BRIC (Brazil, Russia, India, China) group of large emerging economies, is considered a "bright spot as an FDI destination" (UNCTAD 2010, xxiv), and thus makes for a good case study to examine the impact of FDI inflows on intergroup disparities. However, India's attractiveness as a favoured FDI destination needs to be placed in perspective. According to United Nations Conference on Trade and Development (UNCTAD) figures, the annual average FDI inflow into India from 1995 to 2005 was US$4,137 million. The corresponding figure for China was US$48,833 million – more than ten times that of India. These flows were 3.2 percent of gross fixed capital formation (GFCF) over the period for India (annual average), compared with 10.1 percent for China, indicating that not only are FDI inflows into India significantly lower in absolute amounts but also their share in addition to fixed assets in India was about one-third that of China. However, since 2005, this trend seems to have reversed as the proportion of FDI inflows as a percentage for GFCF has been rising for India and falling for China, such that in 2009 the share was 8.4 percent for India and 4 percent for China (UNCTAD, World Investment Report, 2010, factsheet for India).

As stated earlier, this chapter examines the approvals data[3] (and not actual realized inflows); this is because the possibility of identifying the precise location of realized FDI is limited. These data are disaggregated according to which regional office of the Reserve Bank of India (RBI) is used for routing the investment. Each regional office handles investments to a group of states; for instance, the Guwahati office handles the inflows to the entire group of seven northeastern states, thus the regional disaggregation is fairly broad. Table 6.7 in Appendix B gives data on FDI routed through the RBI's regional offices, which shows the level of aggregation at the regional level. For the majority of cases, however, the approvals data enable us to identify the location of the project by district, allowing for a much more nuanced analysis of the impact of FDI inflows.

Of course, there might be a gap between approvals and realized inflows, such that either some of these approvals might not be realized or the actual inflows might be less than approved. The implicit assumption in this chapter is that all these approvals are in fact realized.[4] It should be noted that data on approvals for FDI are compiled on the basis of approvals granted by the Foreign Investment Promotion Board (FIPB) maintained by the DIPP, which are used in the present study. This does not include data from the Special Economic Zones, which are separate bodies.[5] Also, these data reflect approvals for FDI granted by the Indian government (through FIPB); however, nearly 86 percent of FDI inflows today come in through the automatic route, without requiring approval by the FIPB. While these data do not match actual FDI flows, they have the advantage of identifying the precise geographical location.

Methodology

Using these data, the following equation is estimated using Ordinary Least Squares (OLS) on pooled time series cross-section data:

$$lnY_{it} = \beta_i X_{Ti} + \gamma_i Z_{it} + \varepsilon_{it} \quad \text{(Equation 1)}$$

where the standard errors are clustered at the district level and are based on the robust variance estimator, and the district fixed effects are absorbed.

The wage gap, Y_{it}, is calculated as follows. For caste, $Y_{it} = \frac{(W_{Oth} - W_{SC\text{-}ST})}{W_{SC\text{-}ST}}$ where W_{Oth} and $W_{SC\text{-}ST}$ are the daily wages of "Others" and SC-ST, respectively, in district i and time period t, where t can take three values corresponding to the NSS survey years as outlined above.

Analogously for gender, $X_{Ti} = \frac{(W_{male} - W_{female})}{W_{female}}$, where X_{Ti} is the approval rate in the four years *preceding* the given survey years and T refers to the time period classification described above.

Z_{it} are the other controls, and ε_{it} is the error term.

Thus, the approval rate for all approvals during 1995–98 (the first time period) is matched with outcomes in 1999–2000 (NSS-55); the approval rate for all projects during 1999–2003 (the second time period) is matched with outcomes in 2004–05 (NSS-61); and the approval rate for 2004–08 (the third time period) is matched with outcomes in 2009–10 (NSS-66). There is unlikely to be reverse causality here, as there is no evidence to suggest that the FDI approvals at the district level are determined or influenced by relative caste or gender disparities in wages, higher education, or proportions with RWS jobs.

Five models of this equation are estimated and they are listed here from the most parsimonious to the full specification. Model A, the most parsimonious specification, controls only for the approval rate; Model B adds controls for time period (T) and the "sector" of economic activity to Model A; Model C adds controls for the state of India in which the district is located to Model B; Model D further controls for the ratio of caste groups with secondary education (proportion of SC-ST with secondary education/proportion of Others with secondary education) in the equation for castes, and a similar control in the gender equations (proportion of men with secondary education/proportion of women with secondary education); and Model E adds the final control of the ratio of proportions of caste or gender groups in RWS employment.

Descriptive Statistics

Distribution of Approvals by State

While the total number of approvals is spread over twenty-eight states, they are concentrated in a small number of them, as Table 6.1 shows. The top ten states account for 94 percent of approvals over the period.

The bulk of approvals are concentrated in five states: Maharashtra, Delhi, Karnataka, Tamil Nadu, and Andhra Pradesh, in descending order. Maharashtra remains the top destination for FDI approvals in all the years, with the percentage of approvals located in the state rising over the period. In fact, by July 2010, it already accounted for roughly 44 percent of all approvals for that year. Comparing this table with the overall FDI data in Appendix B, we see that the pattern of spatial clustering is similar. The Mumbai office of the RBI handles 35 percent of the FDI flows, followed by the Delhi office, which handles 20 percent. Interestingly, the share of approvals of Gujarat (the state touted for its investor-friendly business climate) not only does not place the state among the top five but barely reaches 5 percent in any of the years. Comparing this figure with the overall FDI figures, we find that Gujarat accounts for 6 percent of the total FDI until 2010. This comparison between distribution of approvals with actual FDI inflows suggests that the approval data, while underestimating the overall volume of FDI, do present a fairly accurate picture of the interstate variation in FDI inflows.

Distribution of Approvals by District

The picture of geographical concentration is further confirmed when we examine the distribution of approvals by district. The approvals are spread over 275 out of 618 districts (as of 2010), but the top 25 districts account for the bulk of the approvals; even within the 25, there is substantial clustering with the top 10 districts, which account for 74 percent of all approvals.

The data reveal that even within the states that are the top five destinations for FDI, the projects are clustered in a small number of districts, giving a picture of high geographical concentration. For instance, within Maharashtra, it is the western belt of Mumbai-Thane-Pune where most of the projects are concentrated. Thus, the distribution of FDI projects is lopsided and highly clustered.

TABLE 6.1

Total approvals by state, July 1995 to 2010

	State	Freq.	%		State	Freq.	%
1	Maharashtra	3,626	26.68	15	Goa	79	0.58
2	Delhi	2,311	17.00	16	Pondicherry	75	0.55
3	Karnataka	2,010	14.86	17	Orissa	61	0.45
4	Tamil Nadu	1,714	12.61	18	Jharkhand	36	0.26
5	Andhra Pradesh	940	6.92	19	Dadra and Nagar Haveli	28	0.21
6	Gujarat	591	4.35	20	Himachal Pradesh	28	0.21
7	Haryana	473	3.48	21	Daman and Diu	26	0.19
8	Uttar Pradesh	430	3.16	22	Uttarakhand	26	0.19
9	West Bengal	427	3.14	23	Bihar	21	0.15
10	Kerala	209	1.54	24	Chhattisgarh	17	0.13
11	Rajasthan	158	1.16	25	Assam	5	0.04
12	Madhya Pradesh	117	0.86	26	Meghalaya	3	0.02
13	Punjab	87	0.64	27	Jammu and Kashmir	2	0.01
14	Chandigarh	80	0.59	28	Punjab	2	0.01
	Total					13,592	100

Table 6.1 confirms the picture from other studies that have found a concentration of FDI inflows in a few states of India. The National Council of Applied Economic Research (2009) reports figures indicating that 97 percent of the total amount of export-oriented FDI and 83 percent of total FDI approvals over 1991–2001 were concentrated in only seven states. All studies have emphasized the importance of infrastructure as a key determinant of FDI, which is also what explains its lopsided concentration. Goldar (2007) suggests that the determinants of the location of plants of foreign and domestic companies are very similar; thus, infrastructure turns out to be a key determinant of domestic industry as well.

Sectoral Distribution of FDI Approvals

The broad sectoral division of FDI approvals shows that 45 percent of FDI approvals are in manufacturing, about 4 percent in the primary sector (agriculture, mining, and quarrying), and the rest in the tertiary sector, within which 26 percent are in the information and technology sector.

Thus, the overall picture is one of sectoral concentration as well as geographical clustering. The spatial concentration suggests that even if FDI has disparity-reducing benefits, they would be highly localized. The fact that over 50 percent of the approvals are in the tertiary sector implies that historically disadvantaged groups would have to acquire English fluency and IT skills in order to take advantage of the new jobs that would presumably be created by FDI. Whether the benefits are spread more widely in the destination states or to other states that do not receive FDI as well as whether, over time, the existence of these opportunities would incentivize members of disadvantaged groups to acquire education to take advantage of these opportunities, are moot points.

Wage Gaps, Relative Education Levels, and RWS Employment

Table 6.2 shows wage gaps, relative education levels, and relative proportions in regular wage/salaried employment by caste and gender over the three time periods used in the estimation.

TABLE 6.2

Summary statistics on selected variables

Variable	Observed	Mean	Variable	Observed	Mean
1995–98			*2004–08*		
castewagegap	497	0.61	castewagegap	141	0.71
gendwagegap	419	0.79	gendwagegap	131	0.57
relRWScaste	510	2.15	relRWScaste	166	1.54
relRWSgender	570	11.09	relRWSgender	169	6.23
releducaste	522	2.42	releducaste	168	1.93
reledugender	554	3.68	reledugender	170	1.53
1999–2003					
castewagegap	381	0.68			
gendwagegap	357	0.78			
relRWScaste	376	2.43			
relRWSgender	471	7.54			
releducaste	287	4.17			
reledugender	472	1.78			

Notes:

castewagegap = caste wage gap as defined under "Methodology" above
gendwagegap = gender wage gap as defined under "Methodology" above
relRWScaste = relative share of the caste groups in regular wage/salaried (RWS) jobs, as a proportion of Scheduled Castes–Scheduled Tribes (SC-ST) in RWS employment relative to proportion of "Others" in RWS employment
relRWSgender = relative gender shares in RWS jobs
releducaste = relative share of the caste groups with secondary education or more
reledugender = The corresponding ratio for gender

In a separate regression used to see whether the change in the caste wage gap is significant over time, we find that, compared with Period 1, the increase in Periods 2 and 3 is mildly significant. We see that the gender wage gap has declined over time, with the change in Period 3 being significant over Period 1 while the change between Periods 2 and 3 is not significant. Proportions of "Others" in RWS employment relative to the proportion of SC-ST (relRWScaste) fluctuate over the period, whereas proportions of men in RWS employment relative to the proportion of women (relRWS-gender) decline over the period. Comparing proportions with secondary education by caste, again we see fluctuations similar to RWS employment, whereas by gender, proportions of women with secondary education relative to proportions of men increase steadily over the period, leading to a decline in the ratio "reledugender."

Empirical Results

Caste Wage Gap

We now examine the correlation between FDI approvals and relative wages of caste groups. Table 6.3 presents the results of Equation 1 estimated for caste groups.

We see that the magnitude is small but the association between the log of the FDI approval rate and the log of the caste wage gap is positive and significant at the 10 percent level in three models; that is, an increase in the approval rate in the four years preceding the wage data is associated with an increase in the caste wage gap.

Gender Wage Gap

Table 6.4 shows the analogous results for the gender wage gap. Here we also see that the association between the log of the approvals and the gender wage gap is positive, that is, an increase in FDI approval rate in the four years preceding the wage data is associated with an increase in the gender wage gap. Compared with the caste wage gap, the results are stronger in that the magnitude of the coefficient is higher and the significance is at 5 or 1 percent in three of the five models.

Discussion

The results indicate that the basic outcome variables, namely, caste wage gap and gender wage gap, are positively correlated with FDI approvals.

TABLE 6.3

Caste wage gaps and FDI approvals

	Model A	Model B	Model C	Model D	Model E
logapprovals	0.0230	0.0575*	0.0575*	0.0638*	0.0523
	(0.0266)	(0.0341)	(0.0341)	(0.0377)	(0.0367)
releducaste	–	–	–	–0.0000967	–0.0266*
	–	–	–	(0.00250)	(0.0138)
relRWScaste	–	–	–	–	0.0661**
	–	–	–	–	(0.0284)
Time period	No	Yes	Yes	Yes	Yes
Sector	No	Yes	Yes	Yes	Yes
State	No	No	Yes	Yes	Yes
_cons	–0.655***	–0.606***	–0.606***	–0.631***	–0.696***
	(0.0591)	(0.176)	(0.176)	(0.793)	(0.195)
N	955	916	916	761	752
R^2	0.722	0.727	0.727	0.795	0.806

Notes: Standard errors are shown in parentheses. The dependent variable is the log of the caste wage gaps.
* $p < .10$, ** $p < .05$, *** $p < .01$

TABLE 6.4

Gender wage gaps and FDI approvals

	Model A	Model B	Model C	Model D	Model E
logapprovals	0.148***	0.0634	0.0634	0.0955**	0.0987**
	(0.0399)	(0.0393)	(0.0393)	(0.0387)	(0.0386)
reledugender	–	–	–	0.0197	0.0181
	–	–	–	(0.0150)	(0.0151)
relRWSgender	–	–	–	0.00793***	(0.00306)
Time period	No	Yes	Yes	Yes	Yes
Sector	No	Yes	Yes	Yes	Yes
State	No	No	Yes	Yes	Yes
_cons	–0.170*	–0.453***	–0.453***	–0.449***	–0.507***
	(0.0870)	(0.122)	(0.122)	(0.132)	(0.133)
N	860	824	824	801	800
R^2	0.671	0.690	0.690	0.723	0.724

Notes: Standard errors are shown in parentheses. The dependent variable is the log of the gender wage gaps.
* $p < .10$, ** $p < .05$, *** $p < .01$

Admittedly, the magnitudes are small, and this analysis is not causal as a number of other factors that would affect the wage gap were not controlled for since data at the district levels are not readily available. However, we did control for variables for which data are available, namely, relative education levels, proportions in RWS employment, and sector of economic activity, in addition to state and time period controls and district fixed effects. Thus, these results provide evidence suggesting that increases in FDI approvals are *not* correlated with a decline in wage gaps.

Geographical Concentration of FDI

In line with other literature on FDI, this chapter shows that FDI is highly concentrated geographically. If this pattern of concentration continues, FDI is likely to have limited, localized impact in terms of employment creation and absorption of the labour force into modern occupations. Lall and Chakravorty (2005) argue that spatial inequality of industrial location is the primary cause of spatial income inequality. They show that new private sector industrial investments are heavily biased toward districts that are already industrialized, whereas state investments are less so. However, given that government investments as a share of total new investments are declining, the policy of privatization and liberalization is associated with an increase in spatial income inequality via greater geographical clustering of industrial projects. This is further confirmed by Nunnenkamp and Stracke (2007), who argue that the concentration of FDI in a few regions might have prevented FDI effects from spreading more widely across the Indian economy.

A later study by Mukim and Nunnenkamp (2010) based on district-level analysis suggests that foreign investors strongly prefer locations with a history of previous presence of other foreign investors. In addition, that study once again confirms the importance of infrastructure as well as existing industrial diversity in attracting FDI. Based on this, the authors suggest that since districts with existing FDI projects are likely to attract more investment, this would lead to an increase in regional inequality.

The unevenness of infrastructure development could be one of the factors that account for India's low performance in several rankings, such as the UNCTAD's FDI performance index, where India was ranked 106 out of a total of 141 countries in 2007 (UNCTAD 2010), or the World Economic Forum's Global Competitiveness Index, where India is ranked 48 out of 131 countries in 2011. Thus, even if FDI increased employment for all, and especially provided employment to individuals from hitherto marginalized sections because it did not discriminate, in the absence of high volumes of FDI, the actual employment generated would not be as high as that needed for FDI to have an emancipatory impact.

FDI through the Automatic Route

Given that the bulk of FDI is through the automatic route, it could be argued that the concerns raised above are valid only for specific kinds of FDI that need approval, and might not hold for FDI coming through the automatic route. However, projects such as the development of new airports; laying of natural gas/liquefied natural gas pipelines; market study, formulation, and investment/financing in the petroleum sector; cash and carry wholesale trading; export trading; power trading, subject to provisions of the *Electricity Act, 2003;* and more are eligible to receive FDI through the automatic route. Given the skill requirements for these sectors, it is reasonable to expect that the same concerns about eligibility of Dalits to get jobs apply equally to FDI coming in through the automatic route.

Types of FDI and Possible Employment Impact

There is a larger issue about the relationship between FDI and employment creation. FDI comprises three components: equity, reinvested earnings, and other capital (although, as explained above and in Appendix A, different data sources use different definitions that vary in the specific component[s] they include). Equity FDI is further subdivided into two components – Greenfield investment and mergers and acquisitions (M&A). Reinvested earnings represent the difference between the profit of a foreign company and its distributed dividend, thus representing undistributed dividends. "Other capital" refers to the intercompany debt transactions of FDI entities. Equity FDI may also include "Brownfield investment," which is a hybrid of Greenfield and M&A foreign investment; although it formally appears as M&A, its effect resembles Greenfield investment. In Brownfield investment, the foreign investor acquires a firm and undertakes a nearly total renovation of plant, equipment, labour, and product lines (UNCTAD 2000). Table 6.5 below shows how Greenfield investments differ from M&A in terms of their short-term impact on capital, on the transfer of technology and skills, on existing assets, and on employment.

TABLE 6.5

Short-term effects of FDI through Greenfield investment versus mergers and acquisitions

Characteristics	Greenfield investment	Mergers and acquisitions
Capital	Adds to productive capacity of the host country	• Initially marked by a change of assets from domestic to foreign hands • In the long term, more sequential investments may follow
Transfer of technology and skills	Likely to transfer new or better technologies or skills	• Less likely to transfer technology or skills • May bring in technology and skills as part of restructuring efforts in later stages
Existing assets	Does not directly reduce technology assets and capabilities in the host economy	• May lead to closure/downgrading/relocation of domestic facilities
Employment	Creates employment	• Does not generate employment at the time of entry • Could conserve employment if the acquired firm is on the verge of closure • Over time, employment generation may occur as a result of sequential investments and retained or strengthened linkages
Market structure	Increases the number of firms in an industry	• Can lead to increased concentration in the host economy

Source: Based on World Investment Report, UNCTAD 2000.

Thus, the employment effect of FDI will depend first on the proportion of equity flows and, within that, on the proportion of Greenfield projects. Table 6.6 shows how the proportionate increase in M&A deals has been higher than in Greenfield projects for India (100 percent versus 50 percent).

However, government reporting of the FDI statistics with comparable information on Greenfield versus M&A investments in numbers or in values is not very clear. According to the available route-wise FDI compiled by

TABLE 6.6

FDI by entry mode

	Greenfield FDI projects		Cross-border M&A deals	
Year	World	India	World	India
2003	9,469	453	4,562	83
2004	10,254	699	5,113	80
2005	10,632	594	8,560	121
2006	12,441	1,026	9,075	161
2007	11,703	682	10,145	167

the Department of Industrial Policy and Promotion, equity investment excluding acquisition of shares may be considered as Greenfield investment in India. Thus, foreign equity inflows under the Secretariat for Industrial Assistance/Foreign Investment Promotion Board route and the RBI route,[6] along with the equity capital of unincorporated bodies, represent the fresh arrival of FDI into India. The DIPP reports a separate category of FDI under inflows through acquisition of existing shares.[7] Kumar (2000) attempts to map the M&A activity between 1993 and early 2000 and finds that if the growing trend of M&A continues to be the preferred form of FDI, as opposed to Greenfield investments, several of the positive effects of FDI might not materialize.

Does FDI Lead to Higher Growth?

Prior to the issue of employment generation is the question of the impact of FDI on growth. Although this topic is outside the scope of this chapter, it is useful to look at the evidence on this relationship. In a regional analysis, Nunnenkamp and Stracke (2007) study whether the link between FDI and economic growth has become stronger in the aftermath of reforms. They find that even though the various categories of FDI are positively correlated with per-capita income growth across Indian states, it is only in the richer states that FDI appears to be associated with higher growth. They also confirm the possibility that FDI might end up exacerbating regional income inequality, a finding from other studies summarized earlier in this chapter.

For this exercise, however, we want to specifically examine employment generation as a result of FDI. The existing literature on FDI inflows has some information on overall employment generation due to FDI. The National Council of Applied Economic Research (2009, 65) reports that "the total number of people employed in FDI plants is about 1,564,920. This amounts to a share of between 4 and 5 percent of the total labour force in the formal sector." Two sectors that provide relatively high shares of total employment in FDI plants include chemical products and growing and processing of crops, including tea and horticulture. Employment originating in FDI manufacturing firms varies widely across states. Eight states – Maharashtra, Karnataka, West Bengal, Haryana, Assam, Tamil Nadu, Gujarat, and Andhra Pradesh – account for about three-fourths of the total manufacturing FDI sector employment (National Council of Applied Economic Research 2009, 65).

The question, then, is whether this employment generation is evenly distributed across social groups and between men and women according to their share in the state populations. The National Council of Applied Economic Research (2009, 18) suggests that India's attractiveness as an investment destination rests on the following factors: "Large and growing market, world-class scientific, technical and managerial manpower, cost-effective and highly skilled labour ... [and] a large English speaking population." The sectoral distribution also suggests that the labour demand generated by FDI would be for workers with a specific educational and skill profile, especially for those with knowledge of English. Given the existing educational and occupational disparities by caste, prima facie, it appears that a large section of Dalits and women would not be prime candidates for these jobs.[8] However, research into the pathways through which caste plays a role in urban, formal sector labour markets suggests that Dalits face direct and indirect discriminatory barriers even after they acquire higher education from reputable, elite institutions (Deshpande and Newman 2007).

Of course, this static picture could change. The growth of certain kinds of jobs could provide the requisite incentives to acquire higher education and English-language skills over time. The education levels of the labour force could thus be both a cause and an effect of FDI; for example, certain kinds of FDI tend to become concentrated in areas that already have the labour force with requisite education and English skills, which then provide further incentives for increasing this skill acquisition. Unless the dynamic spreads to other areas, this could lead to further clustering of FDI.

FDI and Intergroup Disparities

FDI is only one aspect of globalization and liberalization that could affect caste disparities. The broader argument for the emancipatory effect of globalization has several contours. In particular, it hinges on the fact that globalization will make the market salient as well as unleash competition between Indian and foreign firms, impacting Dalits positively in many dimensions. FDI and multinational corporations would be an implicit and important, but not the only, part of this process. Chandra Bhan Prasad, one of the most vocal supporters of globalization and the market economy for its capacity to empower Dalits, argues that one of the ways in which globalization empowers Dalits is by "universalizing access to aspirations." He is referring here to the process of making certain consumer goods (e.g., colour TVs, mobile phones, refrigerators, air conditioners, and so on) plentiful, available, and within reach of the Dalits – goods that are supposed to be considered "material markers of pride." He suggests that this has broken the exclusivity of the "predominantly Upper Caste Consumer Club," a process aided also by the rise of Dalit entrepreneurs.[9]

Omvedt (2015) argues that globalization is an inevitable reality for India and it has many positive aspects. Thus, instead of taking the "blind anti-globalization position" demonstrated, according to her, by the leftist political parties and ecologists in India, she suggests that we need to think about a comprehensive and nuanced response of Dalits and Adivasis to these changing realities. Chandra Bhan Prasad echoes this sentiment by asking Dalits to view globalization as an opportunity rather than as a threat.

Based on a survey of all Dalit households in two blocks of two districts in Uttar Pradesh, Kapur and colleagues (2010, 39) suggest that the shift from a state-led to a market-led path of development has changed patterns of interaction between castes, leading to a "rapid erosion in discriminatory practices that stigmatized Dalits." They also find large shifts in the pattern of economic life, both within and away from the village. They find this change manifesting itself in terms of a change in occupational patterns, with Dalits moving away from traditional occupations, and in the nature of contracts between Dalits and upper castes, such that practices such as bonded labour that tied Dalits to generations of servitude appear to have become obsolete. It is not clear, however, to what extent these outcomes are a result of the regular process of development and not especially attributable to a *shift* from a state-led to a market-led path. In other words, the role of market-oriented liberalization in bringing about these changes needs to be proven, not assumed. These debates are complex and contain many interwoven strands that are not necessarily easy to disentangle. What is noteworthy is that very few of the arguments are backed by hard empirical facts. This chapter seeks to shed some light on these issues, using FDI data and several material indicators.

Conclusion

A discussion on the relationship between globalization, liberalization, and intergroup disparities needs to be informed by an evaluation of the evidence, rather than being based on preconceived notions or wishful thinking. This chapter has attempted to fill the lacunae in the evidence-based assessment of these linkages. Using a unique combination of administrative and survey data, we have evaluated the relationship between FDI approvals and wage gaps between broad caste groups and genders. The analysis presented here does not find any evidence of a negative relationship between FDI approvals and wage gaps. Additionally, given that FDI inflows are very strongly spatially concentrated in a few states, and, within those, in a few districts, the emancipatory effects of FDI inflows, were they to exist, would affect very small segments of the population.

APPENDIX A

Definitions and Basic Information about FDI in India

The term "foreign direct investment" refers to cross-border investments made by a resident in one economy (the direct investor) with the objective of establishing a lasting interest in an enterprise (the direct investment enterprise) that is resident in a country other than that of the direct investor (OECD 2008). The motivation of the direct investor is strategic "lasting interest" in the management of the direct investment enterprise with at least 10 percent voting power in decision making.

The *International Financial Statistics Yearbook* (International Monetary Fund 1995, xix) defines FDI as "the flows of direct investment into the reporting economy. It includes equity capital, reinvested earnings and other capital associated with various intercompany transactions between affiliated enterprises."

FDI statistics in India are officially monitored and published by the Reserve Bank of India and the Secretariat for Industrial Assistance (SIA). While the International Monetary Fund's (IMF) definition of FDI incorporates equity capital, reinvested earnings (retained earnings of FDI companies), and "other direct investment capital" (intra-company loans or intra-company debt transactions), FDI statistics compiled by the RBI in the balance of payments prior to 2000 included only equity capital.

The definition of FDI and computation of FDI statistics used by the RBI does not conform to the guidelines of the IMF. Srivastava (2003) highlights some of the main discrepancies.

First, India excludes reinvested earnings (which are part of foreign investor profits that are not distributed to shareholders as dividends and are reinvested in the affiliates in the host country) while estimating actual FDI inflows. According to IMF guidelines, these reinvested earnings are a part of FDI inflows and should be recorded as inflow on the capital account of the host country's balance of payments.

Second, India does not include the proceeds of foreign equity listings and foreign subordinated loans to domestic subsidiaries, which, according to IMF guidelines, are part of intercompany loans (long- and short-term net loans from the parent to the subsidiary) and should be a part of FDI inflows.

Third, India excludes overseas commercial borrowings, whereas, according to IMF guidelines, financial leasing, trade credits, grants, bonds, and so on should be included in FDI estimates.

Fourth, according to IMF standards, if a shareholding of 10 percent or more is acquired eventually by a non-resident who entered in initially through the portfolio route but holds investment totalling over 10 percent through the purchase of additional shares in subsequent transactions, those additional shares should be regarded as a part of FDI. However, in India some Foreign Institutional Investors (FIIs) hold well over 20 percent of the equity in the form of American Depository Receipts (ADRs) and Global Depository Receipts (GDRs), but these are not considered a part of FDI.

Routes of Entry of FDI into India

Reserve Bank of India (Automatic Route)

Proposals for approval under the automatic route are to be made to the Reserve Bank of India. In a major drive to simplify procedures for FDI under the automatic route, the RBI has given permission to Indian companies to accept investment under this route without obtaining its prior approval. Investors are only required to notify the concerned regional RBI office within thirty days of receipt of inward remittances and to file the required documents with that office within thirty days of issue of shares to foreign investors. This facility is also available to NRI (non-resident Indians)/OCB (Overseas Corporate Bodies) investment. All items/activities for FDI investment up to 100 percent fall under the automatic route except the following:

- all proposals that require an industrial licence
- all proposals in which the foreign collaborator has an existing joint venture/technical collaboration/trademark agreement in the "same" field of activity
- all proposals falling outside notified sectoral policy/caps or under sectors in which FDI is not permitted.

Secretariat for Industrial Assistance/Foreign Investment Promotion Board (Non-Automatic Route)

Non-automatic schemes are referred to the Foreign Investment Promotion Board, which gives clearance on a case-by-case basis. Once the proposal is presented to the FIPB, it consults the concerned ministry and gives clearance based on the quantum of investment and other project details. For the following categories, government approval is necessary:

- proposals attracting compulsory licensing
- items of manufacture reserved for the small-scale sector
- proposals involving any previous joint venture or technology transfer/ trademark agreement in the same or allied field in India
- extension of foreign technology collaboration agreements (including those cases that may have received automatic approval in the first instance)
- proposals not meeting any or all of the parameters for automatic approval.

From the inception of economic reforms in India in 1991 until the year 2000, most of the FDI entered through the non-automatic route as there was strict monitoring of the approvals; FDI entering through the SIA/FIPB route was therefore greater than FDI entering through the RBI route. However, there has been a weakening of this trend since 2005. With the investment boom in India and with different states competing for FDI, the government has eased foreign investment regulations, leading to a spurt in FDI entering through the RBI route, which is a positive sign.

Secretariat for Industrial Assistance (SIA)

The SIA was set up by the government of India in the Department of Industrial Policy and Promotion in the Ministry of Commerce and Industry to provide a single window for providing entrepreneurial assistance and investor facilitation, receiving and processing all applications that require government approval, conveying government decisions on applications filed, assisting entrepreneurs and investors in setting up projects (including liaison with other organizations and state governments), and monitoring implementation of projects. It also notifies all government policies relating to investment and technology, and publishes monthly production data for 209 select industry groups.

Foreign Investment Implementation Authority (FIIA)

The government of India set up the FIIA to facilitate quick translation of FDI approvals into implementation, and to provide one-stop after-care service to foreign investors by helping them obtain necessary approvals, sort out operational problems, and meet with various government agencies to alleviate any issues.

Causes and Reasons for Low FDI (Report of the Steering Group on Foreign Direct Investment, Planning Commission, August 2002)

When a foreign investor considers making any new investment decision, it goes through four stages in the decision-making process and action cycle: screening, planning, implementing, and operating and expanding.

Problems in the FDI entry process include the following:

- A lot of foreign investment proposals are rejected at the screening stage due to poor publicity about India as a business-friendly country.
- Archaic legislation and labour laws lead to cost and time overruns. Reservation of certain sectors of production for small-scale industries (SSI) further limits the possibility of entering labour-intensive sectors for export.

- Levels of realization of FDI inflows are low compared with proposals cleared. Although the realization rate improved to 45 percent in 2000 and 2001 compared with 21 percent in 1997, after hitting a high in 2002, FDI inflows were sluggish during the international financial crisis and seem to have failed to pick up.[10] The precise reason for the low levels of realization can be found in the post-approval procedures. The major implementation problems are encountered at the state level, as this is where project implementation takes place. After approval has been obtained, the applicant may get his unit/company registered with the Registrar of Companies. Subsequently, the company needs to obtain various clearances for land, building designs, pre-construction, or labour (to name a few) from different authorities before beginning its operations. These clearances, moreover, differ from sector to sector and may also differ from state to state.
- Infrastructure is poor.

APPENDIX B
Statement on RBI Regional Offices (with States Covered) Received FDI Equity Inflows (from April 2000 to July 2010)

TABLE 6.7

Received FDI inflows by state

	Regional office	States covered	Cumulative inflows: April–July 2010[1]	Percent of total inflow
1	Mumbai	Maharashtra, Dadra and Nagar Haveli, Daman and Diu	182,920 (40,965)	35
2	New Delhi	Delhi, Uttar Pradesh, Haryana	109,326 (24,128)	20
3	Bangalore	Karnataka	34,650 (7,788)	7
4	Ahmedabad	Gujarat	29,349 (6,640)	6
5	Chennai	Tamil Nadu	26,040 (5,783)	5
6	Hyderabad	Andhra Pradesh	22,773 (5,121)	4

►

	Regional office	States covered	Cumulative inflows: April–July 2010[1]	Percent of total inflow
7	Kolkata	West Bengal, Sikkim, Andaman and Nicobar Islands	5,978 (1,401)	1
8	Chandigarh	Chandigarh, Punjab, Haryana, Himachal Pradesh	3,525 (772)	1
9	Panaji	Goa	3,270 (712)	1
10	Jaipur	Rajasthan	2,246 (475)	0.4
11	Kochi	Kerala, Lakshadweep	1,504 (334)	0.3
12	Bhopal	Madhya Pradesh, Chhattisgarh	1,367 (300)	0.3
13	Bhubaneshwar	Orissa	1,154 (249)	0.2
14	Kanpur	Uttar Pradesh	532 (115)	0.1
15	Guwahati	Assam, Arunachal Pradesh, Manipur, Meghalaya, Mizoram, Nagaland, Tripura	280 (64)	0.1
16	Patna	Bihar, Jharkhand	2 (0.4)	0
17	Region not indicated		100,272 (22,649)	19
Subtotal			526,823 (117,846)	100
Stock swapped (2002–10)			14,962 (3,390)	
Advance of inflows (2000–04)			8,962 (1,963)	
RBIs-NRI schemes (2000–02)			533 (121)	
GRAND TOTAL			551,280 (123,320)	

Note:

1 In INR crores. Numbers in parentheses show the same amount in millions of US dollars.

Source: Modified from http://dipp.nic.in/sites/default/files/india_FDI_July2010_0.pdf.

NOTES

Acknowledgments: Earlier versions of this chapter were presented at the following conferences: on "Indian Inequalities," organized by the University of Michigan at Ann Arbor in Mumbai, 1–4 March 2011; on "New Spatialities of Labour" at the Indira Gandhi Institute for Development Research, Mumbai, July 2012; and on "Economic Growth, Trade and Poverty" at the Institute for Social and Economic Change, Bangalore, 6–7 December 2012. Comments on earlier drafts from conference participants, from Ashok Kotwal, and from an anonymous referee, as well as research assistance by Smriti Sharma and Apoorva Gupta in 2011–12 are gratefully acknowledged. The usual disclaimer applies.

1 Black and Brainerd (2004) make this argument in the context of trade liberalization – while it may lead to increased wage inequality, it reduces the ability of employers to discriminate, thus benefiting women.

2 http://dipp.nic.in/sites/default/files/india_FDI_July2010_0.pdf.

3 These are approvals of FDI cases labelled as "non-technical."

4 It turns out that data do not allow us to match the approvals with the realized investment.

5 The next step would be to extend this analysis to include the impact of FDI in Special Economic Zones.

6 See Appendix A for definitions.

7 While information on acquisition of shares is compiled and provided by the DIPP, there is no explicit information on cross-border mergers occurring in India; however, cross-border mergers effected by swapping of stocks may be included in the stock swaps data provided by the DIPP. Another component of the stock swap, which is simply equity swaps between an Indian and a foreign company, is believed to be much higher, however. Therefore, in the absence of such a breakdown it is not possible to analyze any trends in the cross-border mergers in India.

8 The designation of English as the new "Dalit goddess," as the vehicle that will eventually lead to Dalit emancipation, is easier to understand in the context of the huge advantage that knowledge of English confers in the labour market (Gopinath 2006).

9 https://web.archive.org/web/20090328115348/http://chandrabhanprasad.com:80/.

10 https://www.rbi.org.in/scripts/BS_ViewBulletin.aspx?Id=13224; https://energy.economictimes.indiatimes.com/news/power/indias-fdi-growth-hit-5-year-low-in-2017-18/64820992.

7

Climate Change Mitigation
The Indian Conundrum

MILIND KANDLIKAR and SIMON HARDING

India is a fast-growing economy and the world's fourth-largest contributor to greenhouse gas emissions. It is also an impoverished country with a largely rural, poor population. According to the World Bank, in 2014, 65 percent of India was rural and roughly 60 percent of its population lived on less than $3 per day. Most of its 1.3 billion people depend on agriculture, primarily rain-fed, as their primary means of livelihood. India receives as much as 80 percent of its rainfall from the annual monsoon (Bagla 2006). However, since the monsoons could be influenced by climate change, India's population and economy are extremely vulnerable. The World Bank claimed in 2014 that the current understanding of climate science suggests that increased greenhouse gas (GHG) concentrations will likely result in greater annual precipitation during the monsoon season, but with increased variability. Increases in the frequency of high-rainfall events interspersed with longer dry spells could be potentially devastating for Indian agriculture, as would higher extreme temperatures during the growing season (Aggarwal 2008). Other impacts such as heat waves or rising sea levels near Indian cities could be just as devastating (IPCC 2013).

While vulnerability to climate change has been long recognized in India, the country's own role in contributing to carbon emissions and in finding solutions for climate change has, until recently, been of less concern. The numbers tell part of the story. From 1970 to 2009, a recent period that overestimates the historical responsibility of developing countries, India was responsible for 3.3 percent of global carbon dioxide (CO_2) emissions, whereas China was responsible for 13.5 percent and the United States for 24.4 percent (Jayaraman, Kanitkar, and D'Souza 2011). As the issue of climate change has become more urgent, however, arguments over historical responsibility and per-capita national emissions are being eclipsed by discussions about future responsibility and aggregate national emissions. Consequently, even though India's emissions per capita are still very low,[1] the rapid growth of both its economy and aggregate emissions have led to greater expectations of further reductions in emissions. India finds itself facing a difficult conundrum: it needs to balance the economic aspiration of a growing population while engaging in carbon mitigation and ensuring that nations are on track to keep mean global temperature change to under 2°C by 2100.

This chapter analyzes this conundrum. It examines the evolution of India's position on climate change mitigation in the international arena within the purview of domestic policy. We begin by studying India's changing stance during the negotiations under the *United Nations Framework Convention on Climate Change* (UNFCCC) over the past two decades and how these changes have been influenced by domestic and international considerations.[2] We then focus on "co-benefits," an idea that has emerged recently as a policy focus in India's carbon mitigation efforts, and examine how reducing indoor air pollution in rural India may have indirect benefits for climate mitigation. We conclude with a discussion of how India might meet the twin imperatives of development and climate mitigation as an equal partner in global efforts.

India's Response to Climate Change: A Story of Three Eras

The equity principle has long been the bedrock of India's international climate stance. India is not a major contributor to the climate problem and so not reasonably accountable for emissions reductions. Under this broad equity-based framing of India's role, the Indian response to climate change negotiations can be divided into distinct periods, each with major international and domestic climate mitigation policies. As shown in Table 7.1, these periods can be used to characterize how India's elite and policy makers have viewed climate change.

TABLE 7.1

Timeline of climate change–related events

Event	Year	Outcome	Phase
IPCC[1] First Assessment Report	1990	• Likely existence of anthropogenic climate change identified • 21st-century mean global air temperature will increase by 0.3°C per decade • Global mean surface temperature increased by 0.3–0.6°C in the past century • Sea level will rise by 65 cm by 2100	Pre-Kyoto, "growth first"
IPCC Second Assessment Report	1995	• Confirms continued increases in greenhouse gases (GHG) • Aerosol use produces negative radiative forcing • Discernible human influence on climate change	
COP[2] Berlin	1995	• Industrialized countries commit to legally binding emissions cuts with developing countries exempted • *India breaks ranks with OPEC countries to form a "green group" with Brazil and China*	
COP Kyoto	1997	• Binding emission targets accepted by all industrialized countries except the United States for the periods 2005–12 and 2012–20 • 5.2 percent cut of emissions sought by 2012 • Clean Development Mechanism introduced • *India is a signatory of the Kyoto Protocol but not subject to binding emissions cuts*	Limited engagement; Clean Development Mechanism
IPCC Third Assessment Report	2001	• Confidence in models increased • Sea levels and temperatures rise under all scenarios • Impact of global warming on human life predominantly negative	
COP Delhi	2002	• Agreement to transfer technology to developing countries to mitigate the impact of climate change • Ratification of Kyoto Protocol • *India reiterates equity principle* • *India drops opposition to the Clean Development Mechanism*	
International bilateral agreement	2005	• *India-US Civil Nuclear Agreement signed*	

►

Event	Year	Outcome	Phase
IPCC Fourth Assessment Report	2007	• "Warming of the climate system is unequivocal" published with Indian scientist R.K. Pachauri among the authors • Most of the increase in the global average temperature since 1950 is "very likely" due to anthropogenic GHG emissions	Co-benefits
COP Bali	2007	• Agreement on timeline and structure for the implementation of Kyoto 2012–20 • *India, under pressure from industrialized nations, accepts that developing countries should take mitigation measures*	
Domestic policy	2008	• *India launches National Action Plan on Climate Change*	
COP Copenhagen	2009	• Agreement on Kyoto 2012–20 deferred • Non-binding accord between some nations • BRIC[3] group coalesces • *India participated in the drafting of the accord that was pivotal in obtaining China's agreement* • *India volunteers to cut 2005 emissions by 20–25 percent by 2020* • *India becomes a BRIC member*	
IPCC Fifth Assessment Report	2014	• "Extremely likely" that human influence is the dominant cause of warming since 1950; more certain than previous report • Delays in emissions reductions will be costly to future generations	
COP Paris	2015	• "Extremely likely" that human influence is the dominant cause of warming since 1950; more certain than previous report • Delays in emission reduction will be costly to future generations	

Notes:

1 Intergovernmental Panel on Climate Change

2 Conference of the Parties (to the *United Nations Framework Convention on Climate Change*)

3 Brazil, Russia, India, China

In the earliest period, the Pre-Kyoto period (1990–97), climate change in India was seen as a "Western" problem – one that has been created by the West but whose consequences were being borne by India and other developing countries. The solutions to climate change were to be rightfully and exclusively sought in industrialized economies. During this time, India's aggregate carbon emissions were low, the Indian climate science community was small, and the climate problem generated little policy attention domestically. With the signing of the Kyoto accord in 1997, climate change emerged as a policy problem of modest concern in India. Between 1997 and 2006, there was a period of limited engagement in emissions reduction activities primarily through the vehicle of the Clean Development Mechanism (CDM). By the mid-2000s, as international concern over climate change grew, India's involvement in mitigation took on a *co-benefits framing* (2007 to present). In this view, India is not obligated to reduce CO_2 emissions, but reductions that are a secondary consequence of policy measures that are justified in their own right are to be welcomed. Energy efficiency measures and investment in renewable energy are all examples of activities pursued by India as part of its development. Carbon emissions reductions resulting from these activities are to be counted as a "co-benefit."

Pre-Kyoto Period, 1990–97

India was an enthusiastic signatory to the UNFCCC in Rio de Janeiro in 1992, accepting the reality of anthropogenic climate change as well as the need for significant global mitigation efforts, while arguing, often persuasively, that developing countries should not be subject to any binding emissions reductions. This exemption was justified by the equity principle, according to which industrialized countries that are responsible for the vast majority of excess global atmospheric stocks of carbon have both a greater responsibility to mitigate these emissions and greater capacity to do so. Developing countries, by contrast, were historically minor emitters and remain handicapped by poverty levels. These ideas were incorporated into the UNFCCC principle of "Common but Differentiated Responsibility (CBDR)" in Article 3.1.

India sought to defend its space for growth by recourse to a combination of CBDR and the measurement of emissions on a per-capita basis, which classified India as a low emitter (Baer et al. 2000). As such, its negotiating strategy in this early phase involved making high demands of industrialized countries while taking a moral high ground over emissions and positioning itself as a leader of the G77 group of developing countries. Unwilling to accept compromise, India was regarded as a naysayer in negotiations (Michaelowa and Michaelowa 2012), adhering to the position defined above, known variously as "third worldism" (Isaksen and Stokke 2012), "growth first realism" (Dubash 2013), or "growth first stone-walling" (Dubash 2012). Mohan (2003) likens India's approach to a porcupine: static and defensive, showing its quills to the world. This position was associated with several influential Indian think tanks, such as the Centre for Science and Environment (CSE), and remains the dominant discourse in English-language media (Billet 2009).

India's initial approach to climate talks was heavily influenced by a keen awareness of unequal international relationships rooted in India's colonial experience and consequent lack of trust in the motives of developed nations. If India were to make concessions to the arguments, industrialized countries would use that compromise to shift the burden of mitigation to the developing world in order to maintain their economic dominance. Agarwal and Narain (1991) from the Centre for Science and Environment wrote an influential report titled "Global Warming in an Unequal World," which argued forcefully that the attempt of Washington-based World Resources Institute (WRI) to attribute responsibility for climate change to developing countries by emphasizing agricultural emissions was a "perfect example of environmental colonialism," making countries like India subject to "global rules and discipline" in order to slow their growth.

In addition to a lack of trust in the international process, especially one led by US scientists, the early phase of climate negotiations also came about just as India was moving away from a centralized licence raj economy to a market-oriented one. This shift was in response to a severe balance of payments crisis brought about by the First Gulf War in the early 1990s (Joshi and Little 1996). The implications of this change in the economic climate became a dominant theme in India's politics and international relations. Global climate change was barely discernible on the policy agenda. Institutional resources were limited and administrators were kept busy implementing the liberalization of the economy, leaving little institutional policy capacity for climate change measures (Kandlikar and Sagar 1999). The shortage of state funding also fettered India's scientific research community, which struggled to keep pace with their counterparts in industrialized countries who could successfully integrate science and economics in the service of their own narrow national interests (Sagar and Kandlikar 1997). The resulting participation gap – with Indian negotiators being "outgunned" scientifically – may also have driven the focus on moral arguments such as the equity principle.

The dominance of the porcupine approach did not entirely prevent India from furthering the global climate change negotiation process. For instance, in 1995, India took the lead role in the "Green Group" of G77 countries and secured the establishment of the Berlin Mandate, a precursor to the Kyoto Protocol that proposed binding emissions cuts for industrialized countries (Oberthuer and Ott 1999). At the national level, numerous domestic policies began referring to international comparisons for support. For instance, in 1996, the National Environmental Policy recognized the international nature of several environmental issues and stated India's commitment to international efforts. It also brought domestic environmental laws in line with norms established by international agreements (Atteridge et al. 2012). These shifts foreshadowed changes to come in India's negotiating stance in the late 1990s.

Limited Engagement, 1998–2006

Following India's earlier defensiveness and refusal to consider emissions reductions on equity grounds, the late 1990s saw a shift in India's attitude toward climate change negotiations. During the third Conference of the Parties (COP-3) to the UNFCCC held in Kyoto in December 1997, industrialized countries (Annex 1 countries) agreed to reduce their emissions based on individually negotiated targets and timetables.[3] Industrialized countries could meet these obligations by reducing their own emissions or by buying emissions from other signatories that had surpassed their targets.

Developing countries (Non–Annex 1) were not required to cut their emissions, but industrialized countries could get credit for investments made in developing countries aimed at reducing carbon emissions through the CDM. Market mechanisms had long been championed by rich countries, particularly the United States, as a means of reducing greenhouse gas emissions where it was cheapest to do so. The CDM was a step in that direction and provided the means for industrialized countries to purchase Certified

Emissions Reductions (CERs) at lower costs than paying for equivalent carbon reductions in their own jurisdictions.

The Indian government and policy circles initially greeted the introduction of the CDM with skepticism. Analysts argued that CDM projects would not deliver on development goals and would help industrialized countries pick the low-hanging fruit in terms of cheap emissions reductions. However, Indian industries saw an opportunity to earn revenue, and CDM received the backing of industry groups, including the Confederation of Indian Industry and the Federation of Indian Chambers of Commerce and Industry. Pressure from industry eventually led the government to embrace the CDM, a process that Dubash (2012) refers to as India "dipping half a toe in the water."

The Clean Development Mechanism in India

In the run-up to the COP-8 in New Delhi in 2002, India's refusal to consider participation in global climate change mitigation efforts began to waver. As a host country to the COP, India needed to demonstrate a willingness to engage in climate action. Indian industries were also framing CDM as a win-win. As a medium-sized emitter with a heavy reliance on coal, India could offer cheap and potentially large emissions reductions to industrialized countries seeking to offset their own emissions. Conversely, the transfer of funds and improved technologies would improve the energy efficiency of Indian industry and reduce reliance on non-renewables. Under pressure from the deployment of the win-win argument, Indian negotiators agreed to adopt the CDM framework. The Ministry of Environment and Forestry and a new National CDM Authority became the nodal agencies with the power to approve and monitor India's CDM projects. India soon emerged as the second-largest host of such projects in Asia, second only to China, hosting 27 percent of global new projects in 2005, 30 percent in 2006, and 37 percent in 2007 (Alcamo et al. 2014).

The early emphasis of CDM projects was on reducing the release of non-CO_2 industrial gases, such as hydrofluorocarbons (HFCs) and nitrous oxide, into the atmosphere. These projects represented quick credits because of the high warming impact of HFCs, the inexpensive technology needed (Wara 2007), and the ease with which "additionality" can be demonstrated for end-of-pipe controls of such waste pollutants. Additionality is required in the assignment of CER to CDM projects to ensure that emissions reductions are new and additional – that is, the reductions need to be directly attributable to specific investments. For instance, a project might result in reduced carbon emissions but may be economically viable on its own strength; such projects are not to be funded because the reductions are not considered additional.

Although HFC reduction projects remain the largest emissions reducers to date (and are projected to maintain this status until at least 2030), India's CDM projects began to be distributed more widely. By 2012, India had 942 approved CDM projects, representing 18 percent of the global total. From 2005 to 2014, India issued 13.2 percent of global CERs, second only to China with 59.8 percent (CDM UNFCCC 2014). European Union countries, Switzerland, and Japan are the major buyers of CERs (Alcamo et al. 2014). Table 7.2 shows the number of CDM projects approved in India in each sector in 2007. Wind, biomass energy, and hydropower projects are more numerous, even if small-scale. Geographically, India's larger comparatively more industrialized states have the highest number of CDM projects. Gujarat, Maharashtra, Tamil Nadu, and Andhra Pradesh all have over 100 projects each, as does the poorer Rajasthan. Uptake is lowest in the poor and less industrialized states of Uttar Pradesh and Bihar.

Although India has become a major global recipient of CDM resources, academics and environmentalists have often criticized the way the mechanism has operated in India. First, they have argued that carbon credits, such as those received from HFC reductions, have little impact on development. It is clear that refrigerant manufacturers in India and China were producing *additional* HFC-23 beyond that generated in the manufacturing process in order to receive extra CDM credits for its safe disposal (Wara 2007) Gujarat Fluorochemicals Limited, India's largest HFC producer, earned US$175 million from its CDM credits in 2012, whereas its revenue from refrigerant sales was just US$14.4 million (EIA 2013). In fact, according to the US Energy Information Administration, 93 percent of Gujarat Fluorochemicals' revenue came from carbon credits under the CDM![4] HFC CDM credits were thus being used as a revenue stream by individual firms that reaped windfall profits, instead of as additional funding for the use of sustainable technology.

Critics also point to the difficulties of funding legitimate development-oriented projects, and point to large-scale projects that have CDM funding in return for using technologies that would have been included anyway. An

TABLE 7.2

Numbers of CDM projects and of CERs issued

Area	CDM projects	CERs issued
Afforestation	1	44
Agriculture	1	1
Biomass energy	332	39,361
Cement	14	13,786
CO_2 usage	0	0
Coal bed/mine methane	2	0
Energy distribution	5	0
EE households	62	1,189
EE industry	81	7,090
EE own generation	113	33,463
EE service	24	56
EE supply side	39	4,900
Fossil fuel switch	46	24,835
Fugitive HFC emissions	5	721
Geothermal	0	0
HFCs	9	75,366
Hydro	225	23,341
Landfill gas	29	3,287
Methane avoidance	43	2,400
Mixed renewables	2	0
Nitrous oxide	8	6,135
Perfluorinated chemicals and sulphur hexafluoride	2	1,267
Reforestation	20	4,321
Solar	153	632
Tidal	0	0
Transport	11	1,316
Wind	831	35,350
Total	2,058	278,861

Note: EE = energy efficiency.
Source: CDM Carbon Pipeline database (http://www.namapipeline.org/).

often-cited example is Reliance Power's coal-fired power station built in Jharkhand in 2011, which received US$21 million in credits for using "super-critical" technology that was already required under Indian law. Critics point out that the project will receive support despite estimates that it will have released 240 million tons of CO_2 by 2021.

Overall, India's experience with the CDM has been mixed. While CDM investments have funded many small-scale activities, a large proportion of CERs sold provide windfall revenues to firms developing large industrial projects. The CDM incentivize firms to undermine the aim of the mechanism by pursuing relatively easy and lucrative credit-generating activities with negligible developmental benefits, rather than venturing into more technologically complex and worthwhile areas such as larger-scale renewables (Wara 2007).

The future of the CDM appears to be bleak. The collapse of the carbon credit market brought on by the slowdown in European economies, the primary buyers of CERs, in the aftermath of the global financial crisis of 2008 led to a precipitous drop in the value of CERs. The number and total value of CERs issued dropped by over 50 percent between 2013 and 2014 (Kossoy et al. 2015) and their price on the market has remained under US$1 since. Further, it is unclear whether the rationale for the CDM model exists after the Paris COP. In a post-Paris world, all countries, developing and industrialized alike, will attempt to meet their national contributions to mitigation. In the old Kyoto/CDM model, CERs were credited to private entities in industrialized countries in exchange for financial transfers to private entities in developing countries. Article 6 of the Paris agreement (UNFCCC 2015) explicitly forbids double counting, which gives rise to the tricky question of who owns any new credits transacted in "cash-for-credits" schemes. The future of the CDM or a similar mechanism will depend in large part on how this question is negotiated.

Co-Benefits, 2006–16

Following the acceptance of the CDM, a new attitude toward climate change began to emerge in India. The previous decade had seen rapid economic growth that had left India with a need to balance its international status as a poor country with its emerging identity as a rapidly industrializing economy – one that increasingly saw itself as an associate of the G20 rather than a leader of the G77. Steadfast adherence to the traditional Third World perspective on the global stage no longer reflected India's new ambition. That stance also had domestic limitations: heightened awareness of India's vulnerability to climate change and the growing mismatch between burgeoning demand for resources and dwindling domestic reserves pointed to the need for improved efficiency (Michaelowa and Michaelowa 2012). This concern was especially pressing in the energy sector, which is dependent on low-grade domestic coal and imported oil (Balachandra, Ravindranath, and Ravindranath 2010). The "co-benefits" approach also emerged at a time when research quantifying the regional economic impacts of climate change began getting attention. For example, the Fourth Assessment report of the IPCC quantified annual losses of 2.6 percent by 2100 of India's GDP from climate change–related causes, calling into question the long-held separation between environmental and economic imperatives.

More important than the realization of the domestic impacts of climate change on India's development was the idea that economic growth is not intrinsically linked to emissions. The crux of this new balance between growth and climate action was an increasing emphasis on the "right to growth" rather than the "right to pollute" framing of the earlier equity decade (Mattoo and Subramanian 2010). While the growth imperative continued to be at the heart of the co-benefits approach, it was recognized that some forms of climate change action could be beneficial to the Indian economy. In contrast to the idea that carbon emissions reductions pose an unequivocal threat to growth, some emissions reduction policies could be seen as a potential driver of growth through technological advancement and improved efficiency. These efforts would be in India's self-interest and be the result of well-reasoned choices (Raghunandan 2012); they would also have a positive impact on the economy with the additional benefit of climate change mitigation (Dubash 2013). This is not to imply that the equity arguments and the primacy of CBDRs (Common but Differentiated Responsibilities) in international negotiations were no longer at the centre of India's position (Thaker and Leiserowitz 2014). Rather, there was a dawning awareness that India would need to find a credible way to engage in international negotiations.

In 2008, as part of its domestic response to climate change, the Indian government launched the National Action Plan on Climate Change (NAPCC), a program outlining current and future policies. The NAPCC stated that India would not exceed the average per-capita emission level of the industrialized nations – a non-binding pledge that represents a novel, if rather cynical, spin on the equity principle by appearing to cap India's emissions while effectively allowing India to substantially increase emissions from 2012 emission levels (Olivier, Janssens-Maenhout, and Peters 2012).[5] The NAPCC was an ambitious document. All of its plans addressed climate mitigation and adaptation through a co-benefits frame, and signalled a transition in India's domestic approach to climate change.

External pressures certainly played a role in this transition. The United States had long argued that large emitters like China and India needed to be part of any globally binding treaty. At the COP-13 in Bali in 2007 and in subsequent meetings, developing countries were pressured to articulate plans to reduce emissions within their own economies (Rajamani 2011). In India's case, these climate discussions were also enmeshed in the India-US Civil Nuclear Agreement of 2005. The agreement was ratified by the US Senate in 2008 and transformed India from a nuclear pariah to one that could pursue civilian nuclear power without trade sanctions, as long as it opened its military facilities to inspections by the International Atomic Energy Agency. The pursuit of these broader foreign policy goals may have prompted India's acquiescence to US pressure to engage in climate mitigation, as part of a quid pro quo on nuclear and military deals.

The Copenhagen COP marked a distinct change in India's international climate stance. In the run-up to the meeting in December 2009, the Indian government pledged a 20–25 percent cut in carbon intensity from 2005 levels by 2020.[6] Surprisingly, the pledge was entirely voluntary and the Indian government did not demand any concessions in the form of either emissions reductions on the part of the industrialized world or of funding for new technologies. The Indian position in Copenhagen followed on the heels of a Chinese announcement of 40–45 percent reduction in carbon intensity over the same period. In focusing on carbon intensity and not on absolute emissions, both nations gave themselves the option of increasing their energy use and emissions to suit their growing economies, and, in India's case, its growing population.

Since the Copenhagen meeting, India has continued to engage in the climate negotiations under a co-benefits umbrella. At the 2011 Durban meeting, India agreed, along with other major emitters, to collectively reach an agreement by 2015. Such an agreement, albeit a non-binding one, was reached at the Paris COP in December that year. The Intended Nationally Determined Contribution (INDC) submitted by India included further cuts to its carbon intensity (33–35 percent) from 2005 levels by 2030 and a commitment to increase renewable power to 40 percent of total installed capacity (approximately 175 gigawatts) by 2022 – a 560 percent increase from 2014 levels.

A spillover from the co-benefits approach has been India's influence on discussions on the future of its domestic energy. The Indian government's stated position of simultaneously realizing benefits across multiple development goals has been articulated in national energy plans of the Indian Planning Commission and the NAPCC (Dubash 2013). However, even as the Indian government has discursively used an "equity and development" frame in international negotiations, it has paid less attention to implementing equity within its own borders.

Energy Poverty and Climate Co-Benefits

The equity arguments used by India in international climate negotiations have a sound economic and ethical basis. In order to lift hundreds of millions of people out of poverty, the Indian economy needs "carbon space" to grow. Yet, the idea that India's poor, especially rural, residents who lack basic access to energy, will be disproportionately punished under a carbon-constrained regime ignores an important fact about India's carbon budget: carbon emissions and energy use, like income and wealth in India, are distributed in an extremely unequal manner. On average, urban households use three times the energy that rural households do, and the top quintile of households (by income) consume four times as much as those in the bottom quintile. Chakravarty and Ramana (2011) use 2003 data to show that the top income decile of India's urban population had per-capita carbon emissions that were fifteen and twenty-seven times those of the bottom income decile of urban and rural populations, respectively.

The consequences of energy poverty for development are difficult to overestimate. The lack of access to electricity prevents households from accessing basic necessities and perpetuates poverty. The use of solid fuels such as coal and wood for cooking adds to the daily burden of living in poverty. The products of incomplete combustion (PICs) from indoor cooking are among the largest contributors to ambient air pollution and personal exposure levels. Their impacts are especially high in the poorest developing nations, where extensive indoor use of solid fuels increases exposure to particulate matter and other PICs, making it one of the largest contributors to disease, on par with malnutrition, unprotected sex, and poor sanitation.[7] The World Health Organization (WHO) Global Burden of Disease project estimates that indoor air pollution from the use of such fuels accounted for 3 million deaths globally in 2014. Roughly one-third of these were in India.

Climate agreements have focused on long-lived, well-mixed greenhouse gas species such as CO_2 and methane, two of the six GHGs that are collectively known as the "Kyoto Basket." There is strong evidence that PICs, specifically the light-absorbing black carbon (BC) portion of aerosol particulate matter, make a large contribution to atmospheric warming at regional and global scales. In 2013, the IPCC estimated the range of radiative forcing of the atmosphere from global BC emissions to be 9–48 percent that of global CO_2 emissions. India and China together account for an estimated 25–35 percent of global BC emissions, though the sources of BC in the two countries differ. Eliminating contained-combustion BC emissions such as those from cook stoves, which account for approximately 25–50 percent of total BC emissions from India, represents a significant climate mitigation strategy. The reduction of these emissions provides opportunities for co-benefits through significant improvements in air quality and reduced biomass use.

The 100-year Global Warming Potential (GWP)[8] for BC is estimated to be 900, with a range of 120–1,800 (Bond et al. 2013); thus, the per-unit climate impact of BC is between two and three orders of magnitude greater than that of CO_2. Uncertainties in this estimate result from high scientific uncertainty in the atmospheric heating effects of BC and the short time scales of BC presence in the atmosphere. Despite the potential importance of BC emissions reductions, there has been little discussion within the UNFCCC on adding BC to the Kyoto Basket. The absence of BC from discussions of national mitigation action within the UNFCCC suggests an important disconnect between scientific understanding of the role of aerosols in climate change and policy action. The Fifth Assessment Report of the IPCC equivocates on the BC issue in multiple ways. The Summary to the Policymakers does not directly engage with the question of whether BC and other aerosols should be included in mitigation accounting; and the IPCC's 2013 Scientific Assessment does not provide a value for the GWP of BC and other aerosols. On the other hand, the IPCC 2014 report on mitigation does an extensive assessment of BC across sectors and global regions, particularly in developing countries, where much of the reductions in BC and other aerosols are to be had.

Unsurprisingly, the Paris agreement makes no mention of BC or atmospheric aerosols, and its discussion of mitigation efforts focuses exclusively on the Kyoto Basket. Somewhat more surprising is the Indian government's silence on the exclusion of BC as a recognized greenhouse agent. Given the potency of BC climate forcing, its role in local air pollution, and the fact that including BC reductions as part of climate mitigation accounting would be in India's national interest, there is a powerful basis for arguing for its co-benefits approach. However, the INDC submitted by the Indian government to the Paris meeting in 2015 does not mention BC or cook stoves, while air pollution reductions merit a single desultory mention.[9]

Paris and Beyond

Since the early 1990s, the Indian government has held on to the view that India's carbon emissions need to grow in order to meet the economic expectations of its growing, and largely poor, population. India has since become the fourth-largest global emitter, although its per-capita carbon emissions remain a fraction of those of the top three emitters: China, the United States, and the European Union. India's focus on carbon intensity reductions is not surprising, since reductions in absolute emissions are considered too large given India's current reliance on coal for energy.[10]

India does need "carbon space to grow." Assuming projected growth of 7 percent, India's carbon intensity would have to fall by 64 percent of current levels to stabilize emissions by 2030. Yet it finds itself in a more difficult position than other major emitters. By comparison, the Paris agreement has come at a time when the emissions of other major emitters are stabilizing or falling. The recent discovery of domestic shale gas has been a primary driver in the recent reduction in US emissions. China's peak emissions targets have come after an unprecedented run in coal investment for the past two decades; its peak target simply grandfathers in this increase. India's natural gas options are more limited than those of the United States and China, which have access to domestic and regional natural gas resources.[11] India's argument for carbon space is thus premised on the continued use of coal, yet the Paris agreement does not offer such space.

The agreement reached at the Paris COP in 2015 obligates parties to reduce emissions in order for the global average temperature change from pre-industrial levels to stay below 2°C by 2100. It further urges them to pursue additional efforts to keep the change below 1.5°C. However, there is a substantial disjuncture between the actions necessary to reach this goal and the actual emissions reductions proposed by major emitters in Paris. Peters and colleagues (2015) demonstrate that the INDC reduction commitments of the United States and the European Union would be consistent with the

2°C limit only if the sharing of the remainder of the pie were based on *current* per-capita emissions shares. This means that countries like India would not have any carbon space to grow while countries like the United States would continue to emit at their current high per-capita levels. The Chinese plan is worse since it allows for increases in emissions until 2030. In other words, the EU, US, and Chinese pledges leave little room for other developing nations and require them to limit their per-capita emissions to 7–14 times lower than theirs. The Paris agreement is thus profoundly inequitable, and formally establishes the inequality to which developing countries have long pointed.

India, like other developing nations, finds itself in a bind. Its economy is growing and is dependent on fossil fuels, yet it has a large and poor agrarian population vulnerable to climate change. According to the World Bank in 2014, a two-degree change in global temperature is expected to make the monsoon more variable, resulting in reduced crop yields. If global emissions are allowed to grow beyond this benchmark, India could face potentially catastrophic change, including the threat of rising sea levels to its major coastal cities. How might India then balance the needs of its current population while ensuring that climate change stays within the limits of the Paris agreement, especially when it is responsible for only a relatively small proportion of global emissions? While a detailed assessment of India's climate conundrum calls for a full-fledged research program, we can offer some reflections on ways forward.

First, it is overwhelmingly in India's interest to keep carbon emissions paths under the 2°C benchmark. A fifth of the world's poorest people live in India, and they form the largest group of individuals vulnerable to climate change within a single nation. Credible contributions to carbon mitigation will provide Indian policy makers with a stronger position in negotiating with other large emitters and stressing the need for carbon finance. By taking an international leadership role in climate mitigation and leading by example, India can demand the same of the other signatories.

The second point relates to India's current plan: to reduce carbon intensity through energy efficiency improvements (30–35 percent by 2020); to invest in renewables (increase power to 40 percent of installed capacity by 2030); and to substantially increase forest carbon storage. Using a detailed analysis of India's energy supply sector, Ebinger (2016) argues that India is unlikely to meet intensity and renewable targets unless a variety of economic and governance criteria are met. India will also need sizable investments to modernize its electricity grid and enable it to successfully integrate large volumes of intermittent renewables. A large gap between policy intent and capacity to act has long plagued the Indian energy sector (Ahn and Graczyk 2012).

Domestically, India will need to build the analytical capacity to manage the transition to a modern energy sector. Improved governance in the energy sector, including the removal of regressive subsidies for fossil fuels, among other things (Ghosh and Ganesan 2015), streamlining of land acquisition (Romero 2012), and growth in the financial and institutional capabilities of India's State Electricity Boards will be needed to meet the proposed INDC targets. This point applies more broadly across the economy. Technical solutions for significantly reducing India's carbon emissions using currently available technologies might be available at moderate costs, but implementation of these measures will pose serious challenges.[12]

Third, providing universal access to basic electricity and clean cooking fuels may be less related to growth in carbon emissions than has been imagined. Pachauri (2014) estimates that carbon emissions from improvements in household electricity access contributed only 3–4 percent to carbon emissions growth in India since 1983. Moving all Indian households that use unimproved wood stoves to an improved forced air design could help reduce India's greenhouse gas emissions by 4 percent if only the gases in the Kyoto Basket are considered (Venkataraman et al. 2010).[13] This reduction could more than double if BC reductions are included (Grieshop et al. 2009; Kandlikar, Reynolds, and Grieshop 2009). Consequently, policies aimed at providing clean fuels could save millions of lives in India and result in possible carbon savings. However, in order for carbon-equivalent savings to be fully accounted for and realized, India needs to forcefully make a case for the inclusion of pollutants such as BC in the list of greenhouse agents approved under the UNFCCC.

Solar power provides a second example. India's target of 40 gigawatts of peak installed capacity by 2030 is bold, but much of the focus is likely to be on utility-scale projects aimed at industrial and urban consumers. Micro-grid and off-grid solar will benefit millions in rural India who are either not served or poorly served. A determined policy effort for decentralized solar power could provide universal rural electricity access and carbon reductions.

Finally, there are numerous other ways of realizing climate co-benefits. India is urbanizing rapidly, and urban populations are projected to equal those in rural areas within two decades. Indian cities are locked in a reinforcing feedback loop between greater automobile use and urban sprawl, resulting in long commutes, severe congestion effects, and abysmal air quality. A focus on public transit, pedestrian infrastructure, and management of sprawl will make Indian cities more livable and lessen the country's energy import burden. Solutions to India's climate conundrum will not be easy to realize, but India really has no choice. It will need to a find a way.

NOTES

1 India's per-capita CO_2 emissions were 1.7 tons in 2011, compared with 5.7 tons for China, 17 tons for the United States, and 16.5 tons for Australia (World Bank, IFC, and MIGA 2016).

2 *United Nations Framework Convention on Climate Change,* 1771 UNTS 107; S. Treaty Doc No. 102-38; UN Doc. A/AC.237/18 (Part II)/Add.1; 31 ILM 849 (1992).

3 International agreement did not result automatically in domestic ratification, nor did domestic ratification result in emissions reductions. Some countries, such as the United States, did not ratify the Kyoto Protocol and so ignored its obligations altogether. Others, such as Canada, ratified the deal domestically yet made few attempts to meet their emissions reduction targets.

4 Disposing of HFC-23 under the CDM was highly lucrative. The Energy Information Administration estimates that from 2003 to 2012, four major Indian HFC producers earned US$970 million in carbon credits under the CDM.

5 The NAPCC contains eight missions, representing national priorities: National Solar Mission, Enhanced Energy Efficiency, Sustainable Habitat, Water, Himalayan Ecosystems, Green India, Sustainable Agriculture, and Strategic Knowledge on Climate Change. The scope of the plan is sprawling. There is no inter-mission standardization and the plan lacks a notion of domestic equity, viewing development at the national level only. There is also considerable variation in mission performance, with narrower, more tightly defined missions (e.g., Solar) better able to form succinct, effective intervention strategies than broader ones (e.g., Water, Sustainable Agriculture), which are embedded in existing development debates over dealing with long-standing problems by setting broad priorities (Byravan and Rajan 2012).

6 National carbon intensity measures the amount of CO_2 emissions per unit of economic output. It can be reduced by improving energy efficiency and/or by using sources of energy that are less carbon-intensive, such as renewables, nuclear, or hydropower.

7 Particulate matter (PM) refers to the mixture of airborne particles and liquid droplets suspended in the air (aerosols). They include natural aerosols such as dust, and anthropogenic aerosols released from combustion. Fine particles that are less than

2.5 microns in diameter (PM 2.5) are known to have health effects in humans. PM can also influence the radiative balance of the planet depending on whether it absorbs (when it is black, as is the case with black carbon) or reflects sunlight.

8 GWP is an index that provides a simple way to translate the climatic effects of non-CO_2 greenhouse gases into equivalent CO_2 terms. It measures the climate change potency of a single unit of emissions of non-CO_2 climate drivers relative to a single unit of CO_2 emissions.

9 To the extent that biomass figures in India's INDC, the focus is on its use in distributed electricity generation.

10 About 80 percent of India's electricity comes from coal.

11 Domestic supply has increased in recent years, but demand still exceeds supply by 19 billion cubic metres, with the remainder being supplied by expensive liquefied natural gases. India is close to natural gas sources from the Middle East, but it lives in a "bad neighbourhood" where it is difficult to access these resources via pipelines. Low natural gas prices will help meet rapidly increasing demand.

12 Detailed sector-specific greenhouse gas abatement cost curves for India are scarce. A McKinsey report from 2011 estimates that 37 percent of projected reference 2030 levels could be abated at a negative cost, while an additional 30 percent could be abated at a price of less than 20 euros per ton of CO_2. The report also estimates that only 10 percent of the emissions reductions will be easy to implement, and cites multiple bottlenecks in the Indian economy.

13 There are hundreds of stove designs in use or being piloted. Grieshop and colleagues (2011) found that health and climate impacts span two orders of magnitude across representative sets of technologies. Relative to the simplest technology, the natural draft rocket designs reduce exposures by a factor of two to three. Unvented wood stoves that use a battery-powered fan to enhance combustion performance can reduce exposures by one order of magnitude. Liquefied petroleum gas and kerosene-fuelled stoves were the cleanest along both dimensions.

Conclusion

MOSHE HIRSCH, ASHOK KOTWAL,
and BHARAT RAMASWAMI

The literature on the human rights based approach to economic development presents the experience of India as a prominent example of this approach.[1] The unique combination of widespread poverty, weak institutional capacity, and vibrant democracy has facilitated the development of this approach in India. Thus, active civil society groups, an independent and active judiciary, and a free press may account for the enactment of legislation in India on the right to development.

As elaborated in Chapter 1, the general and "soft" right to development emphasizes the individual person as the central subject of development, highlighting the suffering of poor individuals and their right to human dignity with at least the minimum necessities of life. Individuals who are deprived of such basic needs live in both developed and developing countries, but much more in developing ones. Among the principal characteristics of that right are human-centred development, the realization of which requires the implementation of a wide range of specific and interdependent human rights, and the involvement of considerations of social justice such as fair distribution of benefits and burdens. Implementation of the right to development may be impeded by breaches of a broad range of human rights, including political rights, such as those relating to transparent and accountable governance and democracy. The right to development, however, tends to emphasize the importance of social and economic rights, such as the right to food, education, health, water, clean environment, housing, and work.

The duties emanating from the right to development are attributed to both national governments and international institutions. The governments of countries suffering from a lack of adequate development are urged to undertake the measures needed at the national level in order to realize the right to development. Developed countries as well as international institutions are called on to adopt complementary measures to promote development in developing countries. Though the implementation of the right involves joint and complementary commitments, national authorities bear the primary responsibility for creating conditions favourable to the realization of the right to development. This joint responsibility requires international cooperation to support the efforts of developing countries in resolving their economic and social problems, and to create an environment conducive to the promotion of human development.

The preceding chapters have analyzed Indian legislative measures and administrative programs aimed at promoting economic development, often by conferring legal rights on individuals. This distinctive method is particularly prominent in Chapter 2, addressing the right to food; Chapter 3, with regard to the right to education; and Chapter 4, regarding the right to work in the rural sector. Chapter 7 analyzes the impact of foreign investors on intergroup disparities and illustrates that economic development is threatened by breaches of human rights related not only to activities of government officials but also those of individuals and commercial actors.

The chapters in this book reveal that the human rights approach to economic development is not manifested in a uniform manner but rather through the undertaking of diverse strategies relating to the particular rights and different circumstances prevailing in the specific sector. India's experience in this area is valuable because it also demonstrates some major obstacles to the successful realization of the human rights based approach to development.

The implementation of certain rights related to development may be hindered by inconsistencies with other human rights; however, such inconsistencies have not been found in the areas analyzed in this study. Some links between the right to development and other human rights are revealed, for example, in Chapter 5, which addresses also the link between the right to food, transgenics, and the right to health. Transgenic strategies may rapidly increase access to food in poor countries like India but concerns regarding the perceived impact on the right to health have impeded regulatory decisions on these new techniques. More importantly, while the enactment of comprehensive statutes is important, it does not guarantee effective implementation of the fundamental right that underlies the specific legislation.

Implementation problems are conspicuous in Chapters 3 and 4, which focus on the right to education and right to employment in the rural sector, respectively. Implementation deficiencies identified in these chapters are related to some limitations of the right to development in general. While an active judiciary, civil society groups, and a free press are essential for the human rights based approach, these three factors are not sufficient for the successful planning and execution of comprehensive developmental programs. This is because these significant actors do not possess the required resources to administer large-scale programs, particularly in a vast and extremely diverse country such as India.

Courts generally focus on individual disputes, and the adjudicatory process is characterized by its "piecemeal" quality – courts are ill equipped to devise coherent policies and apply them. The judicial process is also largely passive and courts may intervene where other parties apply to them – legal tribunals do not initiate action ("courts must act when litigants call"). Thus, it is clear that the legislative and executive branches have a much wider range of tools in their toolbox.[2] Courts may sporadically supervise some governmental programs, but realistically they are not always accessible to people belonging to vulnerable groups whose legal rights are breached.

Civil society groups may provide poor people with the necessary financial and legal resources needed to initiate legal proceedings. However, they are not present everywhere and lack the necessary resources to administer court proceedings, which often involve human rights violations. Even where applications to courts are successful, they often cannot overcome deeply entrenched socio-cultural patterns that inhibit economic development in India, such as caste discrimination and gender bias.

In sum, while these actors are valuable for promoting the socio-economic rights of poor people and they may complement governmental programs, they cannot substitute for weak institutions in India.

Finally, the legal rights conferred on Indian residents *may* be challenged by other countries and international institutions as inconsistent with India's international legal obligations. In contrast to arguments that international treaties prevent developing countries from carrying out their domestic mandate and promoting economic development, the chapters here reveal that the principal factors inhibiting economic development in India are related to weak (and occasionally dysfunctional) public institutions. For example, Chapter 2 reveals that the lack of food security in India is not caused by India's obligations under the World Trade Organization (WTO) *Agreement on Agriculture.*

Policy Recommendations

The analyses undertaken in this book may offer some general recommendations to Canadian policy makers.

Common Democratic Values

The point of departure for a productive dialogue between Canada and India is the recognition of India's leading role regarding the human rights based approach to economic development, as well as its long-standing commitment to democratic values. The dialogue between Canada and India should be predicated on the countries' common democratic values and shared heritage.

Implementing Local Legislative Infrastructure

India, like most other developing countries, is sensitive to interference by developed countries and international institutions in its internal affairs, particularly with regard to human rights. Consequently, and in light of India's advanced socio-economic legislation, it is *not* desirable to focus on external human rights norms (either Canadian or international ones) but rather to emphasize the need for effective implementation, and perhaps certain improvements, of local legislation regarding the right to development. The dialogue with India should not neglect civil and political rights, such as the right to information and the prohibition of discrimination (already included in the Indian legislation).

Supporting Local Actors

It is advisable to support and empower local actors in India – governmental and non-governmental alike – engaged in implementing human rights legislation or in strengthening local institutions (including fighting corruption).

It is also desirable to support coordination between governmental agencies and civil society groups active in these spheres.

Joint Consultative Networks

It is advisable to establish joint consultative networks composed of Canadian and Indian public officials (including judges), NGOs, and journalists actively involved in these spheres. The joint forums would discuss challenges encountered by Canadian and Indian officials in these domains, such as implementing the human rights approach to economic development and strengthening domestic institutions. For example, these consultative networks could address innovative strategies to enhance public education and rigorous implementation of Indian and Canadian domestic obligations to fight corruption, including Canadian legislation relating to corrupt practices engaged in by Canadian corporations in India.

Monitoring and Dissemination of Information

The joint networks described above would collect and disseminate information on the achievements, efficiency, and difficulties encountered by governmental and non-governmental bodies aiming to promote the human rights approach to economic development and to strengthen local institutions. Governmental actors and civil society groups in India would undertake to collect and exchange information relating to recent developments in these spheres, while the Canadian bodies would assist by analyzing the information collected in India.

Training Programs

Both countries would initiate joint training programs aimed at implementing the human rights approach to reducing poverty (particularly among disadvantaged groups) as well as strengthening domestic institutions.

Multilateral Economic Institutions

The example of India shows that the claim by developing countries that international treaty obligations are the main obstacle to their development is not always valid. In fact, this sometimes becomes a convenient excuse used by the governments of developing countries to hide their failure to improve their institutions. Instead of accepting such claims, a close scrutiny could, in fact, aid the process of development in developing countries. Both developed and developing countries should support initiatives in multilateral economic institutions (including the WTO) aimed at promoting the right to development. Such efforts may relate to the *establishment of new legal rules* (e.g., new provisions regarding the evaluation of the impact of the states' trade policies on the right to development in the framework of the WTO Trade Policy Review Mechanisms)[3] or the *interpretation of existing rules* in a manner that supports the human rights based approach to economic development (e.g., relating to the conformity of the Indian *National Food Security Act* with the WTO *Agreement on Agriculture*).

Multilateral Economic Treaties

Both countries should support the incorporation of adequate provisions in international trade and investment agreements that realize the right to development and strengthen domestic institutional capacity, including fighting corruption in transnational economic activities.

NOTES

1 See, e.g., Banerjee 2005, 7, 77, 111, 139, 165; Guha-Khasnobis and Vivek 2007; Oestreich 2014; OHCHR 2013, 367, etc.; OHCHR 2006, 3.

2 See, e.g., Horowitz 1977, 22–38.

3 On such recommended reforms to be adopted by the World Trade Organization, see Howse 2013. See also the WTO's "Submission in follow-up to HRC resolution 15/25 'The Right to development,'" http://www.ohchr.org/Documents/Issues/Development/Session12/WTO.pdf.

References

Agarwal, Anil, and Sunita Narain. 1991. *Global Warming in an Unequal World: A Case of Environmental Colonialism.* New Delhi: Centre for Science and Environment.

Aggarwal, P.K. 2008. "Global Climate Change and Indian Agriculture: Impacts, Adaptation and Mitigation." *Indian Journal of Agricultural Sciences* 78 (11): 911.

Ahn, Sun-Joo, and Dagmar Graczyk. 2012. *Understanding Energy Challenges in India: Policies, Players and Issues.* Paris: International Energy Agency. https://www.iea.org/publications/freepublications/publication/India_study_FINAL_WEB.pdf.

Aiyar, Shekhar, and Ashoka Mody. 2011. "The Demographic Dividend: Evidence from the Indian States." Working Paper WP/11/38. Washington, DC: International Monetary Fund.

Alcamo, J., D. Puig, B. Metz, V. Demkine, and T.C. Farrell, eds. 2014. *The Emissions Gap Report 2014: A UNEP Synthesis Report.* Nairobi: United Nations Environment Programme.

Anker, Richard. 1998. *Gender and Jobs: Sex Segregation of Occupations in the World.* Geneva: International Labour Organization.

Arimond, M., and M.T. Ruel. 2004. "Dietary Diversity Is Associated with Child Nutritional Status: Evidence from 11 Demographic and Health Surveys." *Journal of Nutrition* 134: 2579–85.

Artecona, Raquel, and Wendy Cunningham. 2002. *Effects of Trade Liberalization on the Gender Wage Gap in Mexico.* Washington, DC: World Bank, Development Research Group/Poverty Re-education and Economic Management Network.

Athreye, Suma, and Sandeep Kapur. 2001. "Private Foreign Investment in India: Pain or Panacea?" *World Economy* 24: 399–424.

Atteridge, A., M.K. Shrivastava, N. Pahuja, and H. Upadhayay. 2012. "Climate Policy in India: What Shapes International, National and State Policy?" *Ambio* 41 (2012): 68–77.

Baer, P., J. Harte, B. Haya, A.V. Herzog, J. Holdren, N.E. Hultman, D.M. Kammen, R.B. Norgaard, and L. Raymond. 2000. "Equity and Greenhouse Gas Responsibility." *Science* 289 (2000): 2287.

Bagla, Pallava. 2006. "Controversial Rivers Project Aims to Turn India's Fierce Monsoon into a Friend." *Science* 313 (2006): 1036–37.

Bajpai, Nirupam, and Jeffrey Sachs. 2000. *Foreign Direct Investment in India: Issues and Problems.* Discussion Paper No. 759. Cambridge, MA: Harvard Institute of International Development.

Balachandra, P., Darsini Ravindranath, and N.H. Ravindranath. 2010. "Energy Efficiency in India: Assessing the Policy Regimes and Their Impacts." *Energy Policy* 38 (2010): 6428–38.

Balakrishnan, Pulapre, and Bharat Ramaswami. 2015. "Public Intervention and Private Speculation: The Case of Wheat Procurement." *Journal of Quantitative Economics* 11 (1995): 59–83.

Banerjee, Upala Devi. 2005. *Lessons Learned from Rights-Based Approaches in the Asia-Pacific Region: Documentation of Case Studies.* Bangkok: United Nations Development Programme; Office of the United Nations High Commissioner for Human Rights. http://hrbaportal.org/wp-content/files/RBA-in-AP-region3.pdf.

Banga, Rashmi. 2003. "Impact of Government Policies and Investment Agreements on FDI Inflows." Working Paper No. 116. New Delhi: Indian Council for Research on International Economics Relations.

Barwale, R.B., V.R. Gadwal, Usha Zehr, and Brent Zehr. 2004. "Prospects for Bt Cotton Technology in India." *Journal of Agrobiotechnology Management and Economics* 7 (2004): 23–26.

Bedjaoui, Mohammed. 1991. "The Right to Development." In *International Law: Achievements and Prospects,* edited by Mohammed Bedjaoui, 1177. Dordrecht, Netherlands: Martinus Nijhoff.

Bhaumik, Sumon K., P.L. Beena, Laveesh Bhandari, and Subir Gokarn. 2003. "Survey of FDI in India." DRC Working Paper No. 6. London: Centre for New and Emerging Markets, London Business School.

Billet, S. 2009. "Dividing Climate Change: Global Warming and the Indian Mass Media." *Climate Change* 99 (2009): 1–16.

Black, Sandra, and Elizabeth Brainerd. 2004. "Importing Equality? The Impact of Globalisation on Gender Discrimination." *Industrial and Labour Relations Review* 57 (4): 540–59.

Bond, T.C., S.J. Doherty, D.W. Fahey, P.M. Forster, T. Berntsen, B.J. DeAngelo, and S. Kinne. 2013. "Bounding the Role of Black Carbon in the Climate System: A Scientific Assessment." *Journal of Geophysical Research: Atmospheres* 118: 5380–52.

Brown, K.H. 1991. "The Importance of Dietary Quality versus Quantity for Weanlings in Less Developed Countries: A Framework for Discussion." *Food and Nutrition Bulletin* 13: 86–94.

Brown, K.H., K.G. Dewey, and L.H. Allen. 1998. *Complementary Feeding of Young Children in Developing Countries: A Review of Current Scientific Knowledge.* New York: UNICEF.

Bunn, Isabella D. 2000. "The Right to Development: Implications for International Economic Law." *American University International Law Review* 15: 1425–66.

Byravan, S., and S. Rajan. 2012. *An Evaluation of India's National Action Plan on Climate Change.* Madras: Centre for Development Finance, IIT Madras.

Çağatay, N., and G. Berik. 1991. "Transition to Export-Led Growth in Turkey: Is There a Feminisation of Employment?" *Capital and Class* 15 (1): 153–77. https://doi.org/10.1177/030981689104300108.

CDM UNFCCC (Clean Development Mechanism, United Nations Framework Convention on Climate Change). 2014. "Distribution of CERs Issued by Host Party." http://cdm.unfccc.int/Statistics/Public/CDMinsights/index.html#iss.

Chakraborty, Chandana, and Peter Nunnenkamp. 2008. "Economic Reforms, FDI and Economic Growth in India: A Sector-Level Analysis." *World Development* 36 (7): 1192–1218.

Chakravarty, S., and M.V. Ramana. 2011. "Hiding behind the Poor Debate: A Synthetic Overview." In *Handbook of Climate Change and India: Development, Politics and Governance,* 1st ed., edited by N.K. Dubash, 218–29. New Delhi: Oxford University Press.

Chaudhary, A., A. Narain, C. Krishna, and A. Sagar. 2014. *Who Shapes Climate Action in India? Insights from the Wind and Solar Energy Sectors.* Evidence Report 56. Brighton, UK: Institute for Development Studies.

Chinkin, Christine. 2010. "Women, Rights of, International Protection." In *Max Planck Encyclopaedia of Public International Law,* edited by Rüdiger Wolfrum. Oxford: Oxford Public International Law. http://opil.ouplaw.com/home/EPIL.

Cunningham, Clark D. 1987. "Public Interest Litigation in Indian Supreme Court." *Journal of the Indian Law Institute* 29: 494.

Darity, William Jr., and Ashwini Deshpande. 2003. *Boundaries of Clan and Color: Transnational Comparisons of Inter-Group Disparity.* London: Routledge.

Das, Jishnu, Alaka Holla, Michael Kremer, Aakash Mohpal, and Karthik Muralidharan. 2014. "Quality and Accountability in Health: Audit Evidence from Primary Care Providers." Working Paper WPS7334. Washington, DC: World Bank.

De Feyter, Koen. 2013. *Towards a Framework Convention on the Right to Development.* Berlin/Geneva: Friedrich-Ebert-Stiftung.

De Greef, Willy. 2004. "The Cartagena Protocol and the Future of Agbiotech." *Nature Biotechnology* 22 (7): 811–12.

Deshpande, Ashwini. 2011. *The Grammar of Caste: Economic Discrimination in Contemporary India.* New Delhi: Oxford University Press.

Deshpande, Ashwini, and Katherine Newman. 2007. "Where the Path Leads: The Role of Caste in Post University Employment Expectations." *Economic and Political Weekly* 42 (41): 4133–40.

Dewey, K.G., D.A. Finley, and B. Lonnerdal. 1984. "Breast Milk Volume and Composition during Late Lactation (7–20 Months)." *Journal of Pediatrics, Gastroenterology and Nutrition* 3: 713–20.

Ding, Ding, Edward W. Maibach, Xiaoquan Zhao, Connie Roser-Renouf, and Anthony Leiserowitz. 2011. "Support for Climate Policy and Societal Action Are Linked to Perceptions about Scientific Agreement." *Nature Climate Change* 1 (9): 462–66.

Donnelly, Jack. 1985. "In Search of the Unicorn: The Jurisprudence and Politics of the Right to Development." *California Western International Law Journal* 15: 473–509.

Dubash, Navroz K. 2012. "Climate Politics in India: Three Narratives." In *Handbook of Climate Change and India,* edited by N. Dubash, 197–207. Oxford: Routledge.

–. 2013. "The Politics of Climate Change in India: Narratives of Equity and Co-Benefit." *Wiley Interdisciplinary Reviews: Climate Change* 4: 191–201.

Ebinger, Charles. 2016. *India's Energy and Climate Policy: Can India Meet the Challenge of Industrialization and Climate Change?* Washington, DC: Brookings Institution, 2016.

EIA. 2013. *Two Billion Tonne Climate Bomb: How to Defuse the HFC-23 Problem.* Washington, DC and London, UK: Environmental Investigation Agency (EIA). https://eia-international.org/wp-content/uploads/EIA_HFC-23_report_0613_Final1.pdf.

Eriksson, J.G., T. Forsen, J. Tuomilehto, C. Osmond, and D.J. Barker. "Early Growth and Coronary Heart Disease in Later Life: Longitudinal Study." *British Medical Journal* 322: 949–53.

Eswaran, Mukesh, Ashok Kotwal, Bharat Ramaswami, and Wilima Wadhwa. 2009. "Sectoral Labour Flows and Agricultural Wages in India, 1983–2004: Has Growth Trickled Down and How?" *Economic and Political Weekly* 44: 46–55.

Eyhorn, Frank, Mahesh Ramakrishnan, and Paul Mäder. 2007. "The Viability of Cotton-Based Organic Farming Systems in India." *International Journal of Agricultural Sustainability* 5 (1): 25–38.

Felice, William F. 2009. *Encyclopaedia of Human Rights.* Vol. 2, *Right to Development.* New York: Oxford University Press.

Finucane, Melissa L., Ali Alhakami, Paul Slovic, and Stephen M. Johnson. 2000. "The Affect Heuristic in Judgments of Risks and Benefits." *Journal of Behavioral Decision Making* 13 (1): 1–17.

Fischhoff, Baruch, Paul Slovic, Sarah Lichtenstein, Stephen Read, and Barbara Combs. 1978. "How Safe Is Safe Enough? A Psychometric Study of Attitudes towards Technological Risks and Benefits." *Policy Sciences* 9 (2): 127–52.

Fotso, J.C., and B. Kuate-Defo. 2006. "Household and Community Socioeconomic Influences on Early Childhood Malnutrition in Africa." *Journal of Biosocial Science* 38: 289–313.

Freeman, Julia. 2012. "Engineered Debates and Emergent Biosafety: The Social Controversy and Regulatory Challenges Confronting GE Crops in India." PhD dissertation, University of British Columbia.

Freeman, Julia, Terre Satterfield, and Milind Kandlikar. 2011. "Agricultural Biotechnology and Regulatory Innovation in India." *Science and Public Policy* 38 (4): 319–31.

Ghosh, Arunabha, and Karthik Ganesan. 2015. "Policy: Rethink India's Energy Strategy." *Nature* 521: 156–57.

Goldar, Bishwanath. 2007. "Location of Plants of Foreign Companies." Paper presented at India and Globalisation: A Seminar in Honour of Professor N.S. Siddharthan, New Delhi, February.

Gopinath, Vrinda. 2006. "Happy Birthday, Lord Macaulay, Thank You for 'Dalit Empowerment.'" *Indian Express,* 26 October. http://archive.indianexpress.com/news/happy-birthday-lord-macaulay-thank-you-for-dalit-empowerment/15423/0.

Gressel, Jonathan. 2008. *Genetic Glass Ceilings: Transgenics for Crop Biodiversity.* Baltimore: John Hopkins University Press.

Grieshop, A.P., J.D. Marshall, and M. Kandlikar. 2011. "Health and Climate Benefits of Cookstove Replacement Options." *Energy Policy* 39 (12): 7530–42.

Grieshop, A.P., C.C. Reynolds, M. Kandlikar, and H. Dowlatabadi. 2009. "A Black-Carbon Mitigation Wedge." *Nature Geoscience* 2: 533–34.

Gruère, Guillaume P., Purvi Mehta-Bhatt, and Debdatta Sengupta. 2008. *Bt Cotton and Farmer Suicides in India: Reviewing the Evidence.* Washington, DC: International Food Policy Research Institute.

Guha-Khasnobis, Basudeb, and S. Vivek. 2007. "The Rights-Based Approach to Development – Lessons from the Right to Food Movement in India." In *Food Insecurity, Vulnerability and Human Rights Failure,* edited by B. Guha-Khasnobis, S.S. Acharya, and B. Davis, 308–28. London: Palgrave Macmillan.

Gupta, Aarti. 2000. "Governing Trade in Genetically Modified Organisms: The Cartagena Protocol on Biosafety." *Environment: Science and Policy for Sustainable Development* 42 (4): 22–33.

Haas, J.D., E.J. Martinez, E. Murdoch, E. Conlisk, J.A. Rivera, and R. Martorell. 1995. "Nutritional Supplementation during the Preschool Years Influences Body Size and Composition of Guatemalan Adolescents." *Journal of Nutrition* 125: 1078S–89S.

Herring, Ronald J. 2008a. "Opposition to Transgenic Technologies: Ideology, Interests and Collective Action Frames." *Nature Reviews Genetics* 9 (6): 458–63.

–. 2008b. "Whose Numbers Count? Probing Discrepant Evidence on Transgenic Cotton in the Warangal District of India." *International Journal of Multiple Research Approaches* 2 (2): 145–59.

–. 2015. "State Science, Risk and Agricultural Biotechnology: *Bt* Cotton to *Bt* Brinjal in India." *Journal of Peasant Studies* 42 (1): 159–86.

Herring, Ronald J., and N. Chandrasekhara Rao. 2012. "On the 'Failure of Bt Cotton.'" *Economic and Political Weekly* 47 (18): 45.

Herring, Ronald J., and Milind Kandlikar. 2009. "Illicit Seeds: Intellectual Property and the Underground Proliferation of Agricultural Biotechnologies." In *Politics of Intellectual Property: Contestation over the Ownership, Use, and Control of Knowledge and Information,* edited by Sebastian Haunss and Kenneth Shadlen, 56–70. London: Edward Elgar.

Herring, Ronald, J. Wesseler, and S. Scatasta. "Persistent Narratives: Why is the 'Failure of Bt Cotton in India' Story Still with Us?" *AgBioForum* 12 (1) (2009): 14–22.

Hirsch, Moshe. 2010. "Agreement on Rules of Origin." In *Max Planck Commentaries on World Trade: WTO Trade in Goods,* edited by Rudiger Wolfrum, Peter-Tobias Stoll, and Karen Kaiser, 171–88. Leiden, Netherlands: Brill.

Horowitz, Donald L. 1977. *The Courts and Social Policy.* Washington, DC: Brookings Institution.

Horta, B.L., D.P. Gigante, C. Osmond, F.C. Barros, and C.G. Victora. 2009. "Intergenerational Effect of Weight Gain in Childhood on Offspring Birthweight." *International Journal of Epidemiology* 38: 724–32.

Howse, Robert. 2013. "Mainstreaming the Right to Development into the World Trade Organization." In *Realizing the Right to Development: Essays in Commemoration of 25 Years of the United Nations Declaration on the Right to Development.* New York/Geneva: United Nations.

International Monetary Fund. 1995. *International Financial Statistics Yearbook.* Washington, DC. https://books.google.co.in/books/about/International_Financial_Statistics_Yearb.html?id=4g2cMQEACAAJ&redir_esc=y.

IPCC (Intergovernmental Panel on Climate Change). 2013. *Climate Change 2013: The Physical Science Basis. Contribution of Working Group I to the Fifth Assessment Report of the Intergovernmental Panel on Climate Change.* Cambridge: Cambridge University Press.

Isaksen, Kari-Anne, and Kristian Stokke. 2012. "Changing Climate Discourse and Politics in India: Climate Change as Challenge and Opportunity for Diplomacy and Development." *Geoforum* 57: 110–19.

Jacobs, Lesley, and Sarbani Sen. 2012. "The Distinctive Character of Legal Adversarialism in India." *Canada Watch,* Winter. http://robarts.info.yorku.ca/files/2012/02/CW_Winter2012.pdf.

Jasanoff, Sheila. 2005. *Designs on Nature.* Princeton, NJ: Princeton University Press.

Jayaraman, T., T. Kanitkar, and M. D'Souza. 2011. "Equitable Access to Sustainable Development: An Indian Approach." http://citeseerx.ist.psu.edu/viewdoc/summary?doi=10.1.1.684.4372.

Jha, Shikha, and Bharat Ramaswami. 2012. "The Percolation of Public Expenditures: Food Subsidies in India and the Philippines." *India Policy Forum* 8: 95–138.

Jodhka, Surinder, and Katherine Newman. 2007. "In the Name of Globalisation." *Economic and Political Weekly* 42 (41): 4125–32.

Joshi, Vijay, and I.M.D. Little. 1996. *India's Economic Reforms, 1991–2001.* New York: Oxford University Press.

Kandlikar, M., C. Reynolds, and A. Grieshop. 2009. "Alternative Perspective on Black Carbon Mitigation as a Response to Climate Change." In *Smart Solutions to Climate Change: Comparing Costs and Benefits,* edited by Bjørn Lomborg, 159–71. Cambridge: Cambridge University Press.

Kandlikar, M., and Ambuj Sagar. 1999. "Climate Change Research and Analysis in India: An Integrated Assessment of the North-South Divide." *Global Environmental Change* 9: 19–38.

Kapur, Devesh, Chandra Bhan Prasad, Lant Pritchett, and D. Shyam Babu. 2010. "Rethinking Inequality: Dalits in Uttar Pradesh in the Market Reform Era." *Economic and Political Weekly* 45 (35): 39–49.

Kathage, Jonas, and Matin Qaim. 2012. "Economic Impacts and Impact Dynamics of Bt (*Bacillus thuringiensis*) Cotton in India." *Proceedings of the National Academy of Sciences* 109 (29): 11652–56.

Key, Suzie, Julian K.-C. Ma, and Pascal M.W. Drake. 2008. "Genetically Modified Plants and Human Health." *Journal of the Royal Society of Medicine* 101 (6): 290–98. doi:10.1258/jrsm.2008.070372.

Kirchmeier, Felix. 2006. "The Right to Development – Where Do We Stand? State of the Debate on the Right to Development." Occasional Paper No. 23. Geneva: Friedrich-Ebert-Stiftung.

Kleinman, Daniel Lee, Abby J. Kinchy, and Robyn Autry. 2009. "Local Variation or Global Convergence in Agricultural Biotechnology Policy? A Comparative Analysis." *Science and Public Policy* 36 (5): 361.

Klümper, Wilhelm, and Matin Qaim. 2014. "A Meta-Analysis of the Impacts of Genetically Modified Crops." *PLOS ONE* 9 (11): e111629. https://doi.org/10.1371/journal.pone.0111629.

Koo, Bonwoo, Carol Nottenburg, and Philip G. Pardey. 2004. "Plants and Intellectual Property: An International Appraisal." *Science* 306 (5700): 1295–97. doi:10.1126/science.1106760.

Kossoy, A., G. Peszko, K. Oppermann, N. Prytz, N. Klein, K. Blok ... and B. Borkent. 2015. *State and Trends of Carbon Pricing 2015.* Washington, DC: World Bank Group.

Kotwal, Ashok, Milind Murugkar, and Bharat Ramaswami. 2011. "PDS Forever?" *Economic and Political Weekly* 56: 72–76.

Kotwal, Ashok, Bharat Ramaswami, and Wilima Wadhwa. 2011. "Economic Liberalization and Indian Economic Growth: What's the Evidence?" *Journal of Economic Literature* 49: 1152–99.

Kumar, A.K. Shiva. 2013. "National Experience with the Right to Development." In *Realizing the Right to Development: Essays in Commemoration of 25 Years of the United Nations Declaration on the Right to Development,* 367–69. New York/Geneva: United Nations.

Kumar, Nagesh. 2000. "Mergers and Acquisitions by MNEs: Patterns and Implications." *Economic and Political Weekly* 35 (32): 2851–58.

–. 2005. "Liberalization, Foreign Direct Investment Flows and Development: Indian Experience in the 1990s." *Economic and Political Weekly* 40 (14): 1459–69.

Kumar, Sandeep, Amita Misra, Alok Kumar Verma, Ruchi Roy, Anurag Tripathi, Kausar M. Ansari, Mukul Das, and Premendra D. Dwivedi. 2011. "Bt Brinjal in India: A Long Way to Go." *GM Crops* 2 (2): 92–98.

Lall, Somik Vinay, and Sanjoy Chakravorty. 2005. "Industrial Location and Spatial Inequality: Theory and Evidence from India." *Review of Development Economics* 9: 47–68.

Laskey, M.A., A. Prentice, J. Shaw, T. Zachou, S.M. Ceesay, L. Vasquez-Velasquez, and D.R. Fraser. 1990. "Breast-Milk Calcium Concentrations during Prolonged Lactation in British and Rural Gambian Mothers." *Acta Paediatrica* 79: 507–12.

Lenagala, Chakrangi, and Rati Ram. 2010. "Growth Elasticity of Poverty: Estimates from New Data." *International Journal of Social Economics* 37: 923–32.

Levy, Barry S., and Jonathan A. Patz. 2015. "Climate Change, Human Rights, and Social Justice." *Annals of Global Health* 81: 310–22.

Li, H., A.D. Stein, H.X. Barnhart, U. Ramakrishnan, and R. Martorell. 2003. "Associations between Prenatal and Postnatal Growth and Adult Body Size and Composition." *American Journal of Clinical Nutrition* 77: 1498–1505.

Marong, Alhagi. 2010. "Development, Right to, International Protection." In *Max Planck Encyclopaedia of Public International Law,* edited by Rüdiger Wolfrum. Oxford: Oxford Public International Law. http://opil.ouplaw.com/home/EPIL.

Martorell, R., U. Ramakrishnan, D.G. Schroeder, and M. Ruel. 1996. "Reproductive Performance and Nutrition during Childhood." *Nutrition Review* 54: S15–S21.

Martorell, R., J. Rivera, H. Kaplowitz, and E. Pollitt. 1992. "Long-Term Consequences of Growth Retardation during Early Childhood." In *Human Growth: Basic and Clinical Aspects,* edited by M. Hernandez and J. Argente, 143–49. Amsterdam: Elsevier Science.

Mattoo, Aaditya, and Arvind Subramanian. 2010. *Greenprint: A New Approach to Cooperation on Climate Change.* Washington, DC: Centre for Global Development.

Mechlem, Kerstin. 2008. "Food, Right to, International Protection." In *Max Planck Encyclopaedia of Public International Law,* edited by Rüdiger Wolfrum. Oxford: Oxford Public International Law. http://opil.ouplaw.com/home/EPIL.

Michaelowa, Katharina, and Axel Michaelowa. 2012. "India as an Emerging Power in International Climate Negotiations." *Climate Policy* 12: 574–90.

Mohan, Raja. 2003. *Crossing the Rubicon: The Shaping of India's Foreign Policy.* New Delhi: Viking.

MOWCD (Ministry of Women and Child Development). 2006. *National Guidelines on Infant and Young Child Feeding.* New Delhi: Food and Nutrition Board, Government of India.

Mukim, Megha, and Peter Nunnenkamp. 2010. "The Location Choices of Foreign Investors: A District Level Analysis in India." Working Paper No. 1628. Kiel, Germany: Kiel Institute for the World Economy.

Nagaraj, R. "Foreign Direct Investment in India in the 1990s: Trends and Issues." *Economic and Political Weekly,* April 26 (2013): 1702–12.

Narayan, Ambar, and Rinku Murgai. 2016. "Looking Back on Two Decades of Poverty and Well-Being in India." Working Paper No. 7626. Washington, DC: World Bank.

Narayanan, Sudha. 2014. "The National Food Security Act vis-à-vis the WTO Agreement on Agriculture." *Economic and Political Weekly* 49 (5): 40–46.

National Council of Applied Economic Research. 2009. "FDI in India and Its Growth Linkages." New Delhi: NCAER.

Nunnenkamp, Peter, and Rudi Stracke. 2007. "Foreign Direct Investment in Post-Reform India: Likely to Work Wonders for Regional Development?" Working Paper No. 1375. Kiel, Germany: Kiel Institute for the World Economy.

Nußberger, Angelika. 2007. "Work, Right to, International Protection." In *Max Planck Encyclopaedia of Public International Law,* edited by Rüdiger Wolfrum. Oxford: Oxford Public International Law. http://opil.ouplaw.com/home/EPIL.

Oberthuer, Sebastian, and Hermann E. Ott. 1999. *The Kyoto Protocol: International Climate Policy for the 21st Century.* International and European Environmental Policy Series. Berlin: Springer-Verlag.

OECD. 2008. *OECD Benchmark Definition of Foreign Direct Investment, 4th Edition, 2008.* Paris: OECD. https://www.oecd.org/daf/inv/investmentstatisticsand analysis/40193734.pdf.

Oestreich, Joel E. 2014. "The United Nations and the Rights-Based Approach to Development in India." *Global Governance* 20 (1): 77.

OHCHR (Office of the United Nations High Commissioner for Human Rights). 2006. *Frequently Asked Questions on Human Rights–Based Approach to Development Cooperation.* New York/Geneva: United Nations. http://www.ohchr.org/Documents/Publications/FAQen.pdf.

–. 2010. "*Right to Development Report of the High-Level Task Force on the Implementation of the Right to Development on Its Sixth Session (Geneva, 14–22 January 2010).* UN Doc A/HRC/15/WG.2//TF/2, 6. http://www2.ohchr.org/English/issues/development/right/docs/A-HRC-15-WG2-TF-2.doc.

–. 2013. *Realizing the Right to Development: Essays in Commemoration of 25 Years of the United Nations Declaration on the Right to Development.* New York/Geneva: United Nations. https://www.ohchr.org/Documents/Publications/Right DevelopmentInteractive_EN.pdf.

Olivier, Jos G.J., Greet Janssens-Maenhout, and Jeroen Peters. 2012. *Trends in Global CO_2 Emissions: 2012 Report.* Brussels: Institute for Environment and Sustainability, Joint Research Centre.

Omvedt, Gail. 2012. "Will Globalisation Emancipate Dalits?" *Seekingbegumpura,* 13 September 2012. https://seekingbegumpura.wordpress.com/2012/09/13/will-globalization-emancipate-dalits/.

–. 2015. "Capitalism and Globalisation: Dalits and Adivasis." *Economic and Political Weekly* 40 (47): 4881–85.

Osmond, C., D.J. Barker, P.D. Winter, C.H. Fall, and S.J. Simmonds. 1993. "Early Growth and Death from Cardiovascular Disease in Women." *British Medical Journal* 307: 1519–24.

Ozler, Sule, 2000. "Export Orientation and Female Share of Employment: Evidence from Turkey." *World Development* 28 (7): 1239–48. https://EconPapers.repec.org/RePEc:eee:wdevel:v:28:y:2000:i:7:p:1239-1248.

Pachauri, Shonali. 2014. "Household Electricity Access a Trivial Contributor to CO_2 Emissions Growth in India." *Nature Climate Change* 4: 1073–76.

Paine, Jacqueline A., Catherine A. Shipton, Sunandha Chaggar, Rhian M. Howells, Mike J. Kennedy, Gareth Vernon, Susan Y. Wright, Edward Hinchliffe, Jessica L Adams, Aron L. Silverstone, and Rachel Drake. 2005. "Improving the Nutritional Value of Golden Rice through Increased Pro-Vitamin-A Content." *Nature Biotechnology* 23 (4): 482–87. doi:10.1038/nbt1082.

Palit, Amitendu. 2009. "India's Foreign Investment Policy: Achievements and Inadequacies (March 11, 2012)." *Asie Visions, Institut Français des Relations Internationales* (IFRI) 18. https://ssrn.com/abstract=2019897.

Pelletier, David L. 1994. "The Relationship between Child Anthropometry and Mortality in Developing Countries: Implications for Policy, Programs and Future Research." *Journal of Nutrition* 124: 2047S–81S.

Peters, Glen P., Robbie M. Andrew, Susan Solomon, and Pierre Friedlingstein. 2015. "Measuring a Fair and Ambitious Climate Agreement Using Cumulative Emissions." *Environmental Research Letters* 10: 105004.

Planning Commission. 2012. *12th Five Year Plan.* Vol. 2, *Economic Sectors.* New Delhi: Government of India.

Pray, Carl E., Prajakta Bengali, and Bharat Ramaswami. 2005. "The Cost of Biosafety Regulations: The Indian Experience." *Quarterly Journal of International Agriculture* 44 (3): 267–89.

Pray, C.E., L. Nagarajan, J. Huang, R. Hu, and B. Ramaswami. 2011. "The Impact of Bt Cotton and the Potential Impact of Biotechnology on Other Crops in China and India." In *Genetically Modified Food and Global Welfare,* edited by Colin Carter, GianCarlo Moschini, and Ian Sheldon, 83–114. Bingley, UK: Emerald Group.

Pray, Carl E., Bharat Ramaswami, and Timothy Kelley. 2001. "The Impact of Economic Reforms on R&D by the Indian Seed Industry." *Food Policy* 26 (6): 587–98. doi:10.1016/S0306-9192(01)00022-7.

Pritchett, Lant, and Amanda Beatty. 2012. "The Negative Consequences of Overambitious Curriculum in Developing Countries." Working Paper RW12P-035, Harvard Kennedy School. Cambridge, MA: Harvard University.

Pryer, Jane A., Stephen Rogers, and Ataur Rahman. 2004. "The Epidemiology of Good Nutritional Status among Children from a Population with a High Prevalence of Malnutrition." *Public Health Nutrition* 7: 311–17.

Qaim, Matin, and David Zilberman. "Yield Effects of Genetically Modified Crops in Developing Countries." *Science* 299 (5608) (2003): 900-2.

Qayum, Abdul, and Kiran Sakkhari. 2005. *Bt Cotton in Andhra Pradesh: A Three-Year Assessment.* Hyderabad: Booksline.

Raghunandan, D. 2012. "India's Climate Policy: Squaring the Circle." *IDS Bulletin* 43: 122–29.

Rajamani, Lavanya. 2011. "Decoding the Durban Platform." *EJIL: Talk!* 14 December. https://www.ejiltalk.org/decoding-the-durban-platform/.

Ramaswami, Bharat, and Wilima Wadhwa. 2010. "Survey Design and Precision of ASER Estimates." New Delhi: ASER Centre. http://img.asercentre.org/docs/Aser%20survey/Technical%20Papers/precisionofaserestimates_ramaswami_wadhwa.pdf.

Ramessar, Koreen, Teresa Capell, and Paul Christou. 2008. "Molecular Pharming in Cereal Crops." *Phytochemistry Reviews* 7 (3): 579–92. doi:10.1007/s11101-008 9087-3.

Ray, Pradeep K., and Sunil Venaik. 2008. "Foreign Ownership and Subsidiary Performance: Impact on Research and Exports?" *Economic and Political Weekly* 43 (39): 57–65.

Riedel, Eibe. 2011. "Health, Right to, International Protection." In *Max Planck Encyclopaedia of Public International Law,* edited by Rüdiger Wolfrum. Oxford: Oxford Public International Law. http://opil.ouplaw.com/home/EPIL.

Romero, J.J. 2012. "Blackouts Illuminate India's Power Problems." *IEEE Spectrum* 49: 11–12.

Sagar, A., and M. Kandlikar. 1997. "Knowledge, Rhetoric and Power: The International Science and Politics of Climate Change." *Economic and Political Weekly* 32 (49): 3139–48.

Saha, K.K., E.A. Frongillo, D.S. Alam, S.E. Arifeen, L.A. Persson, and K.M. Rasmussen. 2008. "Appropriate Infant Feeding Practices Result in Better Growth of Infants and Young Children in Rural Bangladesh." *American Journal of Clinical Nutrition* 87: 1852–59.

Sahai, Suman. 2003. "Mahyco-Monsanto *Bt* Cotton Fails to Perform." *Current Science* 85 (4): 426–27.

–. 2005. "The Science of Bt Cotton Failure in India." *The Hindu,* 29 August.

Sahai, Suman, and Shakeelur Rahman. 2003. "Performance of Bt Cotton: Data from First Commercial Crop." *Economic and Political Weekly* 38 (30): 3139–41.

Sawadogo, P.S., Y. Martin-Prevel, and M.E. Savy. 2006. "An Infant and Child Feeding Index Is Associated with the Nutritional Status of 6- to 23-Month-Old Children in Rural Burkina Faso." *Journal of Nutrition* 136: 656–63.

Scoones, I. 2006. *Science, Agriculture and the Politics of Policy: The Case of Biotechnology in India.* Himayatnagar, Hyderabad: Orient Blackswan.

Shah, Esha. 2005. "Local and Global Elites Join Hands." *Economic and Political Weekly* 40 (43): 4629–39.

Slovic, Paul. 1987. "Perception of Risk." *Science* 236.4799: 280–85.

Srivastava, Sadhana. 2003. "What Is the True Level of FDI Flows to India?" *Economic and Political Weekly* 38 (7): 608–10. http://www.jstor.org/stable/4413211.

Standing, Guy. 1999. "Global Feminisation through Flexible Labour: A Theme Revisited." *World Development* 27 (3): 583–602.

Stiglitz, J.E. 2007. "Economic Foundations of Intellectual Property Rights." *Duke Law Journal* 57: 1693–1724.

Stone, Glenn Davis. 2011. "Field versus Farm in Warangal: Bt Cotton, Higher Yields, and Larger Questions." *World Development* 39 (3): 387–98.

Sukumar, Arun Mohan. 2013. "The Shaky Geopolitics of India's Food Security." *The Hindu,* 2 August. https://www.thehindu.com/opinion/op-ed/the-shaky-geopolitics-of-indias-food-security/article4978574.ece.

Svedberg, Peter. 2000. *Poverty and Undernutrition: Theory, Measurement, and Policy.* Oxford: Oxford University Press.

Thaker, Jagadish, and Anthony Leiserowitz. 2014. "Shifting Discourses of Climate Change in India." *Climate Change* 123: 107–19.

United Nations. 2009. *World Population Prospects: The 2008 Revision.* New York: Department of Economic and Social Affairs, Population Division, United Nations.

United Nations Conference on Trade and Development (UNCTAD). 2000. *World Investment Report 2000: Cross-Border Mergers and Acquisitions and Development.* New York and Geneva: United Nations. https://unctad.org/en/Docs/wir2000_en.pdf.

–. 2010. *World Investment Report.* Geneva: United Nations.

UNFCCC (United Nations Framework Convention on Climate Change). 2015. "The Paris Agreement." https://unfccc.int/process-and-meetings/the-paris-agreement/the-paris-agreement.

Vagh, Shaher Banu. 2009. "Evaluating READ INDIA: Development of Tools for Assessing Hindi Reading and Writing Ability and Math Skills of Rural Indian Children in Grades 1–5." New Delhi: ASER Centre.

Van Boven, Theo. 2007. "Racial and Religious Discrimination." In *Max Planck Encyclopaedia of Public International Law,* edited by Rüdiger Wolfrum. Oxford: Oxford Public International Law. http://opil.ouplaw.com/home/EPIL.

Vandenbogaerde, Arne. 2013. "The Right to Development in International Human Rights Law." *Netherlands Quarterly of Human Rights* 31: 187–209.

Venkataraman, C., A.D. Sagar, G. Habib, N. Lam, and K.R. Smith. 2010. "The Indian National Initiative for Advanced Biomass Cookstoves: The Benefits of Clean Combustion." *Energy for Sustainable Development* 14 (2): 63–72.

Wadhwa, Wilima. 2009. "Private Schools: Do They Provide Higher Quality Education?" In *Annual Status of Education Report,* 9–11. New Delhi: Pratham Resource Centre and ASER Centre.

–. 2010. "RTE Norms and Learning Outcomes." In *Annual Status of Education Report,* 8–10. New Delhi: Pratham Resource Centre and ASER Centre.

–. 2014. "Government vs. Private Schools: Have Things Changed?" *Annual Status of Education Report,* 19–21. New Delhi: Pratham Resource Centre and ASER Centre.

Wara, M. 2007. "Is the Global Carbon Market Working?" *Nature* 445 (7128): 595–96.

Whelan, Daniel J. 2015. "'Under the Aegis of Man': The Right to Development and the Origins of the New International Economic Order." *Humanity* 6: J93.

Wilfred, Felix. 2007. *Dalit Empowerment*. Delhi: Cambridge Press.

Wolf, Anna-Lena. 2015. "Juridification of the Right to Development in India." *Völkerreschtsblog*, 9 September. http://voelkerrechtsblog.org/juridification-of-the-right-to-development-in-India/.

Wood, Adrian. 1991. "North-South Trade and Female Labour in Manufacturing: An Asymmetry." *Journal of Development Studies* 27 (2): 168–89.

World Bank. 2014a. "Poverty and Equity, Country Dashboard, India." http://povertydata.worldbank.org/poverty/country/IND.

–. 2014b. *Turn Down the Heat: Confronting the New Climate Normal*. Washington, DC: World Bank.

World Bank, IFC, and MIGA. 2016. "World Bank Group Climate Change Action Plan 2016–2020." Washington, DC: World Bank.

World Health Organization Multicenter Growth Reference Study Group. 2006. *WHO Child Growth Standards: Length/Height-for-Age, Weight-for-Age, Weight-for-Length, Weight-for- Height and Body Mass Index-for-Age: Methods and Development*. Geneva: World Health Organization.

Contributors

Ashwini Deshpande is a professor of economics at the Delhi School of Economics, University of Delhi, India. Her PhD and early publications have been on the international debt crisis of the 1980s. She has been working on the economics of discrimination and affirmative action issues, with a focus on caste and gender in India. She has published extensively in leading scholarly journals and is the author of *Grammar of Caste: Economic Discrimination in Contemporary India* (Oxford University Press, 2011) and *Affirmative Action in India* (Oxford University Press, Oxford India Short Introductions series, 2013). She received the EXIM Bank award for outstanding dissertation (now called the IERA Award) in 1994 and the VKRV Rao Award for Indian economists under forty-five in 2007.

Simon Harding obtained his PhD from the Institute for Resources, Environment, and Sustainability at the University of British Columbia. His research focuses on urban sustainability, particularly in the transportation sector. He currently works in Blueprint-ADE in Toronto.

Moshe Hirsch is the Von Hofmannsthal Professor of Law at the Hebrew University of Jerusalem and co-director of the International Law Forum at the Hebrew University. Professor Hirsch specializes in international economic law, public international law, and international legal theory. His recent publications include *Invitation to the Sociology of International Law* (Oxford University Press, 2015); "African Countries in the World Trading System" (co-author, *International and Comparative Law Quarterly*, 2012); "Interactions between Investment and Non-Investment Obligations in International Investment Law," in *Oxford Handbook of International Law on Foreign Investment* (Oxford University Press, 2008); "The Sociology of International Economic Law" (*European Journal of International Law*, 2008); and "Developing Countries," in *The Encyclopedia of Public International Law* (Max Planck Institute, 2008).

Milind Kandlikar is a professor and director at the Institute for Resources, Environment and Sustainability and professor at the School of Public Policy and Global Affairs at the University of British Columbia. He works on policy questions with significant technical content and a particular focus on problems of the global environment.

Ashok Kotwal is a professor of economics at the Vancouver School of Economics, University of British Columbia, and a development economist who has worked on various issues pertaining to the processes of development in India and their impact on poverty. He is also the editor-in-chief of *Ideas for India*, an online newsletter that disseminates research findings on Indian development.

Ashwini Kulkarni belongs to the civil society organization Pragati Abhiyan, based in Nashik, Maharashtra (http://www.pragatiabhiyan.org). She has been associated with rural poverty–related programs for two decades. Pragati Abhiyan works with tribal villages of the Nashik district and is also involved in research and policy work. Ms. Kulkarni has served on government committees seeking to improve the implementation of rural poverty programs. She is also associated with national networks of civil society organizations working in areas related to the *Mahatma Gandhi National Rural Employment Guarantee Act* (MGNREGA) and policies related to rain-fed agriculture.

Nisha Malhotra received her PhD in economics from the University of Maryland at College Park. She is an interdisciplinary social scientist with a strong interest in questions related to population, gender, and health. Her recent work focuses on maternal and child health in Asia. Her other research interests include international trade and development. Dr. Malhotra is a senior instructor at the Vancouver School of Economics at the University of British Columbia.

Milind Murugkar is a policy researcher and activist associated with Pragati Abhiyan, an NGO focusing on rural development. He works to build bridges between grassroots citizen groups and farmers affected by economic and trade policies and the political system that produces the policies. His work fosters understanding of economic and trade policies at the grassroots level through press reports, workshops, and focus group discussions. He works to enhance the knowledge base of political decision makers by sharing his research and results with actors in the political system. He is also involved in the discourse on alternatives for the Public Distribution System (PDS) in India, such as cash transfers. He is widely published in the Marathi-language press and is a well-known commentator on television. He has also published frequently in the English-language dailies, including the *Hindustan Times* and the *Indian Express,* is a columnist for the *Mint,* and has published in academic journals and books.

Bharat Ramaswami is a professor of economics at the Indian Statistical Institute, Delhi. He has held visiting appointments at universities in Canada, Japan, Sweden, and the United States. In 2004, he was awarded the Mahalanobis Memorial Medal by the Indian Econometric Society for his contributions to quantitative economics. His research can be accessed at http://www.isid.ac.in/~bharat/dresearch.html.

Wilima Wadhwa is the director of the ASER Centre. She has been associated with ASER since its inception in 2005 and is the architect of the ASER survey and other primary research studies currently being undertaken by the ASER Centre. ASER's unique approach to measuring learning outcomes has been recognized nationally and internationally and has also been adapted by several other countries in Asia and Africa. Dr. Wadhwa earned her undergraduate degree, with Honours in Economics, from Delhi University, MA degrees in Economics from Delhi University and the University of California, and her PhD in Economics from the University of

California. She has published extensively and teaches statistics and econometrics at the University of California (Irvine) and the Indian Statistical Institute, Delhi. She has also been a member of various government and international committees. Her other research interests include development and economics of education.

Index

Note: "(f)" after a page number indicates a figure; "(t)" after a page number indicates a table; FDI stands for "foreign direct investment"